The Primacy of Politics
*Social Democracy and the Making of Europe's
Twentieth Century*

Political history in the advanced industrial world has indeed ended, argues
this pioneering study, but the winner has been social democracy – an ideology and political movement that has been as influential as it has been
misunderstood. Sheri Berman looks at the history of social democracy
from its origins in the late nineteenth century to today and shows how it
beat out competitors such as classical liberalism, orthodox Marxism, and
its cousins, fascism and National Socialism, by solving the central challenge of modern politics: reconciling the competing needs of capitalism
and democracy. Bursting onto the scene in the interwar years, the social
democratic model spread across Europe after the Second World War and
formed the basis of the postwar settlement commonly but misleadingly
labeled "embedded liberalism." This is a study of European social democracy that rewrites the intellectual and political history of the modern era
while putting contemporary debates about globalization in their proper
intellectual and historical context.

Sheri Berman is an associate professor of political science at Barnard
College, Columbia University. She was previously an assistant professor of
politics at Princeton University. Berman is the author of *The Social Democratic Moment* (1987). She has written articles for top political science
journals including *Perspectives on Politics, World Politics,* and *Comparative Politics,* as well as publications such as *Foreign Affairs, Dissent,* and
World Policy Journal.

T0382386

The Primacy of Politics

Social Democracy and the Making of Europe's Twentieth Century

SHERI BERMAN

Barnard College, Columbia University

CAMBRIDGE
UNIVERSITY PRESS

CAMBRIDGE UNIVERSITY PRESS
Cambridge, New York, Melbourne, Madrid, Cape Town, Singapore,
São Paulo, Delhi, Dubai, Tokyo, Mexico City

Cambridge University Press
32 Avenue of the Americas, New York, NY 10013-2473, USA

www.cambridge.org
Information on this title: www.cambridge.org/9780521521109

First published 2006
Reprinted 2007, 2008, 2010

A catalog record for this publication is available from the British Library.

Library of Congress Cataloging in Publication Data

Berman, Sheri, 1965–
The primacy of politics : social democracy and the making of Europe's twentieth
century / Sheri Berman.
    p. cm.
Includes bibliographical references and index.
ISBN 0-521-81799-4 (hardback) – ISBN 0-521-52110-6 (pbk.)
1. Socialism – Europe – History – 20th century.   2. Democracy – Europe – History –
20th century.   3. Europe – Politics and government – 20th century.   I. Title.
HX239.B47   2006
320.55'1094090904–dc22   2006002125

ISBN 978-0-521-81799-8 Hardback
ISBN 978-0-521-52110-9 Paperback

For those who understood the problem and came up with the answer

Contents

Acknowledgments

This book has been a long time in the making and I owe many debts to many people who made getting through this ordeal easier. First, I want to thank those who provided comments on all or part of the manuscript or who helped move the book along in other ways: Mark Blyth, Consuelo Cruz, Peter Hall, Harold James, Kate McNamara, Bo Rothstein, Anna Seleny, Kathryn Stoner-Weiss, Michael Walzer, and editors at *Dissent*, the editors of *Social Philosophy & Policy*, and the anonymous reviewers at Cambridge University Press. Parts of the argument from this book were also presented to audiences at Georgetown University, Harvard University, McGill University, Princeton University, the Remarque Institute and the Center for European Studies at New York University (NYU), the University of Chicago, and the University of Toronto. I want to thank all those who came to those talks and asked hard-hitting and insightful questions. They pushed me to think more clearly about what precisely I was trying to say and do with this book. Second, I want to thank the many people who helped me prepare the book for publication: Lew Bateman and Andy Saff at Cambridge University Press and, more generally, Johannes Beber Bernd Hilmar, Dan Kurtz-Phelan, Arissa Sidoti, and especially Gideon Rose, whose editing is as slow as it is miraculous. Third, I want to thank those organizations that provided the funding and other support that helped make this book possible: Göteborg University, the Institute for Advanced Study, Princeton University, and the Remarque Institute and the Institute for European Studies at NYU. And in the non-academic realm, I want to thank my family – Gideon, Isaac, Lucy, and the cats – for putting up with the obsessions and endless arguments. Finally, although I can't really thank him, I would like to acknowledge my debt to Karl Polanyi. It was his *The Great Transformation* that got me thinking about this book's issues many years ago.

I

Introduction

For the first half of the twentieth century, Europe was the most turbulent region on earth, convulsed by war, economic crisis, and social and political conflict. For the second half of the century, it was among the most placid, a study in harmony and prosperity. What changed?

Two narratives commonly emerge in answer to this question. The first focuses on the struggle between democracy and its alternatives, pitting liberalism against fascism, national socialism, and Marxist-Leninism. The second focuses on the competition between capitalism and its alternatives, pitting liberals against socialists and communists. In both cases, liberalism triumphed. Democratic capitalism proved the best form – indeed, the "natural" form – of societal organization, and once Western Europe fully embraced it, all was well.

This account obviously contains some truth: The century did witness a struggle between democracy and its enemies and the market and its alternatives. But it is only a partial truth, because it overlooks a crucial point: Democracy and capitalism had been historically at odds. Indeed, this was one point on which classical liberals and traditional Marxists agreed. From J. S. Mill to Alexis de Tocqueville to Friedrich Hayek, liberals have lived in constant fear of the "egalitarian threats of mass society and democratic . . . politics, which, in their view, would lead, by necessity, to tyranny and 'class legislation' by the propertyless as well as uneducated majority." Karl Marx, meanwhile, expressed skepticism about whether the bourgeoisie would actually allow democracy to function (and workers to take power), but felt that if they did, democracy might contribute to bringing about an end to capitalism – a potential, of course, that he, unlike his liberal counterparts, welcomed.[1] The story of the twentieth century, and the reason that its second half was so different from its first, is thus to a large degree the story of how capitalism and democracy were rendered

[1] Clas Offe, "Competitive Party Democracy and the Keynesian Welfare State: Factors of Stability and Disorganization," *Policy Sciences*, 15, 1983, 225–6.

compatible, so much so that we now see them as inextricably linked and as the necessary and sufficient preconditions for social stability and progress.

In practice, this rendering entailed a dramatic revision of the relationship that existed among states, markets, and society up through the early twentieth century; it meant creating a capitalism tempered and limited by political power and often made subservient to the needs of society rather than the other way around. This was as far a cry from what liberals had long advocated (namely, as free a rein for markets and individual liberty as possible) as it was from what Marxists and communists wanted (namely, an end to capitalism). The ideology that triumphed in the twentieth century was not liberalism, as the "End of History" story argues; it was social democracy. This book tells its story.

Capitalism

Before delving into this story, it is worth stepping back a bit to remind ourselves of how contested the relationship among states, markets, and society has been since the onset of capitalism. Most people today take capitalism so much for granted that they fail to appreciate what a recent and revolutionary phenomenon it is. Although trade and commerce have always been features of human societies, only in the eighteenth century did economies in which markets were the primary force in the production and distribution of goods begin to emerge. As these markets spread, they transformed not only economic relationships but social and political ones as well.

In pre-capitalist societies, markets were embedded in broader social relationships and subordinated to politics. Thus, the institutions, norms, and preferences of traditional communities governed markets' reach and operation. From the most traditional societies up through Europe's mercantalist age, decisions about the production and distribution of goods were made not by markets but by those with social and political power. Although markets existed, they were strictly constrained and regulated:

[N]ever before [modern capitalist] time were markets more than accessories of economic life. As a rule, the economic system was absorbed in the social system.... and [w]here markets were most highly developed, as under the mercantile system, they throve under the control of a centralized administration which fostered autarchy both in the households of the peasantry and in respect to national life. Regulation and markets, in effect, grew up together. The self-regulating market was unknown; indeed the emergence of the idea of self-regulation was a complete reversal of the trend of development. It is in light of these facts that the extraordinary assumptions underlying a market economy can alone be fully comprehended.[2]

With the advent of capitalism, in other words, the traditional relationship among states, markets, and society was reversed as the needs of markets came to determine the nature of communal life and the limits of political power; in

[2] Karl Polanyi, *The Great Transformation* (New York: Beacon Press, 1957), 68.

essence, under capitalism, "society [became merely] an adjunct to the market."[3] This is a dynamic, of course, with which any contemporary observer of globalization is familiar, but it did, in fact mark a dramatic historical departure: It was only with the triumph of capitalism in Europe beginning in the late eighteenth and nineteenth centuries that many critical decisions about how people lived their lives were left to the mercy (or lack of it) of impersonal economic forces.

For individuals, capitalism meant an end to a world where one's position and livelihood were defined primarily by membership in a particular group or community, and the transition to a system where identity and sustenance depended on one's position in the market.[4] The shift from traditional to modern societies had, of course, immense liberating potential for individuals: It meant the possibility of a world where one's life chances were not strictly defined by communal identity or family background. It also meant, however, that the web of ties and responsibilities that had tied individuals to their fellows and society more generally was sundered.[5] One critical consequence of this tearing asunder of traditional relationships was that whereas in pre-capitalist society an individual's basic sustenance might be guaranteed as "a moral right of membership in a human community,"[6] under capitalism the threat of starvation – the "economic whip of hunger" – became a necessary and even desirable part of societal arrangements, the ultimate incentive to play by the rules of the game.

Communal life was also up-ended. Throughout Western history, it had been widely believed that societies could be held together only by some shared vision of the public good. It was for precisely this reason that thinkers throughout Western history had long worried about the harmful effects of the pursuit of material gain. Thus Plato had Socrates say in *The Republic* that "the more men value money the less they value virtue," while the Apostle Paul argued, "the love of money is the root of all evils."[7] Capitalism aggravated these tendencies, this argument goes, since in addition to encouraging avarice and amoralism,

[3] Ibid., 52. Also, idem, "The Economy Embedded in Society," in idem, *The Livelihood of Man* (New York: Academic Press, 1977), Harry Pearson, ed., and Allen Morris Sievers, *Has Market Capitalism Collapsed? A Critique of Karl Polanyi's Economics* (New York: Columbia University Press, 1949), 19.

[4] Polyani, *The Great Transformation*, 73. See also Santhi Hejeebu and Deidre McCloskey, "The Reproving of Karl Polanyi," *Critical Review*, 13, 3–4, 1999, and J. R. Stanfield, *The Economic Thought of Karl Polanyi* (New York: St. Martin's Press, 1986).

[5] Marx and Friedrich Engels memorably criticized this shift in the *Communist Manifesto*: "The bourgeoisie, wherever it has got the upper hand, has put an end to all feudal, patriarchal, idyllic relations. It has pitilessly torn asunder the motley feudal ties that bound man to his 'natural superiors,' and has left remaining no other nexus between man and man than naked self-interest." "The Communist Manifesto," reprinted in Robert Tucker, ed., *The Marx-Engels Reader* (New York: W. W. Norton, 1978), 475.

[6] George Dalton, *Essays in Economic Anthropology Dedicated to the Memory of Karl Polanyi* (Seattle: University of Washington Press, 1965), esp. 2–3. See also Sheri Berman, "Capitalism and Poverty," *World Policy Journal*, 22, 5, Spring 2006.

[7] Jerry Z. Muller, *The Mind and the Market* (New York: Alfred Knopf, 2002), 4–5.

market-based societies distracted people from the common purposes and higher ends to which life should be devoted. With the transition to capitalism, self-interest took precedence over communal interest, and temporary and shifting relationships of contract and exchange became the primary bonds between citizens. It is hard for us today to remember how truly revolutionary a transformation this was:

To insist that society is and always has been nothing more than the sum of individuals, that the common end can only be achieved by maximizing individual interests, that the economy is, by definition, a mechanism governed by economic motives for the satisfaction of economic needs, that religious [and moral] standards are at best irrelevant to the economic enterprise, at worst detrimental – this mode of reasoning ... is a peculiarly modern way of thinking, patently at variance with the beliefs most people lived with for most of history.[8]

Perhaps the most influential discussion of this shift was by Ferdinand Tönnies in his path-breaking *Gemeinschaft und Gesellschaft* (*Community and Society*).[9] Here Tönnies argued that there were two basic forms of social life: that which existed before capitalism and after. In the precapitalist world, community reigned supreme. Commitment to the public or communal good was the highest value, and common views and an instinctual, unquestioned sense of social solidarity bound citizens together.[10] Or as another observer noted, "In traditional societies, the principle of social cohesion was part of the very structure of society. Hierarchies and distinctions, as well as equivalences, bound men together organically. The social bond was perceived as natural."[11] The spread of markets, in contrast, destroyed the traditional elements holding together communal life and created a type of social organization where self-interest rather than communal interest reigned supreme. As Tönnies famously noted, "In community people remain essentially united in spite of all separating factors, whereas in society they are essentially separated in spite of all uniting factors."[12] "Re-creating through political means the social unity which modernization has

---

[8] Gertrude Himmelfarb, *The Idea of Poverty: England in the Industrial Age* (New York: Alfred Knopf, 1984), 23–4.

[9] Ferdinand Tönnies, *Gemeinschaft und Gesellshaft* (Leipzig: Fues, 1887). Not everyone, of course, agreed with such views. See, most importantly, Adam Smith's discussion of "self-interest properly understood" in both *The Theory of Moral Sentiments* (New Rochelle, NY: Arlington House, 1969) and *The Wealth of Nations* (New York: R. R. Smith, 1948).

[10] One should not, as Tönnies and others had a tendency to do, romanticize pre-capitalist life. The "public" or "communal" good was not one that people got to vote on; it was determined by tradition and, for the most part, suited best the needs of the most powerful. Nonetheless, what is important to note here is the powerful sense that communities took precedence over individuals and that, although unequal, all members of a community had certain responsibilities toward each other.

[11] Pierre Rosanvallon, *The New Social Question: Rethinking the Welfare State* (Princeton, NJ: Princeton University Press, 2000), 11.

[12] Quoted in Muller, *The Mind and the Market*, 230.

destroyed" has thus been, as we will see, one of the main challenges facing modern societies.[13]

In short, the transition to capitalism brought a tragic irony: "At the heart of the Industrial Revolution of the eighteenth century there was an almost miraculous improvement in the tools of production, which was accompanied by catastrophic dislocations in the lives of the common people" and the organization of human communities.[14] These dislocations were so radical and destabilizing that they prompted an almost immediate backlash: an effort to limit the reach of markets and protect society from their destabilizing consequences. Thus began what Karl Polanyi called a "double movement," a battle between opposing principles that would shape modern life from that point forward:

[O]ne was the principle of economic liberalism, aiming at the establishment of a self-regulating market, relying on the support of the trading classes, and using largely laissez-faire and free trade as its methods; the other was the principle of social protection aiming at the conservation of man and nature as well as productive organization, relying on the varying support of those most immediately affected by the deleterious action of the market... and using protective legislation, restrictive associations, and other instruments of intervention as its methods.[15]

This dialectic came to a head in the 1920s and 1930s. With economic collapse and social chaos threatening much of Europe, publics began to renew their demands for the stability, community, and social protection that modern capitalist societies seemed unable to provide. At this point fascism and national socialism charged onto the stage, offering a way out of the downward spiral, a new vision of society in which states put markets in their place and fought the atomization, dislocation, and discord that liberalism, capitalism and modernity had generated. For many fascism and national socialism thus represented "real but barbaric solution[s]" to the contradictions and problems of market society.[16] The fascist and National Socialist cures, of course, were worse than the original disease, and Europeans emerging from the tragedy of the interwar years and the Second World War confronted the challenge of creating a world in which the market's reach and excesses could be controlled and people's longing for social solidarity could be satisfied – without the sacrifice of democracy and the trampling of freedom that fascism and Nazism brought in their wake.

Just such a system, of course, is precisely what emerged during the postwar period. And although it is most often understood today as a modified or "embedded" form of liberalism, this is a dramatic misreading of both its

---

[13] Samuel Huntington, *Political Order in Changing Societies* (New Haven, CT: Yale University Press, 1968), 73.

[14] Muller, *The Mind and the Market*, 33.

[15] Polanyi, *The Great Transformation*, 132.

[16] E.g. Ibid. Also Fred Block and Margaret Somers, "Beyond the Economistic Fallacy: The Holistic Science of Karl Polanyi," in Theda Skocpol, ed., *Vision and Method in Historical Sociology* (New York: Cambridge University Press, 1984), 61, and John Lewis, Karl Polanyi, and Donald Kitchen, eds., *Christianity and the Social Revolution* (London: Victor Gallancz, 1935).

roots and nature. In fact, rather than some updated form of liberalism, what spread like wildfire after the war was really something quite different: social democracy. By the end of the Second World War, social democracy had already been busy for a decade winning its first major political victories on Europe's northern periphery. Rejecting the economism and passivity of liberalism and orthodox Marxism, and eschewing the violence and authoritarianism of fascism and national socialism, social democracy was built on a belief in the primacy of politics and communitarianism – that is, on a conviction that political forces rather than economic ones could and should be the driving forces of history and that the "needs" or "good" of society must be protected and nurtured – and represented a non-Marxist vision of socialism. It was the most successful ideology and movement of the twentieth century: Its principles and policies undergirded the most prosperous and harmonious period in European history by reconciling things that had hitherto seemed incompatible – a well-functioning capitalist system, democracy, and social stability.

If this sounds surprising or overblown, it is perhaps first and foremost because, as noted previously, we have forgotten how unprecedented an achievement the postwar order was. Many, particularly in the United States, assume the natural compatibility of capitalism, democracy, and social stability when in fact they have historically not gone together. This lack of perspective is reflected in social scientific research as well. We have many excellent analyses of the constituent elements of Europe's postwar political economies. We know a lot, for example, about how and why democracy developed in Europe and elsewhere[17]; the nature and development of welfare states[18]; and the evolution, logic, and

---

[17] The literature of the development of democracy in Europe and elsewhere is huge. This book will in particular build on the work of scholars such as Barrington Moore and Gregory Luebbert, who have argued that there are fundamentally different paths to modernity, Barrington Moore, *The Social Origins of Dictatorship and Democracy* (Boston: Beacon Press, 1993), and Gregory Luebbert, *Liberalism, Fascism or Social Democracy* (New York: Oxford University Press, 1991).

   This book will also address the much debated question of which socioeconomic groups and political actors should be seen as the fundamental bearers of democratic aspirations. In particular, it will argue against those who overemphasize the role of middle classes and liberal parties as opposed to workers and parties of the left, but it also takes issue with those who view the aspirations of workers and leftist parties as a unified whole. As we will see, it was only a very particular part of the socialist spectrum – the revisionist and social democratic part – that wholeheartedly stood behind the democratic project in the late nineteenth and early twentieth centuries. On the role of workers and parties of the left in the struggle for democracy, see Geoff Eley, *Forging Democracy: The History of the Left in Europe* (New York: Oxford University Press, 2002), and Dietrich Rueschmeyer, Evelyn Huber Stephens, and John Stephens, *Capitalist Development and Democracy* (Chicago: University of Chicago Press, 1992).

[18] The literature on the development of European welfare states is also huge, and accordingly this book will address only certain parts of it directly. So, for example, it will only in passing engage the debates concerning the origins or correct characterization of welfare states. E.g., Peter Baldwin, *The Politics of Social Solidarity* (New York: Cambridge University Press, 1990); Gøsta Esping-Andersen, *Three Worlds of Welfare Capitalism* (Princeton, NJ: Princeton University Press, 1990); Peter Flora and Arnold Heidenheimer, eds., *The Development*

consequences of Keynesianism, planning, and other tools of economic management.[19] What we have thought less about is the postwar order's overall historical role and philosophical significance.[20] This book will therefore build on the existing literature on Europe's twentieth century political economies but also go beyond it. In addition to chronicaling the "back story" of the postwar order, I will argue that this order must be understood as a solution to the problems unleashed by capitalism and modernity. During the nineteenth and first half of the twentieth centuries, the liberal, Marxist, and fascist/national socialist solutions to these problems were tried and found wanting. Once the catastrophe of the Second World War was over, a new order began to emerge based on an understanding of the relationship among states, markets, and societies that differed radically from that advocated by liberals, Marxists, and fascists/national socialists. Based on a belief that political forces should control economic ones and aiming to "re-create through political means the social unity which modernization has destroyed,"[21] this order was, as we will see, a fundamentally social democratic one.

If one reason why social democracy's key role in twentieth century history has been obscured is that we have for the most part not thought about the postwar order holistically and historically, a second is that few scholars or commentators have given social democracy itself either the respect or in-depth ideological analysis it deserves. As a result, a force that has altered the course of European politics in the past and could do so again in the future remains strangely obscure.

of Welfare States in Europe and America (New Brunswick, NJ: Transaction, 1981); Evelyn Huber and John Stephens, *Development and Crisis of the Welfare State* (Chicago: University of Chicago Press, 2001); Isabela Mares, *The Politics of Social Risk* (New York: Cambridge University Press, 2003). Instead, the book focuses on the larger question of how to best understand the role or function played by welfare states in postwar political economies and builds upon the work of the "power resources" school and others who have written on the overall political and social implications of the welfare state. E.g., Gøsta Esping-Andersen, *Politics Against Markets* (Princeton, NJ: Princeton University Press, 1985); Walter Korpi, *The Democratic Class Struggle* (London: Routledge and Kegan Paul, 1983); idem, *The Working Class in Welfare Capitalism* (London: Routledge and Kegan Paul, 1978); Rosanvallon, *The New Social Question;* John Stephens, *The Transition from Capitalism to Socialism* (Chicago: University of Illinois Press, 1986).

[19] Carlos Boix, *Political Parties, Growth and Inequality* (New York: Cambridge University Press, 1998); John Goldthorpe, ed., *Order and Conflict in Contemporary Capitalism* (New York: Oxford University Press, 1984); Peter Gourevitch, *Politics in Hard Times* (Ithaca, NY: Cornell University Press, 1986); D. A. Hibbs, The *Political Economy of Industrial Democracies* (Cambridge, MA: Harvard University Press, 1987); Alexander Hicks, *Social Democracy and Welfare Capitalism* (Ithaca, NY: Cornell University Press, 1999).

[20] But see Mark Blyth, *Great Transformations: Economic Ideas and Institutional Change in the Twentieth Century* (New York: Cambridge University Press, 2002); Charles Maier, "The Two Postwar Eras," *American Historical Review*, 86, 2, April 1981; T. H. Marshall, *Class, Citizenship and Social Development* (New York: Anchor Books, 1965); Offe, "Competitive Party Democracy and the Keynesian Welfare State."

[21] Huntington, *Political Order in Changing Societies*, 73.

One reason for this neglect is a simple confusion of terms. During the late nineteenth and early twentieth centuries, many socialists adopted the label "social democrat" to differentiate themselves from other socialists who did not accept democracy. But these figures often agreed on little beyond the rejection of an insurrectionary or violent route to power, making their grouping of limited analytical use. Thus in Germany, for example, both Karl Kautsky and Eduard Bernstein claimed the social democratic label, even though they espoused dramatically different versions of socialism. Today the situation is similar, with a wide range of individuals and very different political parties identifying themselves as social democratic and having little in common save some vaguely leftist sentiments and a fervent desire not to be identified as communist.

Modern scholars, meanwhile, have often failed to appreciate social democracy's ideological distinctiveness. Most work on the subject in recent decades adopts one of two perspectives. The first, often espoused by critics, sees social democracy as an unstable halfway house between Marxism and liberalism, cobbled together from elements of incompatible traditions. In this view, social democrats are socialists without the courage of revolutionary conviction or socialists who have chosen ballots over bullets.[22] The second perspective, often held by supporters, sees the movement as an effort to implement particular policies or uphold certain values. In this view, social democrats are basically the champions of the welfare state, "equality," or "solidarity."

Each of these views contains some truth, but both miss the larger picture. This book will argue that social democracy is far more than a particular political program. Nor is it a compromise between Marxism and liberalism. And neither should it apply to any individual or party with vaguely leftist sympathies and an antipathy to communism. Instead, social democracy, at least as originally conceived, represented a full-fledged alternative to both Marxism and liberalism that had at its core a distinctive belief in the primacy of politics and communitarianism. The key to understanding its true nature lies in the circumstances of its birth. But before we can tell its story, a few words are necessary about the study of political ideologies more generally.

Ideology

Most contemporary political scientists tend to shun the study of ideology because they consider the concept too vague and amorphous to have a place

---

[22] Thus Vladimir Lenin fervently attacked Eduard Bernstein and other forefathers of social democracy for what he saw as their attempt to sully socialism with "bourgeois liberalism." True revolutionary socialists, he argued, recognized the "antithesis in principle between liberalism and socialism." See Lenin, "What Is to Be Done?" in Robert Tucker, ed., *The Lenin Anthology* (New York: W. W. Norton, 1975). For the notion that social democracy is distinguished by its belief in the possibility of a "parliamentary road" to socialism, see Adam Przeworski, *Capitalism and Social Democracy* (New York: Cambridge University Press, 1988), and idem with John Sprague, *Paper Stones: A History of Electoral Socialism* (Chicago: University of Chicago Press, 1986).

in rigorous analysis. Political scientists prefer to work with things that can be easily observed and quantified, and ideologies do not fit the bill. Yet even the skeptics would find it hard to deny, if pressed, that ideologies exist and exert a profound influence on politics. It would be impossible to discuss twentieth century history without using terms such as "fascist," "communist," or "liberal," and one would be laughed at if one tried. The result is a gap between academic theory and political reality that calls to mind the drunk looking for his lost keys under the lamppost because that was where the light was: The barren but easily searchable areas of political life receive lots of attention, while important subjects lie ignored in the dark a few feet away.[23]

Some social scientists justify the lack of attention paid to ideologies because they view them as mere epiphenomena, rising and falling thanks to changes in underlying economic interests or material conditions without exerting any significant independent impact along the way. For many Marxists, rational-choice scholars, and realists, for example, ideologies are best understood as mere tools or "covers" – adopted and used by political actors for various reasons, but not determining outcomes on their own. While this may often be the case, such a blanket rejection of ideologies' import is clearly wrong. Even a cursory reading of history shows that ideologies have played an important role in driving events down paths they would otherwise not have taken. They link people who would not otherwise have been linked and motivate them to pursue political goals they would not otherwise have pursued.

Another part of the problem is that many scholars who actually study ideology have been so narrowly focused on them that they haven't paid much attention to how ideologies are affected by other factors. Intellectual historians, for example, have produced rich and fascinating accounts of the content and advocates of ideologies, but they are often less good at telling us something about where ideologies come from or how they are shaped by the wider social, political, and economic contexts out of which they spring. Yet another problem is that many students of ideology work with a sort of status quo bias, treating ideologies as preexisting parts of a landscape and focusing on how they influence actors' behavior over time. Students of culture and certain kinds of institutionalists, for example, have a lot to tell us about how ideas and norms shape decisions and behavior, but especially, until recently, they have been less good at analyzing periods of change – times when belief systems and ideologies come under attack and new ones begin to emerge.[24]

---

[23] In recent years, political scientists have begun to remedy this situation, yet even within the new and promising literature on ideas, topics such as the rise and fall of ideologies remain relatively understudied. Sheri Berman, "Ideas, Norms, and Culture in Political Science," *Comparative Politics*, 33, 2, 2001; Mark Blyth, "Any More Bright Ideas?," *Comparative Politics*, 29, 2, 1997; Stephen Hanson, "From Culture to Ideology in Comparative Politics," *Comparative Politics*, 35, 3, April 2003.

[24] Berman, "Ideas, Norms, and Culture in Political Analysis"; Blyth, "Any More Bright Ideas?"; Harry Eckstein, "A Culturalist Theory of Political Change," *American Political Science Review*, 82, 3, September 1988, 790; Jonas Pontusson, "From Comparative Public Policy to Political

The starting point for a more satisfying literature is the recognition that ideologies exist at the juncture of theory and practice, with one foot in the realm of abstract ideas and the other in everyday political reality. They have their greatest impact when they can seamlessly relate the one to the other, offering adherents both a satisfying explanation of the world and a guide to mastering it.

Even if a perfect fit does emerge between an ideology and its environment, it rarely lasts for long. The political, social, or economic landscape changes, and the ideology becomes less useful. Sometimes it can be tinkered with or updated to suit the new conditions; sometimes it just stagnates, opening the way for an alternative to vault into prominence and power. The story of each period of ideological hegemony, therefore, truly begins with the decline of its predecessor.

Ideologies, in other words, rise and fall through a two-stage process. In the first stage, existing ideologies are questioned and tarnished, opening up a political space that competitors aspire to fill.[25] In this phase, in other words , the perceived failures or inadequacies of the reigning intellectual paradigm(s) create a *demand* for new ideologies. Once a political space has begun to open, the second stage of the process begins, as some political actors start to develop and embrace alternative approaches. In this phase, that is, a *supply* of new ideologies begins to appear, with contenders competing for mindshare and political power.

This book will trace such patterns over time, treating the fate of twentieth century ideologies as an extended case study. During the late nineteenth and early twentieth centuries, Western European nations underwent massive change. New social groups increased in size and power; old political patterns and forms of social organization began to crumble; economies were transformed. These developments led many across the continent to question existing political ideologies and search for new ways of understanding and responding to the rapidly evolving world around them. The crises that buffeted the continent during 1910s through 1940s accelerated the process of reconsideration. Two world wars and a massive depression discredited many of the institutions, organizations, and approaches that had long dominated European politics, giving added impetus to the ideological reexamination and reformulation that was already under way.

Economy," *Comparative Political Studies*, 28, 1, April 1995; William H. Sewell, Jr., "A Theory of Structure: Duality, Agency and Transformation," *American Journal of Sociology*, 98, 1, July 1992. However, there has been some real progress of late in this regard. See Rawi Abdelal, *National Purpose in the World Economy* (Ithaca, NY: Cornell University Press, 2001); Blyth, *Great Transformations*; Craig Parsons, *A Certain Idea of Europe* (Ithaca, NY: Cornell University Press, 2003); Paul Pierson, *Politics in Time* (Princeton, NJ: Princeton University Press, 2004).

[25] Peter Gourevitch, *Politics in Hard Times* (Ithaca, NY: Cornell University Press, 1984); Ernst B. Haas, *When Knowledge Is Power* (Berkeley, CA: University of California Press, 1990); Stephen Krasner, "Approaches to the State: Alternative Conceptions and Historical Dynamics," *Comparative Politics*, 16, January 1984; Bo Rothstein, "Political Institutions," in Robert E. Goodin and Hans-Dieter Klingemann, eds., *A New Handbook of Political Science* (New York: Oxford University Press, 1996).

In response to such massive changes and external shocks, political actors in all European societies not only began questioning existing ideologies, they also began developing a variety of powerful alternatives to the ideological status quo. That the questioning took place across Western Europe at around the same time and in a broadly similar way indicates that something beyond the borders of each country was at work. But the fact that the precise nature of political battles and their outcome varied greatly from country to country shows that one needs to go beyond broad structural changes and cross-national exogenous shocks and examine local political contexts and local political actors to get the full story. In particular, this book will stress the crucial role played by political parties in the development and fate of ideologies. In recent years, political parties have been understudied and undertheorized in political science, but, as we will see, it is impossible to understand twentieth century political developments without a focus on them.[26] In particular, we will see that political parties functioned as what the ideational literature calls "carriers."[27] Ideologies do not achieve political prominence on their own; they must be championed by "carriers" capable of persuading others to reconsider the ways they think and act. This is, as we will see, one critical role played by many political parties during the twentieth century: They promoted or diffused ideologies to a mass audience and provided the political vehicle through which true believers strove to implement particular political projects.

If the fate of ideologies cannot be understood without a focus on political parties, it is also the case that the development of parties cannot be understood without a focus on ideology. In particular, we will see that the organizations, political strategies, and electoral coalitions that defined particular parties were all crucially shaped by the ideological projects they championed. It is impossible to understand, for example, the cross-class coalitions, "people's party" strategies, and "principled pragmatism" that characterized social democrats, fascists, and national socialists without reference to their distinctive ideologies.[28] The

---

[26] Indeed, the classic works on the role of political parties in political development were done at least a generation ago. E.g., Mauric Duverger, *Political Parties* (New York: John Wiley, 1954); Otto Kirchheimer, "The Transformation of the Western European Party System," in Joseph LaPolombara and Myron Weiner, eds., *Political Parties and Political Development* (Princeton, NJ: Princeton University Press, 1966); Seymour Martin Lipset and Stein Rokkan, eds., *Party Systems and Voter Alignments* (New York: Free Press, 1967).

[27] See Berman, "Ideas, Norms and Culture in Political Analysis"; Blyth, "Any More Bright Ideas?"; James Kloppenberg, "Institutionalism, Rational Choice and Historical Analysis," *Polity*, 29, 1, Fall 1995, esp. 126; Judith Goldstein, "The Impact of Ideas on Trade Policy," *International Organization*, 43, 1, 1989; G. John Ikenberry, "Creating Yesterday's New World Order: Keynesianism 'New Thinking' and the Anglo-American Postwar Settlement," in Judith Goldstein and Robert Keohane, eds., *Ideas and Foreign Policy* (Ithaca, NY: Cornell University Press, 1993); William Sewell, Jr., *Work and Revolution in France* (New York: Cambridge University Press, 1980).

[28] There has been some good recent work on the changing organization and strategies of political parties. E.g., Mark Blyth and Richard S. Katz, "From Catch-all Politics to Cartelisation: The Political Economy of the Cartel Party," *West European Politics*, 28, 1, January 2005; Herbert

precise way in which these processes and dynamics played out is the subject of the chapters that follow, but the book's basic argument can be summarized briefly as follows.

The Story of Social Democracy

With the onset of the industrial revolution, liberalism took center stage as the first modern political and economic ideology. As capitalism spread across Europe during the nineteenth century, liberalism provided both an explanation of and a justification for the transformations the new system brought. Liberals promulgated a faith in progress: a belief that the market could deliver the greatest good to the greatest number, and the conviction that government should interfere as little as possible in the forward march of history. Indeed, there was such a match between the times and the ideology that the nineteenth century has often been called the "age of liberalism."[29]

Yet by the end of the century, the bloom was already off the rose. The practical consequences of early capitalism – especially the dramatic inequalities, social dislocation, and atomization it engendered – led to a backlash against liberalism and a search for alternatives.[30] The most important and powerful challenge on the left came from Marxism, and by the last decades of the nineteenth century, a scientific and deterministic version of Marxism (which was largely codified by Friedrich Engels and popularized by Karl Kautsky) had established itself as the official ideology of much of the international socialist movement.

The most distinctive features of this doctrine were historical materialism and class struggle, which combined argued that history was propelled forward not by changes in human consciousness or behavior but rather by economic development and the resulting shifts in social relationships. As Engels put it:

The materialist conception of history starts from the proposition that . . . the final causes of all social changes and political revolutions are to be sought, not in men's brains, not in man's better insight into eternal truth and justice, but in changes in the modes of production and exchange. They are to be sought, not in the *philosophy* but in the *economics* of each particular epoch.[31]

As one observer noted, what historical materialism offered was an "obstetric" view of history: Since capitalism had within it the seeds of the future socialist

Kitschelt, *The Transformation of European Social Democracy* (New York: Cambridge University Press, 1994); Kay Lawson, ed., *How Political Parties Work: Perspectives from Within* (Westport, CT: Praeger, 1994).
[29] E.g., L. T. Hobhouse, *Liberalism* (New York: Oxford University Press, 1964), 110.
[30] Within the liberal camp itself, unease with the effects of unfettered markets on society led liberal "revisionists" to strike out on their own in the hope of creating a new synthesis. James Kloppenberg, *Uncertain Victory: Social Democracy and Progressivism in European and American Thought, 1870–1920* (New York: Oxford University Press, 1986).
[31] Friedrich Engels, *Anti-Dühring: Herr Eugen Dühring's Revolution in Science* (Moscow, 1962), 365–6.

society, socialists had only to wait for economic development to push the system's internal contradictions to the point where the emergence of the new order would require little more than some midwifery.[32] And in this drama the role of midwife was played by class struggle and in particular by the proletariat. As Kautsky put it, "economic evolution inevitably brings on conditions that will compel the exploited classes to rise against this system of private ownership."[33] With each passing day, ever larger would grow the group of "propertyless workers for whom the existing system [would become] unbearable; who have nothing to lose by its downfall but everything to gain."[34]

As time passed, however, orthodox Marxism began to run into trouble. To begin with, many of Marx's predictions failed to come true. By the fin-de-siècle, European capitalism had developed renewed vigor after a long depression and bourgeois states had begun undertaking important political, economic, and social reforms. Just as Marxism's failings as a guide to history were becoming clear, moreover, criticism arose within the international socialist movement regarding its inadequacy as a guide to constructive political action. Parties acting in Marx's name had become important political players in a number of European countries by the end of the nineteenth century, but orthodox Marxism could not furnish them with a strategy for using their power to achieve any practical goals. Orthodox Marxism in general had little to say about the role of political organizations, since it considered economic forces rather than political activism to be the prime mover of history.

Around the turn of the twentieth century, therefore, many on the left faced a troubling dilemma: Capitalism was flourishing, but the economic injustices and social fragmentation that had motivated the Marxist project in the first place remained. Orthodox Marxism offered only a counsel of passivity – of waiting for the contradictions within capitalism to bring the system down, which seemed both highly unlikely and increasingly unpalatable.

Orthodox Marxism's passive economism also did little to meet the psychopolitical needs of mass populations under economic and social stress. The forward march of markets had caused immense unease in European societies. Critics bemoaned the glorification of self-interest and rampant individualism, the erosion of traditional values and communities, and the rise of social dislocation, atomization, and fragmentation that capitalism brought in its wake. As a result, the fin-de-siècle witnessed a surge in communitarian thought and nationalist movements that argued that only a revival of national communities could provide the sense of solidarity, belonging, and collective purpose that Europe's divided and disoriented societies so desperately needed. Many

---

[32] The term comes from G. A. Cohen, *If You're an Egalitarian, How Come You're So Rich?* (Cambridge, MA: Harvard University Press, 1999).

[33] Karl Kautsky, *The Class Struggle* (Chicago: Charles Kerr, 1910), 90.

[34] Ibid., 119. One can find these views presented in any number of Kautsky's popular writings. See, for example, Kautsky, *The Capitalist Class* (New York: National Executive Committeee of the Socialist Labor Party, 1918); idem, *The Economic Doctrines of Karl Marx* (New York: Macmillan, 1936); idem, *The Working Class* (New York: New York Labor News Co., 1918).

nationalists came to see socialism as a necessary component of their larger
political program, but this was a socialism divorced from Marxism, based on
a deep suspicion of capitalism and a firm belief that something had to be done
for those most discomfited by it, but vehemently rejecting historical materialism and class struggle. It was against this backdrop and in response to these
frustrations that the social democratic movement emerged.

As the nineteenth century drew to its close, several socialists realized that
if their desired political outcome was not going to come about because it was
inevitable (as Marx and even more so Engels and many of their influential
followers believed), then it would have to be achieved as a result of human
action. Some of the dissidents, such as Lenin, felt it could be *imposed*, and set
out to spur history along through the politico-military efforts of a revolutionary
vanguard. Others felt that it could be made *desirable*, and thus emerge through
the collective efforts of human beings motivated by a belief in a higher good.

Within this latter "revisionist" camp, two distinct strands of thinking
emerged. The first was revolutionary and epitomized by the work of Georges
Sorel.[35] For Sorel, a radical and perhaps violent overthrow of the existing order
seemed the surest path to a better future. Socialism, in this view, would emerge
from "active combat that would destroy the existing state of things."[36] The
second strand of revisionism was democratic and epitomized by the work of
Eduard Bernstein. Like Sorel, Bernstein believed that socialism would emerge
from an active struggle for a better world, but unlike Sorel he thought this struggle could and should take a democratic and evolutionary form. Where Sorel's
work would help lay the groundwork for fascism, Bernstein's would help lay
the groundwork for social democracy.

Bernstein attacked the two main pillars of orthodox Marxism – historical
materialism and class struggle – and argued for an alternative based on the
primacy of politics and cross-class cooperation. His observations about capitalism led him to believe that it was not leading to an increasing concentration
of wealth and the immiseration of society, but rather was becoming increasingly
complex and adaptable. Instead of waiting until capitalism collapsed for socialism to emerge, therefore, he favored trying actively to reform the existing system. In his view, the prospects for socialism depended "not on the decrease but
on the increase of ... wealth," and on the ability of socialists to come up with
"positive suggestions for reform" capable of spurring fundamental change.[37]

Bernstein's loss of belief in the inevitability of socialism led him to appreciate the potential for human will and political action. Orthodox Marxists'
faith in historical materialism, he felt, had bred a dangerous political passivity

[35] Zeev Sternhell, *Neither Right nor Left* (Princeton, NJ: Princeton University Press, 1986), and
   idem with Mario Sznajder and Maia Asheri, *The Birth of Fascist Ideology* (Princeton, NJ:
   Princeton University Press, 1994).
[36] Georges Sorel, *Reflections on Violence* (London: Collier Macmillan, 1950), 50.
[37] Eduard Bernstein, "The Struggle of Social Democracy and the Social Revolution," *Neue Zeit*,
   Jan. 19, 1898.

that would cost them the enthusiasm of the masses. He felt the doctrine of inevitable class struggle shared the same fatal flaws, being both historically inaccurate and politically debilitating. There was actually a natural community of interest between workers and the vast majority of society who suffered from the injustices of the capitalist system, he argued, and socialists should regard dissatisfied elements of the middle classes and peasantry as potential allies ready to be converted to the cause.

Bernstein's arguments were echoed by a small but growing number of dissident socialists across Europe, who shared an emphasis on a political path to socialism rather than its necessity, and on cross-class cooperation rather than class conflict. During the last years of the nineteenth and the first years of the twentieth century, revisionism progressed in fits and starts, within and across several countries, and against continued opposition from both orthodox Marxists and atheoretical pragmatists (who wanted to pursue reforms without rocking the boat). Although Bernstein and his fellow revisionists insisted that they were merely "revising" or "updating" Marxism, their fiercest critics – the defenders of orthodoxy – saw clearly what the revisionists themselves were loath to admit: that they were arguing for a replacement of Marxism with something entirely different. By abandoning historical materialism and class struggle, they were in fact rejecting Marxism as thoroughly as Marx had rejected liberalism a half-century earlier. But the revisionists were not yet ready to accept fully the implications of their views and make a clean break with orthodoxy. The result was growing tension and confusion, which left the international socialist movement, like many of its constituent parties, a house divided against itself. World War I and its aftermath brought the house down.

The vast changes unleashed by the Great War led many on the West European left to reject explicitly the twin pillars of orthodox Marxism – class struggle and historical materialism – and embrace openly their antitheses – communitarianism and the primacy of politics. Revolutionary revisionists finally rejected class struggle upon their realization that workers alone would not make an effective revolutionary vanguard and their recognition of the vast mobilizing power of nationalism. Democratic revisionists' similar conclusions followed from their recognition that workers alone could never yield an electoral majority and that cooperation with non-proletarians was the price of political power. They also recognized the power of nationalism and worried that clinging to orthodox Marxism's emphasis on class conflict and proletarian exclusivity would prevent them from responding to the needs of ordinary citizens. Historical materialism, meanwhile, fell by the wayside when both camps decided that rather than agitating for capitalism's collapse, it made more sense to use the state to fetter the market's destructive and anarchic potential, while exploiting its ability to produce unprecedented material bounty. They thus came to champion a real "third way" between laissez-faire liberalism and Soviet communism, based on a belief that political forces must triumph over economic ones.

Meanwhile, on the other side of the political fence, the nationalist, right-wing protests against the atomization, amoralism, and materialism of the modern liberal, capitalist world that had been growing for decades gained a mass base during the interwar years, and many within these movements began to recognize a community of interest with some of their left-wing counterparts. A common emphasis on "the people" and the nation, a rejection of liberalism and democracy, and a desire for a non-Marxist socialism drew revolutionary revisionists and disgruntled rightists together to produce fascism in some parts of Europe.[38] Indeed, across Europe nationalists began openly referring to themselves as "national" socialists to make clear their commitment to ending the insecurities, injustices, and instabilities that capitalism brought in its wake, while clearly differentiating themselves from their competitors on the left.

Democratic revisionists, running scared of the fascist and national socialist right as well as the communist left, argued that clinging to orthodox Marxism would doom the mainstream left to political oblivion. What was needed was a democratic leftist program that would tap into the needs and demands of the disoriented and discontented European masses. To develop such a program, they returned to the themes and critiques offered by Bernstein and others a generation before: the primacy of politics and the imperative of cross-class cooperation.

Across much of Western Europe by the late 1920s, the two great political movements and ideologies of the nineteenth century, liberalism and Marxism, were out of new ideas and irrelevant to contemporary problems.[39] Fascists, national socialists, and social democrats were active, aggressive, and hungry. The ideological stage was thus set for a transition.

Although obviously differing in critical ways, fascism, national socialism, and social democracy had important similarities that have not been fully appreciated. They all embraced the primacy of politics and touted their desire to use political power to reshape society and the economy. They all appealed to communal solidarity and the collective good. They all built modern, mass political organizations and presented themselves as "people's parties." And they both adopted a middle ground with regard to capitalism – neither hoping for its demise like Marxists nor worshiping it uncritically like many liberals, but seeking a "third way" based on the belief that the state could and should

[38] In some countries (such as France and Italy), an explicit symbiosis occurred, creating, in the words of Zeev Sternhell, a new type of political movement that was neither "right nor left." In other countries, such as Sweden and Germany, left and right merged in somewhat different ways. In the former, the left essentially coopted the themes of the right, producing social democratic hegemony, while in the latter, the Nazis' "reactionary modernism" and emphasis on the "primacy of the political" reflected a distinctively German version of a broader European pattern. The term "reactionary modernism" comes from Jeffrey Herf; see his *Reactionary Modernism* (New York: Cambridge University Press, 1984). In addition, a group of "National Bolsheviks" in Germany developed very similar criticisms of liberal capitalism and democracy as did their counterparts in the "conservative revolution," leading to a convergence around a "German" version of socialism during the Weimar Republic. This will be discussed in Chapters 4 and 6.

[39] Communism was, of course, still a powerful force in many West European countries. However, as later chapters, particularly Chapter 5, will argue, by this time communism had little to offer on either a practical or theoretical level to West European leftists.

control markets without destroying them. These similarities are reflected in the posters shown on the cover of this book. Both come from electoral campaigns in the early 1930s and offer comparable messages: Vote for us and we will provide a new socioeconomic order where the state will guarantee work for all citizens – regardless of class background. (The top poster is from the Swedish Social Democrats and the bottom from the German National Socialists.)

Once one recognizes such similarities, and the ways that these movements represented a rejection of *both* Marxism and liberalism, it becomes easy to understand not only why they were able to exert such a hold over European publics during the interwar years, but also how so many prominent intellectuals could make the seemingly irrational journey from (revisionist) left to (fascist or national socialist) right during the period.

Fascism and national socialism, of course, went down in flames during World War II, at which point social democracy went on to its period of greatest success. Although many have interpreted the postwar settlement as a triumph for liberalism, albeit in a somewhat chastened form, what made Europe work after 1945 actually had far more to do with social democracy. The postwar consensus was based on a dramatic revision in the relationship among states, markets, and society. Unchecked markets were now viewed as dangerous; societal interests were now viewed as trumping private prerogatives; and states were seen as having the right – indeed the duty – to intervene in the economy and society to protect a "common" or "public" interest. After 1945, in other words, people began to perceive states as the guardian of society, and economic imperatives were often forced to take a back seat to social ones. The result was the reconciliation of things long viewed as incompatible: a well-functioning capitalist system, democracy, and social stability. This new order had little grounding in any honest reading of traditional liberal or Marxist doctrine. What it did resemble were the principles and policies advocated by social democrats, and, to a lesser degree, fascists and national socialists, from the 1920s through the 1940s.

The notion that the key to the postwar settlement was its ability to reconcile capitalism, democracy, and social stability is not new. What was once nearly a truism, however, has been forgotten as the old battles between markets and publics have passed into history. As noted previously, one goal of this book, accordingly, is to remind younger generations of just what that settlement consisted of, why it was necessary, and how it came about. A second goal is to reassign some of the credit for it to those who deserve it most, the relatively unknown continental European pioneers of social democracy. Social democracy, this book will show, must be understood as a distinctive ideology and movement, built on the primacy of politics and communitarianism, and representing a non-Marxist socialism. It must also be recognized as the most successful ideology and movement of the twentieth century: Its principles and policies undergirded the most prosperous and harmonious period in European history. And finally, this book will show how a proper understanding of social democracy's history can offer a guide for tackling contemporary

political challenges, which have more in common with those of a century ago
than is generally realized.

The Plan of the Book

The following chapters sketch out this story in detail. The book relies on both
secondary and primary source material, but is envisioned first and foremost as a
work of synthesis and comparative political science rather than original historical research. It presents what might be called a qualitative analytical narrative,[40]
a story that draws on both political and intellectual history to show the interplay
of ideological supply and demand. It is not a comprehensive treatment of the
entire left, but instead focuses on those actors and factors that contributed to
the emergence and evolution of democratic revisionism and social democracy.
It is also not a treatment of the entire labor movement, but rather concentrates
on political parties since they were the key carriers of ideology as well as the
most directly engaged in the struggle for political power. The book focuses on
Germany, Austria, France, Italy, and Sweden rather than on Western Europe
more generally, for a number of reasons. First, since social democracy emerged
out of a revision of orthodox Marxism, I exclude from my study countries such
as England and Spain, where Marxism remained overshadowed by other types
of socialist thinking (such as laborism and anarchism). Second, these five countries include the most important and the most innovative individual socialist
parties within the Second International, and analyzing them as a group provides
a good sense of both the general trends and particular, country-level tendencies
that shaped the development of the international socialist movement during
the late nineteenth and twentieth centuries. Third, since I engage in an explicit
comparison of social democracy and fascism/national socialism, I include those
countries considered to be the birthplace of fascist and national socialist thinking and movements: Germany, Italy, and France. The five countries together
thus offer a varied but coherent picture of Europe's nineteenth and twentieth
century ideological battleground and provide an empirical foundation upon
which arguments with broad historical and geographical scope can be built.

   Chapter 2 explores the background to and foundations of the social democratic movement. It details the growing dissatisfaction with orthodox Marxism
toward the end of the nineteenth century, the consequent opening up of a political space, and the first stirrings of the revisionist movements that arose to
fill it.

   Chapter 3 focuses on how and why democratic revisionism spread throughout Western Europe in the years before the First World War, and how it began to
reshape individual socialist parties, the international socialist movement, and
European politics more generally.

---

[40] Compare with Robert Bates et al., *Analytic Narratives* (Princeton, NJ: Princeton University
   Press, 1998).

Chapter 4 recounts what was happening simultaneously on the other side of the political fence, focusing on the rise of revolutionary revisionism and tracing how and why figures on the European right began agitating for a non-Marxist, "national" socialism.

Chapter 5 discusses the First World War and its consequences, showing how the new political landscape of the 1920s and 1930s helped turn democratic revisionists into full-fledged social democrats. Chapter 6, in turn, discusses how similar factors helped turn revolutionary revisionists into fascists and "socially" minded nationalists into national socialists.

Chapter 7 offers an in-depth examination of the paradigmatic Swedish case, showing how the origins and strength of social democratic hegemony there were rooted in the early conversion of the country's socialist party (the SAP) to social democratic principles and its concomitant ability to coopt many issues and tropes on which the nationalist right rode to power elsewhere.

Chapter 8 takes the story into the second half of the twentieth century, reassessing the nature and significance of Europe's postwar settlement and examining how and why social democracy began to lose its way during the last quarter of the century.

Chapter 9, finally, highlights the implications of the book's central arguments for various scholarly literatures and the contemporary political scene. Far from a topic of mere antiquarian interest, I contend, getting the story of social democracy straight is an indispensable prerequisite for understanding the contours of politics in both the advanced industrial democracies and the developing world today.

2

The Background and the Foundations

In the nineteenth century, Europe underwent an economic, political, and social transformation. The spread of capitalism increased the continent's wealth and dynamism, which in turn fostered the diffusion of European culture and civilization across the globe. The forces that were driving Europe to the height of its power, however, were also generating social and political turmoil. Dissatisfaction with the reigning liberal order grew over the course of the nineteenth century. Ultimately, the practical consequences of unfettered capitalism – dramatic inequalities, social dislocation, and atomization – generated a backlash against liberalism and a search for ideological alternatives. As one of the great observers of the liberalism of the era, L. T. Hobhouse, noted, if "The nineteenth century might be called the age of Liberalism... its close saw the fortunes of that great movement brought to its lowest ebb."[1]

The most important challenge from the left came in the form of Marxism, which during the second half of the century gathered enough adherents to spawn its own political movement. By the time of the Second International, (1889–1914), orthodox Marxism had become the dominant doctrine within most socialist parties.[2] The most distinctive features of this orthodox Marxism were historical materialism and class struggle, which combined to produce a view of history as being propelled forward by economic development and the ever-sharpening class conflict generated by it. Yet by the end of the century, orthodox Marxism was itself in crisis, challenged on both a practical and theoretical level by a growing number of socialists across the continent. Orthodoxy met its earliest and most powerful practical challenge in France, where the existence of democracy and the temptations of cross-class cooperation and participation in bourgeois governments forced many socialists to question it. As the

---

[1] L. T. Hobhouse, *Liberalism* (New York: Oxford University Press, 1964), 110.
[2] This is not true of England and parts of southern Europe, where orthodox Marxism never developed the hold over workers movements that it did in other parts of Western Europe. As noted in Chapter 1, that is one reason why these countries are excluded from this book's analysis.

turn of the century approached, the practical challenge from France fused with an intensifying theoretical challenge from Germany, led by Eduard Bernstein, who attacked orthodoxy's main pillars head on. The combined result of these challenges was that by the beginning of the twentieth century the foundations for an entirely new, non-Marxist version of socialism had been laid.

The Rise and Decline of Orthodox Marxism

Although rooted in Marx's writings, orthodox Marxism really emerged in the years after Marx's death in 1883. What most socialists across the continent came to know, and what the revisionists would later react against, was not so much the work of Marx himself but a particular interpretation of it propagated by his key disciples: Friedrich Engels, his collaborator, and Karl Kautsky, the "pope" of socialism. In simplifying and popularizing Marx's thought for the socialist movement, Engels and Kaustky accentuated (and perhaps exaggerated) the deterministic and scientific aspects of the master's thought and created a doctrine based on the primacy of economic forces in history and the inevitability of class struggle. Indeed, these became the two main pillars of orthodoxy that dominated socialist parties by the late nineteenth century.

The most distinctive aspect of Marx's thought – and the one that lay at the heart of orthodox Marxism – was historical materialism. Marx argued that history was propelled forward by economic development and the class conflict it generated. He thus characterized the ultimate aim of his life's work as "laying bare the economic law of motion of modern society"[3] – showing how economic forces determined the logic and direction of historical evolution.[4] "It is a question of . . . laws," he once put it, "tendencies working with iron necessity towards inevitable results."[5] Since this view implied that the only thing required for achieving socialism's goals was "calm recognition of the historically inevitable,"[6] Marx's view was profoundly comforting. But it also led Marx to devote little time to worrying about the actual transition from

---

[3] Marx, "Preface to the First German Edition of *Das Kapital*, Vol. 1," reprinted in Robert Tucker, ed., *The Marx-Engels Reader* (New York: W. W. Norton, 1978), 297.

[4] Not surprisingly, Marx saw in Charles Darwin a kindred spirit and claimed to have found in his work the "basis in natural history for our view." See Marx's letters to Engels of December 19, 1860, and Ferdinand Lassalle of January 16, 1861, quoted in Alvin W. Gouldner, *The Two Marxisms: Contradictions and Anomalies in the Development of Theory* (New York: Seabury Press, 1980), 72. See also Lawrence Krader, "Theory of Evolution, Revolution and the State: The Critical Relation of Marx to His Contemporaries Darwin, Carlyle, Morgan, Maine, and Kovalevsky," in Eric Hobsbawm, ed., *The History of Marxism*, Vol. 1 (Bloomington, IN: Indiana University Press, 1982).

[5] Marx, "Preface to the First German Edition of *Das Kapital*, Vol. 1," in Tucker, ed., *The Marx-Engels Reader*, 296.

[6] Robert A. Nisbet, *The Quest for Community: A Study in the Ethics of Order and Freedom* (New York: Oxford University Press, 1953), 5.

capitalism to socialism[7] or how socialist parties might encourage or manage it.[8] In Marx's view of history, revolutionaries "did not have to plan ahead or think about how a just society should be organized...because they knew the solution was contained in the problem, and would appear in due course through the inevitable process of dialectical transformation. Midwives do not have to design the babies they deliver."[9] In this vision of socialism, in other words, politics was at best a secondary activity.

Historical materialism was not the only reason Marx neglected politics. He also believed that until the demise of capitalism, politics would be driven by narrow economic interest and the quest for domination. The state would remain at the service of the dominant (bourgeois) class, he believed, so there was little point in devoting much attention to analyzing its functioning or logic.[10] And since society was neatly dividing into two separate and opposed camps, cooperation with other social and political groups made little long-term sense for workers. Furthermore, with the transition to socialism, politics itself would disappear – as the elimination of classes and economic scarcity created harmonious and prosperous communities with no need for political institutions to suppress and mediate conflict.

Marx held, in short, a "negative" view of politics – he believed that with the achievement of economic abundance, the need for politics would wither away. This conviction was something he shared with his liberal antagonists. As Michael Walzer has written:

...it has been the assumption of liberal theorists ever since Hobbes and Locke that once security and welfare were assured, once the utilitarian purposes of politics were achieved, men would turn away from public to private life, to business and family, or to

---

[7] Although Marx himself distinguished between socialism and communism (with the former being an intermediate stage along the way to the latter), especially after the Soviets appropriated the latter term, socialism was most often used to refer to the accepted end state of the international socialist movement. I will thus adhere to that convention here.

[8] The obvious contradiction here, of course, is that if all that was required was a little "midwifery," why build up large, powerful socialist parties in the first place? This is a dilemma that Marxist scholars have grappled with ever since. This contradiction is dealt with throughout his book. See also, for example, Perry Anderson, *In the Tracks of Historical Materialism* (Chicago: University of Chicago Press, 1983); Gouldner, *The Two Marxisms*; James Gregor, *A Survey of Marxism: Problems in Philosophy and the Theory of History* (New York: Random House, 1965); F. R. Hansen, *The Breakdown of Capitalism* (London: Routledge and Kegan Paul, 1985).

[9] Thomas Nagel, "Review of G. A. Cohen's, *If You're an Egalitarian, How Come You're So Rich?* (Cambridge: Harvard University Press, 1999)," in the *Times Literary Supplement*, June 23, 2000, 6.

[10] In addition to the view of the state as the "executive committee of the bourgeoisie," there is also present in some of Marx's writings a view of the state as occasionally having a degree of relative autonomy from the dominant class (relative in the sense that the state must still strive to maintain the ultimate viability of capitalism). See Norbert Bobbio, *Which Socialism? Marxism, Socialism and Democracy* (Oxford, UK: Polity Press, 1987), 61; Martin Carnoy, *The State and Political Theory* (Princeton, NJ: Princeton University Press, 1984), 47; Robert C. Tucker, *The Marxian Revolutionary Idea* (Princeton, NJ: Princeton University Press, 1970), esp. 85ff.

religion and self-cultivation. Indeed, it was this turning away – which might be called legitimate apathy since it rests on the satisfaction of all recognized needs and desires – that would assure the stability of the liberal achievement. Conflict would disappear; the state would become a neutral agency for the administration of security and welfare. This was a liberal even before it was a Marxian vision.[11]

Marx's historical materialism also led him to dismiss the importance of morality and idealism in human history. Capitalism would be overthrown not because it was unjust, but because its internal contradictions made it unsustainable. "Communism," he wrote, "is not for us a *state of affairs* which is to be established, an *ideal* to which reality [will] have to adjust itself"; it was inscribed in the historical process.[12]

This emphasis on the necessity rather than the desirability of socialism was a source of conflict between Marx and other socialist theorists of his day.[13] In *Capital*, for example, Marx scorned Pierre Proudhon's appeal to justice, asking what opinion should "we have of a chemist, who instead of studying the actual laws of the molecular changes in the composition of matter, and on that foundation solving definite problems, claimed to regulate the composition and decomposition of matter by means of 'eternal ideas'?"[14] Marx thought appeals to morality or idealism misleading, since they had no independent existence or validity and were "dependent on and relative to changing material circumstances."[15] Once one realized the primacy of economic forces and structures, the dependent or contingent nature of "morality, religion, metaphysics, [and] all the rest of ideology" would become clear, and "empty talk about consciousness [would] cease, and real knowledge [would] take its place."[16] Those who based the case for socialism on capitalism's immorality, injustice, and corruption thus got the historical causal chain backward. Such conceptions were the product rather than the cause of fundamental social change. "When people speak of ideas that revolutionize society," Marx wrote, "they do but express the fact, that within the old society, the elements of a new one have been created, and that the dissolution of the old ideas keeps even pace with the dissolution of

[11] Michael Walzer, "Politics in the Welfare State," in Irving Howe, ed., *Essential Works of Marxism* (New York: Holt, Rinehart and Winston, 1970), 389. See also Joseph Schwartz, *The Permanence of the Political: A Democratic Critique of the Radical Impulse to Transcend Politics* (Princeton, NJ: Princeton University Press, 1995), esp. 15, 199.

[12] Karl Marx, "The German Ideology," in Tucker, ed., *The Marx-Engels Reader*, 162. Emphasis in the original.

[13] Of course, even though Marx stressed the scientific nature of his critique of capitalism and the materialist nature of his philosophy of history, it is impossible to read his work and not be struck by his moral critique as well. Throughout his writings, one finds powerful descriptions and denunciations of how capitalism violated human freedom, dehumanized workers, and quashed the achievement of human potential.

[14] Quoted in Steven Lukes, *Marxism and Morality* (Oxford, UK: Clarendon Press, 1985), 6–7.

[15] Ibid., 5. See also Marshall Cohen, Thomas Nagel, and Thomas Scanlon, eds., *Marx, Justice, and History* (Princeton, NJ: Princeton University Press, 1980), esp. the essays by Ziyad Husami and Alan Wood.

[16] Marx, "The German Ideology," in Tucker, ed., *The Marx-Engels Reader*, 154–5.

the old conditions of existence.... Life is not determined by consciousness, but consciousness by life."[17]

Friedrich Engels, Marx's collaborator and leading apostle, was especially important in promoting a scientific, deterministic version of Marxism squarely based on the primacy of economic forces in history and the inevitability of class struggle. Although he occasionally bemoaned the vulgarization of Marxism that occurred after Marx's death and (in private) expressed his displeasure with those who put forward overly dogmatic interpretations of the master's teachings,[18] it was through Engels' writings that Marxism "came to mean... a materialist evolutionism.... [where] historical evolution is an aspect of general (natural) evolution, and basically subject to the same 'laws.'"[19] At Marx's funeral, Engels indicated where he believed Marx's true legacy lay by characterizing his friend as the Darwin of socialism – the man who "discovered the laws of development of human history."[20] Economic determinism led Engels to emphasize (again perhaps more than Marx himself) the at best secondary or subsidiary nature of political activity. As he once famously put it, revolutions were "not intentionally and capriciously made, but rather have universally been the necessary consequence of conditions completely independent of the will and leadership of individual parties and entire classes."[21] And once revolution occurred, all politics would fade away:

As soon as there is no longer any social class to be held in subjection... nothing more remains to be repressed and a special repressive force, a state, is no longer necessary. The first act by virtue of which the state really constitutes itself as the representative of the whole of society... is its last independent act as a state. [Under socialism] state interference in social relations becomes... superfluous... and the government of persons is replaced by the administration of things.... The state is not 'abolished.' *It dies out.*[22]

By the time of his death in 1895, Engels had succeeded in establishing this doctrine – aggressively scientific and deterministic and firmly grounded in the

---

[17] Ibid., 155, and Marx and Engels, "The Communist Manifesto," 489, in Tucker, ed., *The Marx-Engels Reader*.

[18] For example, in an oft-quoted letter to J. Bloch, Engels rejected the idea that either he or Marx had ever meant that the "economic element is the only determining one," which he described as a "meaningless, abstract, senseless, phrase." Lucio Colletti, *From Rousseau to Lenin* (New York: New Left Books, 1972), esp.64, and idem, *Bernstein und der Marxismus der Zweiten Internationale* (Frankfurt: Europa Verlag, 1971), 28. Nonetheless, as even the few quotes presented here make clear, there is no doubt that Engels (as well as Marx) consistently insisted on the primacy of economic forces and that in his popular writings in particular Engels presented a view of historical development that was deterministic and materialistic and payed little attention to the role of conscious human action.

[19] George Lichtheim, *Marxism* (London: Routledge and Kegan Paul, 1961), 245–6.

[20] Engels, "Speech at the Graveside of Karl Marx," reprinted in Tucker, ed. *The Marx-Engels Reader*.

[21] Engels, "Socialism, Utopian and Scientific" (selections from Anti-Dürhing), reprinted in Carl Cohen, ed., *Communism, Fascism and Democracy* (New York: Random House, 1968), 125.

[22] Ibid., 139.

primacy of economic forces and the concomitant necessity of class struggle – as orthodox Marxism.

If Engels was responsible for codifying this Marxist orthodoxy, Karl Kautsky was largely responsible for its popularization. (Indeed, some trace the origins of the terms "Marxist" and "Marxism" to Kautsky.[23]) After Engels' death, Kautsky became the dominant intellectual of the Second International, and his writings were often the first, and sometimes the only, interpretation of Marx available to an entire generation of socialists in Germany and elsewhere.[24] Although Kautsky's views evolved over time, "it was thanks to his interpretive works that the stereotype known as scientific socialism – the evolutionist, determinist, and scientific form of Marxism – became universally accepted in its main lines."[25]

Before he was a Marxist, Kautsky had been a Darwinist, and this inheritance shaped his interpretation. "No one could or would even wish to dispute," he wrote in an obituary, "that [Marx's theory] gave science the same importance as Darwin's theory, and just as the latter dominated the natural sciences, so Marx's theories dominate the social and economic sciences."[26] Similarly, in explaining the significance of Marx's materialist conception of history, Kautsky noted that, "Capital turned theoretical socialism into a distinct science which one can perhaps define as the study of the laws of evolution of modern society."[27] Kautsky continually stressed the "scientific" nature of Marxism not only to differentiate it from utopian socialism and other "idealistic" ideologies, but also because, like Marx and Engels, he had a boundless faith in the capacity of science to point the way toward fundamental truth.

Influenced by the experience of the Great Depression of 1873–95, Kautsky's writings depict a capitalist system characterized by increasing class conflict, chronic depressions, and recurring crises and careening toward its own demise.

[23] E.g., Georges Haupt, *Aspects of International Socialism, 1871–1914* (Cambridge, UK: Cambridge University Press, 1986), 13.
[24] The amount of work on Kautsky and his interpretation of Marxism is huge. Ingrid Gilcher-Hotley, *Das Mandat des Intellektuellen: Karl Kautsky und die Sozialdemokratie* (Berlin: Siedler, 1986); Walter Holzheuer, *Karl Kautskys Werk als Weltanschauung* (München: C. H. Beck, 1972); Hans Kelsen, *Sozialismus und Staat: Eine Untersuchung der Politischen Theorie des Marxismus* (Leipzig: C. L. Herschfeld, 1923); Leszek Kolakowski, "German Orthodoxy: Karl Kautsky," in Kolakowski, *Main Currents of Marxism*, Vol. 2: *The Golden Age* (New York: Oxford University Press, 1978); Erich Matthias, "Kautsky und der Kautskyanismus: Die Funktion der Ideologie in der deutschen Sozialdemokratie vor dem ersten Weltkrieg," *Marxismusstudien*, 2, 1957; David Morgon, "The Orthodox Marxists: The First Generation of a Tradition," in R. J. Bullen, H. Pogge von Strandmann, and A. B. Polonsky, eds., *Ideas into Politics* (London: Croom Helm, 1984); Massimo Salvadori, *Karl Kautsky and the Socialist Revolution, 1880–1938* (London: NLB, 1979); Gary Steenson, *Karl Kautsky: Marxism in the Classical Years* (Pittsburgh, PA: University of Pittsburgh Press, 1978).
[25] Kolakowski, "German Orthodoxy," 31–2.
[26] Obituary of Marx in *Die Neue Zeit*, 1, 1883, quoted in Haupt, *Aspects of International Socialism* 11.
[27] Quoted in Rogers H. Kendell, *Before the Revisionist Controversy: Kautsky, Bernstein and the Meaning of Marxism* (New York: Garland, 1992), 22.

"Irresistible economic forces," he wrote, "lead with the certainty of doom to the shipwreck of capitalist production."[28] The role of socialist parties was thus not to drive the transition to socialism but to help workers understand the nature of capitalist society and prepare them for the inevitable class struggle that would bring it crashing down. Hence Kautsky's famous characterization of the German socialist party as

...a revolutionary party, but not a revolution-making one. We know that our goal can only be achieved through a revolution [and] we also know how little it is within our power to make this revolution, as little as it is possible for our opponents to hinder it.... [T]he revolution can not be arbitrarily made by us...and we are just as incapable of saying when and under what conditions and in what form it would appear.[29]

Although it is perhaps hard for us to understand today, if one looks back at the conditions both inside and outside the socialist movement during the 1870s and 1880s, the appeal of orthodox Marxism becomes easier to comprehend. In order to eliminate the continuing hold of the "immature" philosophies of anarchists, Lassaleans, Proudhonians, Saint Simonians, and others on socialist movements, Marx and his disciples needed to put forward a simple, powerful, and optimistic vision capable of winning converts across the globe. Thus orthodox Marxism's two pillars – historical materialism and class struggle – together provided a clear and dramatic vision of history working inevitably toward socialism's victory.[30] In addition, a long-lasting depression took a heavy toll on European societies during this period and made orthodox Marxism's stress on the misery, inefficiency, and imminent collapse of capitalism easy to believe. Repression of socialist parties, meanwhile, gave plausibility to the view that class conflict was inevitable and the bourgeois state was of little value. In short, by providing workers with a conviction that history was on their side and with a collective identity as the group tasked with propelling history forward, orthodox Marxism helped many socialists weather dark and depressing times and united and strengthened the young movement for the struggle ahead. As one contemporary observer noted, "The theory that socialism was bound to come, like some unpreventable natural phenomenon; that to spread its teaching was to spread the 'truth,' gave the socialist movement a propelling force that it could not otherwise have obtained."[31]

---

[28] Kautsky, *The Class Struggle* (Chicago: Charles Kerr, 1910), 119. One can find these views presented in any number of Kautsky's popular writings. See, for example, Kautsky, *The Capitalist Class* (New York: National Executive Committee of the Socialist Labor Party, 1918); idem, *The Economic Doctrines of Karl Marx* (New York: Macmillan, 1936); idem, *The Working Class* (New York: New York Labor News Co., 1918).

[29] Kautsky, *Der Weg zur Macht* (Berlin, 1920), 57.

[30] As Engels himself once noted, he and Marx had perhaps focused so heavily on the economic determinants of historical development because they felt they "had to emphasize the main principle vis-à-vis [their] adversaries, who denied it, and we had not always the time, the place or the opportunity to give their due the other elements involved in the interaction." Letter from Engels to J. Bloch, in Colletti, "Bernstein and the Marxism of the Second International," in idem, *From Rousseau to Lenin*, 64.

[31] Werner Sombart, *Socialism and the Socialist Movement* (London: J. M Dent, 1909), 90.

But as the turn of the century neared, the situation confronting socialists across the continent began to change – prompting many to question whether the orthodox view was still appropriate. One source of dissatisfaction was the fact that many orthodox Marxist predictions were simply not coming true. After the depression of the 1870s and 1880s, capitalism developed renewed vigor in the 1890s. Helped by revolutions in both transportation and communication, a version of globalization swept the world, swelling trade and capital flows to levels that were not reached again until the end of the twentieth century; European firms grew and expanded their global reach, while labor movements gained enough traction to press for changes in the political economy. Such trends made prophecies of general economic collapse increasingly unbelievable. Other orthodox Marxist predictions regarding capitalist development – such as the immiseration of workers, the disappearance of small farming and businesses, and the contraction and eventual collapse of the middle classes – were also belied by the era's economic realities.

Orthodox Marxism also had real failings as a guide to constructive political action. Socialist parties had become powerful actors in a number of European countries by the end of the nineteenth century, yet orthodoxy could not furnish them with a strategy for using their power to achieve their ultimate goals. To socialist intellectuals and activists eager to play a role in the formation of a better world, orthodoxy offered only a counsel of passivity – of waiting for the contradictions within capitalism to emerge and bring the system down, which was coming to seem both increasingly unlikely and increasingly unpalatable.

A final problem stemmed from the widening gulf between orthodox Marxism's laissez-faire economism and the psychopolitical needs of mass populations under economic and social stress. The economic development and globalization of the late nineteenth and early twentieth century generated immense social dislocation, fragmentation, and atomization. The result of such societal upheavals was a renaissance of communitarian thought and the rise of nationalist movements, as Europeans searched for ways to reintegrate their societies and restore a sense of purpose to the "disenchanted" world in which they now lived.[32] These developments placed orthodox Marxism – with its conviction that capitalist development must be allowed to transform societies ruthlessly; its concomitant lack of concern for history's losers (for example, the peasants and the "old" middle classes); its emphasis, even welcoming, of societal conflict; and its denigration of nationalism – increasingly out of touch with many of the most powerful intellectual and cultural trends of the day.

It was in response to such frustrations that socialist revisionism emerged. Two main strands were put forward, each of which attempted to "correct"

---

[32] Another interesting outgrowth of this era was the birth of sociology – the academic study of society. Concerned with understanding and counteracting the societal problems of the day, many prominent intellectuals and academics engaged in path-breaking studies of modern society. Nisbet, *The Quest for Community*; idem, *The Sociological Tradition* (New York: Basic Books, 1966); Steven Siedman, *Liberalism and the Origin of European Social Theory* (Berkeley, CA: University of California Press, 1983).

orthodox Marxism and form the basis for a new movement capable of meeting contemporary challenges. Revolutionary revisionism, which was epitomized by Georges Sorel and which played a key role in the development of fascism, will be discussed in Chapter 4. The following section discusses the practical and theoretical orgins of the other, democratic strand of revisionism.

France: The Beginnings of Democratic Revisionism in Practice

France's first truly Marxist party, the Parti Ouvrier Français (POF), was born in 1879 under the tutelage of two of France's best-known Marxists, Jules Guesde and Paul Lafargue.[33] Guesde and Lafargue championed a particularly crude version of orthodox Marxism in which the primacy of economic forces in history and the inevitability of class conflict were front and center.[34] Both insisted that "the capitalist mode of production would give way to socialism not because of its injustice, but because of its self-destructive internal logic,"[35] and claimed that earlier French socialists who believed that "man could be changed by moral sermons"[36] simply did not understand the logic of historical development. As one observer put it, "French Marxists envisaged themselves as mere thermometers indicating the boiling point reached by the masses under the pressure of the economic phenomena which victimize them."[37] This led them, predictably, to denigrate political work and argue that existing political institutions (in this case, the democracy of the French Republic) were of little value. As Lafargue once put it with his characteristic bluntness, "The bourgeois republican order is the most corrupt and dishonest regime which could possibly exist."[38] To believe, therefore, that it could be used to fundamentally improve the life of

---

[33] Interestingly, despite their being among France's best-known advocates of Marxism, neither Guesde nor Lafargue had extensive firsthand knowledge of Marx's oeuvre nor much in the way of sophisticated economic or philosophical training (this despite the fact that Lafargue was Marx's son-in-law). On the third of the POF's founding fathers, see Joy Hudson Hall, "Gabriel Deville and the Development of French Socialism" (Ph.D. Dissertation, Auburn University, 1983).

[34] Typical is Robert Wohl's characterization of Guesde as representing "a distorted French reflection of Kautsky's Marxist orthodoxy," and Leszek Kolakowski's assessment of Lafargue as "the French Marxist...closest to German orthodoxy." See Wohl, *French Communism in the Making, 1914–1924* (Palo Alto, CA: Stanford University Press, 1966), 435, and Kolakowski, *Main Currents of Marxism*, Vol. 2: *The Golden Age*, 141.

[35] George Lichtheim, *Marxism in Modern France* (New York: Columbia University Press, 1966); Thomas Moodie, "The Parti Ouvrier Français, 1871–1893" (Ph.D. Dissertation, Columbia University, 1966); Aaron Noland, *The Founding of the French Socialist Party* (Cambridge, MA: Harvard University Press, 1956); Robert Stuart, *Marxism at Work: Ideology, Class, and French Socialism During the Third Republic* (New York: Cambridge University Press, 1992), 332.

[36] Paul Lafargue, *Economic Evolution* (Chicago: Charles Kerr, 189?), 3–4.

[37] Stuart, *Marxism at Work*, 60, 330.

[38] Guesde (1886), quoted in Louis Levine, *Syndicalism in France* (New York: Columbia University Press, 1912), 56.

workers, was an illusion. Or, as Guede put it, "in multiplying reforms, one only multiplies shams."[39]

The hardline orthodox Marxism of the POF and in particular its denigration of democracy and reform work set the stage for a dynamic that would plague French socialism through the late nineteenth and early twentieth centuries: the splitting (and concomitant weakening) of the movement over differing views of the viability of orthodox Marxism and the value of democracy. Already by 1882, a group of socialists led by Benoît Malon and Paul Brousse, who believed that the POF's insistence on the primacy of economic forces and inevitability of class conflict was leading French socialists to ignore the real possibilities for reform and even fundamental change offered by the Republic, split off to found a new party, the Fédération des Travailleurs Socialistes de France. Because of their faith in the possibilities offered by the Republic, Guesde mockingly referred to Malon, Brousse, and their followers as "Possibilists," a label that they in turn embraced.

The differences between the Possibilists and the POF were highlighted by the Boulanger crisis of 1889.[40] In response to a de facto slow-motion coup attempt by General Georges Boulanger, the Possibilists rushed to the defense of the Third Republic, attacking Boulanger and working against his candidates at the polls; they also committed themselves to supporting whatever pro-Republic candidate had the best chance of success, even if that meant helping another party. The POF, in contrast, refused to expend political capital defeating Boulanger, since it claimed not to see much difference between his dictatorial aims and "bourgeois" democracy. Guesde, for example, argued that "The shoulder strapper Boulanger and the employer Jacques both belong to the same enemy class which for a century has kept you, proletarian France, under a regime of hunger and lead."[41] And Lafargue claimed that while reactionaries like Boulanger were "wolves in wolves' clothing," Republicans were simply "wolves in sheep's clothing [who] camouflaged the mechanisms of exploitation behind false promises of universal freedom and equality."[42] Indeed, the POF saved most of its ire for defectors from orthodoxy, spending more time attacking the Possibilists, as one observer notes, than "all the other [French] political movements combined."[43]

Despite having become a successful political force in France during the 1880s, in later years the Possibilists fractured and declined.[44] The POF, on the other

[39] Ibid.
[40] On the Boulanger crisis and the threat to the Third Republic, see J. P. T. Bury, *France 1814–1940* (London: Methuen, 1949); Alfred Cobban, *A History of Modern France*, Vol. 3 (Middlesex, UK: Penguin, 1986); Theodore Zeldin, *France: 1848–1945* (Oxford, UK: Clarendon Press, 1973).
[41] Quoted in Harold Weinstein, *Jean Jaurès* (New York: Columbia University Press, 1936), 18.
[42] Lafargue (1900), quoted in Stuart, *Marxism at Work*, 230.
[43] Ibid., 35.
[44] In fact, Possibilism's very success contributed to its decline. In particular, the election of several Possibilists to the Paris municipal council in 1887 led to dissension within the party. Some began to believe that the party was becoming too heavily focused on elections and reform work and was, as a result, ignoring the larger goals of socialist organizing and transformation. These dissidents

hand, remained, but the reality of French political life forced the party to accept many of the stances that the Possibilists had urged on it years before. In particular, although the POF managed to survive, it suffered electorally, and to ensure its political survival the party realized it needed to spend more time on practical politics, particularly at the local level. A reorientation proved successful, and the POF captured a growing number of municipal governments during the 1890s. The party thereby found itself increasingly drawn into developing and managing local welfare policies and institutions, practices for which its leaders had vociferously attacked the Possibilists only a few years earlier. In fact, in the municipalities in which it ruled, the POF devoted itself wholeheartedly to providing libraries, soup kitchens, school lunches, old-age and sickness pensions – the whole range of policies and services associated with the welfare state.[45]

The reality of French politics also led the POF to move away from orthodox views of societal development and relations, particularly with regard to the peasantry. By the early 1890s, it had become increasingly clear that, contrary to Marx's predictions, the peasantry in France was not declining and therefore represented a major source of potential votes. At the POF's 1892 congress in Marseilles, accordingly, the party put forward a program of agrarian reforms that among other things promised small peasants that their land would not be collectivized. At the party's 1894 congress in Nantes, the POF went even further, pledging to expand its efforts on behalf of the peasantry.[46] Lafargue delivered the key address on the agrarian issue, and argued that "the small field is the tool of the peasant as the plane is to the carpenter and the scalpel is to the surgeon. The peasant, carpenter, and surgeon exploit no one with their instruments of labor; thus [they should] not fear seeing [these instruments] taken away from them by . . . socialist[s]."[47]

Lafargue and Guesde tried to claim that this new agrarian program did not represent any fundamental deviation from orthodoxy, but few were convinced by such protestations, and leading orthodox figures in the Second International criticized the POF accordingly.[48] Engels characterized the POF's program as

grouped themselves around J. Allemane and became known as "Allemanists"; in 1890, they left and formed a socialist party of their own (Parti Socialiste Ouvrier Revolutionnaire, PSOR). This division increased confusion within the workers' movement. By the early 1890s, there were four socialist parties in France: the POF, the Possibilists, the Allemanists, and the insurrectionary Blanquists, as well as a number of independent socialist deputies.

[45] On the party's municipal socialism and its implications for party development, see R. Baker, "A Regional Study of Working Class Organization in France: Socialism in the Nord, 1870–1924" (Ph.D. Dissertation, Stanford University, 1967).

[46] Raymond Anthony Jonas, "From Radical Republic to the Social Republic: On the Origins and Nature of Socialism in Rural France, 1871–1914" (Ph.D. Dissertation, University of California, Berkeley, 1985); Carl Landauer, "The Guesdists and the Small Farmer: Early Erosion of French Marxism," *International Review of Social History*, 6, 1961; Hans Georg Lehmann, *Die Agrarfrage in Der Theorie und Praxis der Deutschen und Internationalen Sozialdemokratie* (Tübingen: J. C. B. Mohr, 1970).

[47] Quoted in Barbara Mitchell, *The Practical Revolutionaries: A New Interpretation of French Anarchosyndicalism* (New York: Greenwood Press, 1987), 162.

[48] Ibid., 163, and Moodie, "The Parti Ouvrier Français," 222ff.

"inconsistent, futile, and opportunistic." "Bluntly speaking," he wrote, "in view of the small farmers' economic position . . . we can win him now or in the near future only by giving him promises which we know we cannot keep. . . . But it is not in our interest to win the farmer . . . and to have him defect from our ranks . . . when we fail to keep our promises. The farmer who expects us to perpetuate his dwarf property is not acceptable to us as a party member."[49] Yet despite such (correct) criticisms of the party's program as representing a dramatic break with orthodoxy, the POF refused to change course and indeed many now found themselves criticizing the defenders of orthodoxy for being out of touch with the actual needs and demands of the party. As one party member wrote to Guesde about the attacks by Engels and Kautsky. "This is always the trouble with those who oppose our program . . . they never offer anything positive. . . . the fundamentalists have produced no idea, no plan, nor have they told us what their method would be."[50]

But if the reality of electoral politics and nature of French society caused the POF to abandon some hardline positions, the Dreyfus Affair caused an even more extensive and open questioning of many of the key components of orthodoxy. In 1894, Alfred Dreyfus, a Jewish captain in the French army, was found guilty of treason in a secret court martial and sent off to life imprisonment on Devil's Island.[51] There he probably would have died, but for a later investigation by a new chief of army intelligence who uncovered strong evidence that a Major Esterhazy was guilty of the crimes of which Dreyfus had been accused. Since the army was more interested in protecting its image than in getting to the truth of the matter, Esterhazy was acquitted despite the new evidence. Once again the story might have ended there, but in January 1898 Émile Zola published his famous condemnation of the army's actions (*"J'accuse!"*) and set off a political firestorm. The right viewed the controversy over Dreyfus as a conspiracy by Jews, Freemasons, and other "enemies" of France to discredit the army and the country's other traditional structures and institutions, while the left saw in the right's reaction a potentially deadly attack on the foundations of the Third Republic. At the height of the controversy, the battle lines in French society – between monarchists and Republicans, the Church and secularists, and anti-Semites and humanists – were drawn more sharply than ever. What was at issue in the Dreyfus Affair, therefore, was less the guilt or innocence of a particular individual than the desirability and future of the Republic.

---

[49] Friedrich Engels, "Die Bauernfrage in Frankreich und Deutschland," *Die Neue Zeit*, 10, 13, 1894–5, reprinted in Karl Marx and Friedrich Engels, *Werke* (Berlin: Dietz Verlag, 1972), Vol. 22, 3, 501, and Landauer, "The Guesdists," 215.

[50] Quoted in Landauer, "The Guesdists," fn. 2, 217.

[51] The literature on the Affair is huge. Recent entries include Michael Burns, *France and the Dreyfus Affair* (Boston: St. Martin's Press, 1999); Eric Cahm, *The Dreyfus Affair in French Society and Politics* (New York: Longman, 1996); Leslie Derfler, *The Dreyfus Affair* (Westport, CT: Greenwood Press, 2002); Alain Pagès, ed., *Emile Zola, The Dreyfus Affair: J'accuse and Other Writings* (New Haven, CT: Yale University Press, 1996).

The controversy thus forced socialists to confront head on their views about democracy. Should they defend the Republic because democracy was critical to the achievement of socialism, or stay on the sidelines because the fate of the bourgeois state did not really concern them and had little to do with socialism's ultimate victory in any case? On one side stood Guesde and Lafargue, who simply could not bring themselves to defend the bourgeois Republic and accept the open modification of their understanding of socialism which that defense would entail. They insisted that "the proletarians have nothing to do with this battle which is not theirs."[52] On the other side stood those for whom the institutions and ideals of the Republic were a critical component of their social-ist vision. The undisputed leader of this camp was Jean Jaurès, who argued that

...the democratic Republic is not, as our self-styled doctrinaires of Marxism so often say, a purely bourgeois form...it heralds Socialism, it prepares for it, contains it implic-itly to some extent, because only Republicanism can lead to Socialism by legal evolution without break of continuity.[53]

Jaurès' defense of the Republic during the Dreyfus Affair brought him into the political spotlight. Indeed, from then until his assassination in 1914, he became one of the most important and beloved figures in the French and international socialist movements – and a champion of a vision of socialism that, although he himself often denied it, diverged fundamentally from orthodox Marxism.

Jaurès argued that socialism should be viewed not as the consequence of inevitable economic development and class conflict, but rather as a possible result of the work of socialists themselves – who, motivated by their belief in a higher good, would use the democratic system to attract adherents and begin changing society from within. Indeed, Jaurès viewed socialism as the nat-ural expansion of the principles of the French Revolution; it would, he argued, "give the declaration of the Rights of Man its full meaning,"[54] transforming bourgeois ideals "into a higher form of social and economic justice."[55] Jaurès believed that it was "contrary to common sense to suppose that the social-ist idea could assert itself automatically, without the aid of human faith and enthusiasm.... Socialism would not exist without the forces set in motion by capitalism...but it would also not exist if it were not for the conscious will of humanity, a thirst for freedom and justice and inspired by the energy to transform the opportunities offered by capitalism into reality."[56]

[52] Quoted in J. P. Mayer, *Political Thought in France: From the Revolution to the Fourth Republic* (London: Routledge and Kegan Paul, 1943), 99.

[53] Quoted in David Thomson, *Democracy in France: The Third Republic* (New York: Oxford University Press, 1946), 49–50.

[54] Jean Jaurès, "From the Rights of Man to Socialism," in Irving Howe, ed., *Essential Works of Socialism* (New York: Holt, Rinehart and Winston, 1970), 103.

[55] Quoted in Joel Colton, *Lèon Blum: Humanist in Politics* (New York: Alfred Knopf, 1966), 19.

[56] Kolakowsi, *Main Currents of Marxism*, Vol. 2: *The Golden Age*, 127.

Jaurès argued that in the struggle for socialism, democracy was the movement's most valuable "instrument of progress [since it represented] the best means ever devised for peaceful social change."[57] Socialists could use the democratic system to effect a peaceful, gradual transformation of the existing order – a process that Jaurès referred to as "revolutionary evolution."[58] To set this process in motion, socialists needed to focus their attention on winning the support of the great mass of French citizens: "The great social changes that are called revolutions," Jaurès noted, "cannot, or rather can no longer, be accomplished by a minority. A revolutionary minority, no matter how intelligent and energetic, is not enough in modern times to bring about a revolution. The co-operation and adhesion of a majority, and an immense majority, is needed."[59]

Jaurès' conviction that socialism could and should have broad appeal was based on his belief that at its core, socialism contained "an impassioned moral appeal, a new and more perfect expression of man's eternal thirst for justice, unity and brotherly love."[60] For this and other reasons, Jaurès rejected orthodoxy's vision of class struggle. "For the first time since the beginning of human history," he wrote, "a great social upheaval will have for its aim not the substitution of one class for another, but the destruction of class and the inauguration of a universal humanity."[61] Rightly understood, socialism should appeal "not to a narrow faction" of society, but to humanity itself, and its achievement should be the consequence not "of a violent and exclusive agitation of a social fraction, but . . . of a national movement."[62] Jaurès thus urged socialists to focus their attention not merely on workers, but rather on the myriad groups suffering most directly from the injustices of capitalism (such as small producers and peasants), and he believed socialists should work with almost any group genuinely committed to positive change – including the bourgeoisie, whom he often argued had been a force for progress.

Although Jaurès maintained that his vision of socialism did not contradict orthodoxy, its defenders thought differently and heaped nothing but scorn on him. In a famous debate on this topic, Lafargue correctly pointed out the fundamental difference between Jaurès' and the orthodox view of socialism, noting that:

The course of history, the line of progress from earliest origins to the eve of socialism had been determined by material evolution alone – by economic transformations and their consequent social struggles. . . . in their drive toward communism, the masses responded not to the misty ideal of justice but to hard economic realities . . . and

---

[57] Quoted in Harvey Goldberg, *The Life of Jean Jaurès* (Madison, WI: University of Wisconsin Press, 1962), 289.

[58] Jaurès derived the term from his reading of Marx.

[59] Jaurès, "Revolutionary Majorities" in Jean Jaurès, *Studies in Socialism*, Mildred Minturn, ed. and trans. (New York: G. P. Putnam's Sons, 1906), 51.

[60] Kolakowski, *Main Currents of Marxism*, 116.

[61] Jaurès, "The Necessity for a Majority," in Minturn, ed. and trans., *Studies in Socialism*, 102.

[62] Weinstein, *Jean Jaurès*, 54.

their success was assured not by their moral claims but by the relentless dialectic of history.[63]

Yet ultimately the obvious attractions of the Republic won out and Jaurès was able to convince a majority of French socialists that their overriding goal should be protecting it from anti-Dreyfus forces. With socialist support, a new pro-Republic government was elected in 1899 under René Waldeck-Rousseau, who then paid back the favor by asking a socialist named Alexandre Millerand to join his cabinet. This request, however, triggered a full-fledged crisis within the socialist movement, since the cross-class cooperation and acceptance of the bourgeois state that this would entail challenged orthodoxy head on.

Millerand was a protégé of Jaurès (with roots in the Possibilism of Malon) and had long advocated a dramatic revision of socialism. He rejected orthodox Marxism's emphasis on economic developments and class struggle, arguing instead that the achievement of socialism required "the Socialist party endeavor[ing] to capture the government through universal suffrage." He believed that those who recoiled from full engagement with the institutions of the "bourgeois" state ran the risk of dooming socialism to insignificance: "To put the people off to the mysterious date when a sudden miracle will change the face of the world, or day by day, reform by reform, by a patient or stubborn effort to win step by step all progress – those are the two methods we must choose between."[64] Joining a non-socialist government was the natural consequence of such views, and so he accepted Waldeck-Rousseau's offer, thereby becoming the first European socialist ever to join a bourgeois government.[65] This move outraged Guesde, Lafargue, and many others. Since ministrialism – the policy of socialists joining a bourgeois government – implied the viability of a political path to socialism and the desirability, if not necessity, of alliances with non-proletariat groups, it constituted, as one opponent noted, "an egregious violation of the fundamental doctrine of the class struggle," and an implicit rejection of the view that socialism would come about only as a result of the working of ineluctable economic forces.[66]

The seriousness of Millerand's move was reflected in the convocation in 1899 of France's first all-socialist congress since the split between the POF and the Possibilists back in 1882. Not surprisingly, at the congress Jaurès emerged as the strongest defender of Millerand and his larger strategy, reminding his audience

---

[63] Goldberg, *The Life of Jean Jaurès*, 81, 113, 284–5. See also Jean Jaurès, "Idealism in History," in Albert Fried and Ronald Sanders, eds., *Socialist Thought: A Documentary History* (Edinburgh, UK: Edinburgh University Press, 1964), 410.

[64] Millerand, "French Reformist Socialism," reprinted in R. C. K. Ensor, *Modern Socialism* (New York: Harper and Brothers, 1904), quote on 64.

[65] In fact, there had been a previous example of this occurrence in France in 1848 but it happened under exceptional circumstances when Louis Blanc joined a government formed as the result of revolution. It is also important to note that Millerand accepted this role in the government as an individual and not in direct consultation with or with the support of his party or the socialist movement more generally.

[66] Édouard Valliant, quoted in Noland, *The Founding of the French Socialist Party*, 106.

that Guesde had been so convinced of the righteousness of orthodoxy and the inevitability of capitalism's collapse that he had predicted that socialism would arrive by 1900. "If we can't predict exactly when and how capitalism will collapse," Jaurès argued, "[we need to] work for those reforms which... will prepare the way" for socialism.[67] Guesde and other opponents of Millerand needed to take account of changing times and update their views accordingly: "Once we had to cut through the false teaching of the iron law of wages, which would have discouraged the workers from struggling to improve their conditions; now we have to cut through the equally false notion of the iron law of the State.... We must fight not from a futile distance, but from the very heart of the citadel."[68]

The outcome of the congress was ambiguous. Two resolutions were adopted, the first declaring the participation of socialists in a bourgeois government incompatible with the principle of class struggle, and the second saying that under "exceptional circumstances" such a tactic might be permitted. The controversy thus continued to simmer, and in fact spread from France across the European continent – since it crystallized in practice the theoretical challenge to orthodox Marxism that Eduard Bernstein was simultaneously raising in Germany.

Germany: The Origins of Democratic Revisionist Theory

As was the case in France, a large gap between the theory and practice of the socialist movement opened up in Germany during the last years of the nineteenth century. The gap had its origins in the early years of SPD's history, particularly during the period of the antisocialist laws (1878–90). Repression by the government had strengthened those who viewed the bourgeois state as socialism's implacable enemy, and a lengthy depression served to convince many that the collapse of capitalism was right around the corner. At the same time, however, the SPD's electoral fortunes improved greatly and the involvement of party activists in day-to-day politics increased. This somewhat schizophrenic combination was reflected in the program that the party adopted at its congress at Erfurt in 1891.

The most striking feature of the SPD's Erfurt program was its dualism.[69] The first, theoretical section was drafted mainly by Karl Kautsky and adhered closely

---

[67] Goldberg, *The Life of Jean Jaurès*, 261–2. Also Noland, *The Founding of the French Socialist Party*, 103–5.

[68] Goldberg, *The Life of Jean Jaurès*, 261–2.

[69] Helga Grebing, *The History of the German Labour Movement* (Dover, NH: Berg, 1969), 75–80; Harry Marks, "The Sources of Reformism in the Social Democratic Party of Germany, 1890–1914," *Journal of Modern History*, 11, September 1939; Hans-Josef Steinberg, *Sozialismus und deutsche Sozialdemokratie: Zur Ideologie der Partei vor dem 1. Weltkrieg* (Berlin: J. H. W. Dietz, 1979), 40–70. For an English translation of the program, see Bertrand Russell, *German Social Democracy* (New York: Simon and Schuster, 1965), 137–41.

to the orthodox Marxism he championed.[70] It consisted largely of an analysis of the deleterious consequences of economic development for the proletariat and painted a grim picture of the future of capitalism. The program's second section, written primarily by Eduard Bernstein, concentrated on the practical demands of the party. It was essentially a laundry list of reforms (including universal manhood suffrage for all elections, compensation for elected officials, the liberalization of labor laws, a declaration that religion was a private affair, the secularization of schools, and graduated income and property taxes), most of which could be supported by progressive liberals. No real attempt was made to tie the two halves of the program together, and so the relationship between the orthodox Marxism that the party espoused and the practical demands that it made on behalf of its constituents remained unclear. Commenting on this divergence between the party's theory and praxis, Paul Kampffmeyer noted that: "On the one hand they heap anathema after anathema upon bourgeois society; on the other they labor with burning zeal to patch up and improve it."[71]

As long as the SPD was under the shadow of the antisocialist laws and did not play a significant role in German political life, the contradiction was relatively unproblematic. But as the restrictions were removed, the German economy recovered, and the SPD's electoral fortunes continued to wax, increasing numbers of socialists began to chafe at orthodox Marxism's limitations on political action. Even though the SPD firmly rejected insurrectionary activity, it did not really value parliamentary work either. Kautsky, for example, argued that "demanding the democratization of all public institutions and improving the social conditions of workers within the existing state and social order [is] at the same time nonsense as well as an abandonment of the entire earlier character of our movement."[72] And the party's leader, August Bebel, asserted, "[W]hoever believes that we can reach the final goal of socialism through the present-day parliamentary-constitutional means, either doesn't know [this system] or is a charlatan [*Betrüger*]."[73] He further stated, "The purpose of our participation in the Reichstag was merely to demonstrate to the masses that the bourgeoisie will not even satisfy their most elementary needs."[74]

As time passed, party leaders began to appreciate the advantages electoral and parliamentary participation offered and thus began to soften their views. But despite this shift to "ambivalent parliamentarism,"[75] the party continued

---

[70] In fact, it was an almost verbatim recapitulation of chapter 4, paragraph 7, of Marx's *Capital*.

[71] Paul Kampffmeyer, "Schrittweise Sozialisierung Oder Gewaltsame Sprengung der Kapitalistischen Wirtschaftsordnung," *Sozialistische Monatshefte*, 10, 1899, 466.

[72] Quoted in Gilcher-Hotley: *Das Mandat des Intellektuellen*, 109.

[73] Quoted in Gustav Seeber, "Wahlkämpfe, Parlamentsarbeit und Revolutionäre Politik," in Horst Bartel, ed., *Marxismus und Deutsche Arbeiterbewegung* (Berlin: Dietz, 1970), 282.

[74] Quoted in David Rosen, "German Social Democracy Between Bismarck and Bernstein: Georg von Vollmar and the Reformist Controversy, 1890–1895" (Ph.D. Dissertation, University of Wisconsin, 1975), 95.

[75] Vernon Lidtke, *The Outlawed Party: Social Democracy in Germany, 1878–1890* (Princeton, NJ: Princeton University Press, 1966).

to reject the idea that political work could be the primary motor of socialist transformation. A similar gulf grew between the party's official view of the class struggle and the political realities of fin-de-siècle German political life. For example, making arguments similar to those winning out in France at the same time, Bavarian SPD leader Georg von Vollmar argued strenuously that the party needed to expand its appeal and turn its attention to the peasantry.[76] In 1892, he got his regional party to adopt its own agricultural program, which put peasants and workers on a par with each other and declared the SPD to be the party of all laboring people.[77] In 1894, the national party set up a commission to study the issue, and when its recommendations came up for discussion at the SPD's 1895 Breslau congress, a storm broke out. The party's leaders, Bebel and Karl Liebknecht, were willing to consider some changes, but Kautsky and Engels, less concerned with practical concerns and worried about similar trends toward accommodation with peasants elsewhere in Europe, held the line and turned the debate over revisions to the agricultural plank into one about orthodox Marxism.

They warned of dire consequences if the SPD were to sully its ranks "with ultimately unreliable peasants."[78] Kautsky reminded his colleagues that the "very first line of the Erfurt program asserts that economic developments necessarily lead to the decline of small enterprise."[79] The new agrarian program, he said, would change the very nature of the SPD, since "it emphasizes not what divides us from democrats and social reformers but what we have in common with them, and it thereby arouses the impression that social democracy is simply a kind of democratic party of reforms."[80] Similarly, Engels argued that

... it is the duty of our party to make clear to the peasantry again and again that their position is absolutely helpless so long as capitalism holds sway, that it is absolutely

---

[76] See, for example, his pamphlet "Bauernfrage und Sozialdemokratie in Bayern" (Nuremberg 1896), reprinted in Athar Hussain and Keith Tribe, eds., *Paths of Development in Capitalist Agriculture: Readings from German Social Democracy, 1891–1899* (London: Macmillan, 1984).

[77] Athar Hussain and Keith Tribe, *Marxism and the Agrarian Question* (London: Macmillan, 1983), 94–5. Another important protagonist in the fight for a change in attitude toward agriculture was Eduard David. In a series of articles in the mid-1890s and later in his influential book *Sozialismus and Landwirtschaft*, David asserted that by not differentiating among agricultural groups, the theoretical section of the Erfurt program hindered the SPD's growth. He argued that small peasants were not disappearing and that, as workers of their own property, they did necessarily contradict social democratic tenets. Some of the articles are reprinted in Hussain and Tribe, eds., *Paths of Development in Capitalist Agriculture*. See also Eduard David, *Sozialismus und Landwirtschaft* (Berlin: Sozialistische Monatshefte, 1902).

[78] Salvadori, *Karl Kautsky and the Socialist Revolution, 1880–1938*, 51–5; Gary Steenson, *"Not One Man! Not One Penny!" German Social Democracy, 1863–1914* (Pittsburgh, PA: University of Pittsburgh Press, 1981), 201.

[79] Lehmann, *Die Agrarfrage*, 165–6.

[80] Kautsky, "Our Latest Program," (1895) reprinted in Hussain and Tribe, eds., *Paths of Development in Capitalist Agriculture*, 111. Also Karl Kautsky, *Die Agrarfrage* (Stuttgart: J. H. W. Dietz, 1899), and the general discussion of Kautsky's views on agriculture in Hussain and Tribe, eds., *Marxism and the Agrarian Question*, 104–36.

impossible to preserve their holdings as such, and that capitalist large scale production is absolutely sure to run over their impotent and antiquated system of small scale production as a train runs over a pushcart.[81]

In the end, such arguments won out and the Breslau congress rejected the proposed changes as well as any broader attempts to reach out to other bourgeois groups.

Even though these official challenges were beaten back, discontent within the party continued to grow as the century drew to a close. The party found itself drawn further and further into political work and the incentives for cooperation with non-proletariat groups increased, further amplifying the tension between the party's principles and its praxis. It was against this background of a growing gap between the party's official ideology and the reality it faced that Eduard Bernstein launched the most comprehensive and formidable theoretical critique of the orthodox position that the continent had yet seen.[82]

Bernstein was no ordinary socialist. He was one of the SPD's most important leaders and intellectual figures, a trusted and early colleague of Marx and Engels, and a good friend of Kautsky's. As such, his views had to be taken seriously. As one observer noted, "when Bernstein challenged the accuracy of Marxian prophecy it was as if the pope declared there would be no Second Coming."[83] In addition to his background, the fact that Bernstein's home base was the continent's most powerful socialist party and one that viewed its identity as being tied up with orthodox Marxism also gave his theoretical critique added weight.

Bernstein's apostasy originated with his conviction that historical materialism could no longer explain the dynamics of either contemporary capitalism or the transition to socialism:

No one will deny that the most important part in the foundation of Marxism, the basic law, so to speak, that penetrates the whole system, is the particular *theory of history* known as the materialist conception of history. In principle, Marxism stands

---

[81] Friedrich Engels, "The Peasant Question in Germany and France," reprinted in Hussain and Tribe, eds., *Marxism and the Agrarian Question*, 17–18.

[82] One way to characterize the differences betweeen Bernstein and some of the other early critics of orthodoxy is by using the term "revisionist" for the former and "reformist" for the latter. Broadly defined, revisionism refers to the attempt made by Bernstein and others to change the praxis of socialist parties by grounding it in a reevaluation of orthodox Marxism and developing a more suitable socialist theory. Reformists, on the other hand, were interested in the changing the praxis of socialist parties but, unlike the revisionists, were relatively uninterested in theory.

For a discussion of reformist challenges to the SPD, see Stanley Pierson, *Marxist Intellectuals and the Working-Class Mentality in Germany, 1887–1912* (Harvard University Press, 1993); Rosen, "German Social Democracy Between Bismarck and Bernstein; Steenson, "*Not One Man! Not One Penny!*"; Hans-Josef Steinberg: *Sozialismus und Deutsche Sozialdemokratie. Zur Ideologi der Partei vor Dem 1. Weltkrieg* (Bonn: J. H. W. Dietz Nachf. GmbH, 1979).

[83] Joshua Muravchik, *Heaven on Earth. The Rise and Fall of Socialism* (San Francisco: Encounter Books, 2002), 95.

or falls with this theory; and insofar as it suffers modification, the relationship of the other parts to each other will be affected. Any investigation into the correctness of Marxism must therefore start with the question of whether or how far this theory is valid.[84]

According to Bernstein, his questioning of historical materialism began with a lecture he gave to the Fabian Society in January 1897. At some point during the talk, he realized that he was no longer convinced of the veracity of many of Marx's arguments and prognostications. "I told myself secretly that this could not go on," he later recounted:

It is idle to attempt to reconcile the irreconcilable. The vital thing is rather to clarify for oneself the points on which Marx is still right, and the points on which he is not. If we jettison the latter, we serve Marx's memory better than when (as I did and many still do) we stretch his theory until it will prove anything. Because then it proves nothing.[85]

By the time Bernstein was done, however, few of the elements of the materialist conception of history were left standing.

Bernstein questioned almost every prediction about capitalism and economic development postulated by the reigning orthodoxy of his day. He argued against the view that capitalism was leading to the immiseration of the proletariat and most of society. "Proof for actual immiseration has never been and will never be offered," he noted. Instead, over the past years, the "wealth of society has increased enormously, and its wide distribution makes it possible to fight the danger of stagnation more effectively. Vast market expansion has created previously unimagined possibilities for balancing conflicting forces." As a result, "the revisionist claim that the way to socialism leads via the ascent, and not the immiseration of the proletariat, has been achieving greater recognition all around."[86] Bernstein also rejected the assertion that capitalism was leading to an ever-increasing concentration of wealth and property:

That the number of property owners increases rather than diminishes is not an invention of bourgeois "harmony economists" but a fact, which ... can now no longer be disputed. But what does this fact signify for the victory of socialism? Why should the achievement of socialism depend on its denial? Well, simply because ... a plank threatens to break away from the scaffolding if one admits that the social surplus product is appropriated by an increasing instead of a decreasing number of property-owners.[87]

---

[84] Eduard Bernstein, *The Preconditions of Socialism*, Henry Tudor, ed. (New York: Cambridge University Press, 1993), 12. Emphasis in the original.

[85] Idem in a letter to August Bebel, October 20, 1898, in F. Adler, ed., *Victor Adler, Briefwechsel mit August Bebel und Karl Kautsky* (Vienna: Wiener Volksbuchhandlung, 1954), 260–3.

[86] Idem, "Lecture to the Student Association for Social Studies in Amsterdam," and idem, "From Someone Pronounced Dead," both reprinted in Manfred Steger, ed., *Selected Writings of Eduard Bernstein* (New Jersey: Humanities Press, 1996), 62, 77.

[87] Idem, *The Preconditions of Socialism*, 200–1.

And Bernstein also cast doubt on the picture of capitalism as crisis-prone and doomed to demise. This view may have seemed plausible during an earlier phase of capitalism, he noted, but what socialists faced at the turn of the century was a capitalist system that seemed to be entering a new and more robust phase:

We impute to business relationships a rigidity and narrowness which might pertain to the age of manufacture or the beginning of the machine age ... but which are blatantly at odds with the characteristic features of modern industrial life.... [What we have witnessed recently is in fact [a] steadily growing number of different kinds of business.... and [a] growing adaptability and flexibility [in] the contemporary business world.[88]

Since orthodoxy's predictions about and picture of capitalism were flawed, then so too must be its assertion that socialism would come about only on the heels of its demise. Socialists could not, Bernstein argued, allow their "tactics to be determined by, or made dependent upon, the prospect of any forthcoming major catastrophe,"[89] because this would leave them waiting around for an event that might never occur. Instead socialists had to face up to the reality that it was "neither possible nor necessary to give the victory of socialism a purely materialistic basis."[90]

Bernstein's observations about capitalism and economic development led him to reject one of the main pillars of orthodox Marxism – historical materialism – and argue instead for an activist, political path to socialism. If socialism was not something that *had* to be, he concluded it should be "something that *ought* to be."[91] He called orthodox Marxists "Calvinists without God"[92] and argued that their faith in the inevitability of socialism bred a dangerous political passivity that would cost them the enthusiasm of the masses. Over the long term, he felt, individuals were motivated by their ideals and a vision of a better world; they could not be convinced to struggle for something that was merely the historically inevitable result of economic laws. "What draws [the masses] to socialism," Bernstein argued, "is the aspiration towards a more practical and a more equitable social order."[93]

Since movement toward this new order would not be the inevitable result of economic development, the task facing socialists was to come up with

---

[88] Idem, "The Struggle of Social Democracy and the Social Revolution," *Neue Zeit*, January 19, 1898. Reprinted in H. Tudor and J. M. Tudor, eds., *Marxism and Social Democracy: The Revisionist Debate 1896–1898* (New York: Cambridge University Press, 1988), 164–5.

[89] Idem, "Letter to the Stuttgart Party Congress," in *Protokoll über die Verhandlungen des Parteitages der Sozialdemokratische Partei Deutschlands*, Stuttgart, October 3–8, 1898 (Bonn: J. H. W. Dietz Verlag, c. 1898), 122–6.

[90] Idem, *The Preconditions of Socialism*, 200.

[91] Idem, "How Is Scientific Socialism Possible?" Lecture, May 1901, reprinted in Steger, ed., *Selected Writings of Eduard Bernstein*, 95. Emphasis added. See also, Robert S. Wistrich, "Back to Bernstein," *Encounter*, 50, 6, 1978, 79.

[92] Bernstein, *The Preconditions of Socialism*, 13.

[93] Ibid., 240.

"positive suggestions for reform capable of spurring fundamental change."[94] These reforms, in turn, should aim "not at the decrease but the increase in social wealth" – at improving the living conditions of the great masses of society: "With regard to reforms, we ask, not whether they will hasten the catastrophe which could bring us to power, but whether they further the development of the working class, whether they contribute to general progress."[95] This progress would consist of the "steady expansion of the sphere of social obligations (i.e. the obligations of the individual toward society, his corresponding rights, and the obligations of society toward the individual), the extension of the right of society, as organized in the nation or state, to regulate economic life; the growth of democratic self-government in municipality, district, and province; and the extended responsibilities of these bodies – for me all these things mean development toward socialism, or, if you will, piecemeal realization of social-ism."[96] Bernstein thus believed that "revisionism translated into the political realm means consequent reformism."[97]

Although less dramatic than the vision of revolutionary collapse and rebirth propagated by orthodox Marxists, the revisionist view of the transition to socialism, he argued, was more likely to achieve concrete results:

There has never yet in history been a radical change of such widespread significance as that which [revisionism] strives to achieve.... Such a change demands long and thor-ough work. And let it not be thought that, because everyday work is concerned with little things it is of less value than large-scale campaigns. It is precisely the little things which are often of the greatest significance. In the modern working class movement, what matters is not the sensational battles but the ground gained piecemeal by hard, unremitting struggle.[98]

This belief led Bernstein to make his (in)famous comment that "what is usually termed the final goal of socialism is nothing to me, the movement is everything."[99] By this he simply meant that constantly talking about some abstract future outcome was of relatively little value; instead socialists needed to focus their attention on the "political and economic agitation and organization" that would underpin the long-term struggle to create a better world.[100]

---

[94] Ibid., 61, and idem, "General Observations on Utopianism and Eclecticism," *Neue Zeit*, October 28, 1896. Reprinted in Tudor and Tudor, eds., *Marxism and Social Democracy*, 74, and idem, *The Preconditions of Socialism*, 61.

[95] Idem, "Critical Interlude," *Neue Zeit*, March 1, 1898, reprinted in Tudor and Tudor, eds., *Marxism and Social Democracy*, quote on 222.

[96] Idem, "The Struggle of Social Democracy and the Social Revolution: 2," *Neue Zeit*, January 19, 1898, in Tudor and Tudor, eds., *Marxism and Social Democracy*, 168.

[97] Manfred Steger, *The Quest for Evolutionary Socialism* (New York: Cambridge University Press, 1997), 175.

[98] Bernstein, "Critical Interlude," *Neue Zeit*, March 1, 1898, reprinted in Tudor and Tudor, eds., *Marxism and Social Democracy*, quote on 222.

[99] E.g., idem, *The Preconditions of Socialism*, 190.

[100] Idem, "The Struggle of Social Democracy and the Social Revolution: 2," in Tudor and Tudor, eds., *Marxism and Social Democracy*, 169.

This belief in a gradual, political path to socialism led Bernstein to view democracy as "both a means and an end. It is a weapon in the struggle for socialism and it is the form in which socialism will be realized."[101] Democracy provided socialists with "the most effective tool for implementing profound, step-by-step reforms without bloodshed.... Universal suffrage and parliamentary action must be seen as the apex, the most comprehensive form of class struggle – a permanent organic revolution that is fought within legal parameters, reflecting a level of cultural development that corresponds to modern civilization."[102] But democracy was more than simply the best instrument socialists had for achieving their goals. It also embodied many of the most important ideals of socialism, such as classlessness, equality, and freedom.

Alongside his rejection of historical materialism, Bernstein also attacked the second pillar of orthodox Marxism, class struggle. In his view, the doctrine of inevitable class struggle shared the same fatal flaws as the belief in economic determinism: It was both historically inaccurate and politically debilitating. By the end of the nineteenth century, Bernstein had become convinced that class structures were not developing along the lines predicted by orthodox Marxism. In particular, he came to believe that social relations were becoming more differentiated and complex. For example, in contrast to the orthodox Marxist predictions of growing proletarianization, Bernstein recognized that workers were not on their way to becoming the vast majority of society. He also took issue with the orthodox Marxist prediction that the logic of capitalism would eventually lead to the demise of small businesses and agricultural enterprises and their replacement by larger, more efficient industrial units. And he realized that rather than disappearing, the middle classes were growing and becoming increasingly complex and differentiated. From these trends, he concluded that the increasing social polarization and class conflict predicted by orthodox Marxism was simply not coming to pass and that socialists therefore needed to develop a new view of class relations and societal dynamics:

If society were constituted, or if it had developed, in the manner socialist theory has hitherto supposed, then indeed it would be only a short space of time before economic collapse occurred. But that...is precisely not the case.... [Indeed, we socialists must recognize] that the intensification of social relations predicted by [Marx and Engels] has not in fact occurred.... It is not only useless but extremely foolish to conceal this fact from ourselves.... The number of property owners has grown, not diminished. The enormous increase in social wealth has been accompanied, not by a fall in the number of capitalist[s], but by an increase in the number of capitalists.... The middle classes are changing in character, but they are not disappearing.... [In short], everywhere in the more advanced countries we see the class struggle assuming more moderate forms, and our prospects for the future would hold little hope if this were not the case.[103]

---

[101] Idem, *The Preconditions of Socialism*, 142.
[102] Idem, "Political Mass Strike and Romanticizing Revolution," *Sozialistische Monatshefte*, 12, 1, 1906, in Steger, ed., *Selected Writings of Eduard Bernstein*, 139.
[103] Idem, "Letter to the Stuttgart Party Congress," and idem, *The Preconditions of Socialism*, 62.

Instead of viewing history as moving inexorably toward increasing social polarization and class conflict, Bernstein believed that a community of interest was being created between workers and others suffering from the injustices and dislocations generated by capitalism. He recognized that many outside the working classes were feeling economically threatened and socially adrift, and argued that such people should be seen as potential allies or even recruits. Bernstein thus urged socialists to ground their appeals not on the distinctive needs of the proletariat and the inevitability of class conflict but rather on "the feeling of common humanity [and a] recognition of social interdependence."[104] Indeed, Bernstein was convinced that underneath the social conflicts of the day there existed a fundamental common interest or good that socialists should recognize and promise to protect. He thus presented socialism as a fundamentally cooperative, even communal endeavor, that could and should offer the vast majority of citizens a vision of a better life.[105]

In short, during the last years of the nineteenth and the first years of the twentieth century, Bernstein developed a wide-ranging critique of the main tenets of orthodox Marxism. In essence, he advocated replacing historical materialism and class struggle with a belief in the primacy of politics and the value of cross-class cooperation – a conviction that individuals, motivated by their ideals and by a vision of a better world, could band together and use the power of the democratic state to reshape gradually the world around them:

This new vision [of the transition to socialism] takes place in the daily life of the working class, struggling anew against exploitation. It shows the proletariat growing in numbers and in social power – not merely pushing forward, but upward as well, elevating its economic, ethical, and political standards and becoming increasingly capable of co-governing state and economy. This vision is alive and well among those... commonly called "revisionists."[106]

When Bernstein first began his public questioning of Marxism, the party leadership had hoped that a controversy could be avoided. As time passed and Bernstein continued to press and even expand his critique, however, this became increasingly difficult to avoid. Many came to see him as a stalking horse for a more widespread threat to the movement's traditions, coherence, and future – a threat that party leaders decided they had to face directly.

The opportunity presented itself in 1898, when Bernstein sent a letter to the SPD's Stuttgart congress setting out his views. Despite some conciliatory gestures, he once again presented a frontal assault on the main tenets of Marxism, arguing that economic development was not turning out as planned and that presenting socialism as the result of an inevitable capitalist collapse and

---

[104] Idem, "Political Mass Strike and Romanticizing Revolution," reprinted in Steger, ed., *Selected Writings of Eduard Bernstein*, 152.

[105] Henry Tudor, introduction to Bernstein, *The Preconditions of Socialism*, xxi.

[106] Bernstein, "Lecture Presented to the Student Association for Social Studies in Amsterdam," in Steger, ed., *Selected Writings of Eduard Bernstein*, 79.

ever-sharpening class struggle was a major mistake. Instead, the time had come
for socialists to turn their attention to the political arena; it was there that the
coming battle for socialist transformation would be fought. This proved to be
the final straw for many. Kautsky, for example, had hitherto been hesitant to
criticize Bernstein publicly, although he had made clear in private correspondence that he felt his old friend had separated himself from and perhaps even
betrayed the movement that they had both long served. "You declare as false,"
Kautsky wrote to Bernstein, "the theory of value, the dialectic, [historical] materialism, the class struggle, the proletarian character of our movement . . . well,
what remains then of Marxism? To characterize what you are trying to do as the
'surmounting' of Marxism is too weak a term. What it really means is the collapse of Marxism."[107] In his correspondence with others, Kautsky made clear
that he felt that what Bernstein was doing was working toward the "ruination"
(*Verhunzung*) of Marxism.[108] "There is no point," he concluded "in trying to
hide [this] or . . . resist drawing the necessary consequences."[109]

After Stuttgart, pressure began to build for a public condemnation. In order
to prepare his old friend for this, Bebel wrote Bernstein explaining that the
party leadership had been forced to conclude that "we are divided not only
by profound differences on tactical matters, but also by fundamental concep-
tual differences. Karl [Kautsky] was quite right when he declared . . . that if the
views reiterated in your statement on bourgeois society and its development
were correct, then we must cease to be" socialists.[110] Bernstein thanked Bebel
for his honesty and in particular for making clear that "while you do not say
so in so many words . . . [I see that it is] your honest opinion [that] I cannot,
with my views as they are, remain a member of the party."[111] But remain he
did, which served only to keep the controversy alive. But rather than coming
from his old friends, the most public and powerful criticism of Bernstein during this time came from a young rising star in the socialist movement, Rosa
Luxemburg.[112]

In 1899, Luxemburg published *Reform or Revolution* to answer Bernstein's
Evolutionary Socialism. Luxemburg urged socialists to recognize that if Bernstein was correct, the whole edifice of orthodox Marxism would be swept
away: "Up until now," she argued, "socialist theory declared that the point

---

[107] Kautsky to Bernstein, October 23, 1898, reprinted in Friedrich Alder, ed., *Victor Adler
Briefwechsel mit August Bebel und Karl Kautsky* (Vienna: Wiener Volksbuchhandlung, 1954),
273.
[108] Kautsky to Victor Adler (leader of the Austrian Socialist Party), March 7, 1899, in ibid., 293.
[109] Kautsky to Bernstein, October 23, 1898, reprinted in ibid., 273.
[110] Bebel to Bernstein, October 16, 1898, in ibid., 258.
[111] Bernstein to Bebel, October 20, 1898, in ibid., 258–63.
[112] Bernstein himself recognized Luxemburg as his most powerful and effective critic, calling her
writings "on the whole among the best of those that were written against me." Bernstein, *The
Preconditions of Socialism*, 200. Luxemburg's attack appeared in articles in the *Leipziger Volkszeitung* in September 1898 and in a response to the publication of Bernstein's *Voraussetzungen*
in April 1899. Together the articles were published in 1900 as Rosa Luxemburg, *Reform or
Revolution* (New York: Pathfinder, 1996).

of departure for a transformation to socialism would be a general and catastrophic crisis." Bernstein, however, "does not merely reject a certain form of the collapse. He rejects the very possibility of collapse.... But then the question arises: Why and how...shall we attain the final goal?"[113] Bernstein's answer, of course, was that the final goal could be attained politically, through the active efforts of a majority. This, Luxemburg, correctly noted, represented a fundamental break with both Marxism and the party's long-standing strategy:

> According to the present conception of the party, trade-union and parliamentary activity are important...because such activity prepares the proletariat, that is to say, creates the *subjective* factor of the socialist transformation, for the task of realizing socialism. But according to Bernstein, trade unions and parliamentary activity gradually reduce capitalist exploitation itself. They remove from capitalist society its capitalist character. They realize objectively the desired social change.[114]

Luxemburg urged socialists to recognize that Bernstein's revisionism presented the movement with a simple question: Either "socialist transformation is, as before, the result of the objective contradictions of the capitalist order...and at some stage some form of collapse will occur," or capitalism really has changed, becoming more adaptable and capable of being fundamentally altered by the active efforts of inspired majorities. If this latter vision were correct, then "the objective necessity of socialism, the explanation of socialism as the result of the material development of society, falls to the ground,"[115] taking orthodox Marxism with it.

Driven by the growing recognition of just how fundamental Bernstein's apostasy was, and that such views were acquiring support elsewhere, the leaders of the SPD finally decided to strike back. At the party's 1899 Hanover congress, for example, Bebel attacked Bernstein, arguing that he was strengthening the party's opponents with "his attack on all the basic positions of Marxism."[116] The congress ultimately adopted a resolution stating that "now as ever," the SPD based itself on the class struggle and believed that the "liberation of the working class can be won only by the working class itself." Furthermore, "the development of bourgeois society gives the party no reason to change or

---

[113] Ibid., 11–12, 35.
[114] Ibid., 30. Emphasis in the original.
[115] Ibid., 12–13.
[116] Sozialdemokratischen Partei Deutschlands, *Protokoll über die Verhandlungen des Parteitages der Sozialdemokratischen Partei Deutschlands*, Hanover, October 9–14, 1899, 96. Even those who supported practical positions similar to Bernstein's recognized the importance of orthodox Marxist theory to the party's identity and unity, and so hesitated in their defenses of him. Thus leading reformists such as Georg von Vollmar and Ignaz Auer urged the party to take what it wanted from Bernstein and leave party ideology to be debated by Kautsky, Luxemburg, and other theorists. (Auer wrote privately to his friend, "Do you really think that a party, resting on fifty years of literature and forty years of organization, can reverse its theory at the snap of your fingers? What you demand my dear [Eduard] one does neither openly admit nor formally vote on; one simply does it." Auer repeated the last part of this at the congress; see ibid., 208.

give up its . . . principles . . . its basic demands, its tactics, or its name." [117] Such a ringing endorsement of ideological traditionalism, many felt, would surely be the final word in what had already been a painful and divisive battle against revisionism. Little did they know that Hanover would not mark the end of the revisionist controversy, nor even the beginning of the end. But it would be the end of the beginning.

[117] Ibid., 243–4.

3

Democratic Revisionism Comes of Age

In the last chapter, we saw how democratic revisionism emerged during the late nineteenth century out of frustration with orthodox Marxism's inability to explain or respond to the needs and demands of the day. In particular, we saw that in France, Socialists found it hard to resist reaching out to peasants, defending democracy, and participating in government – all of which challenged the reigning orthodoxy. In Germany, a gap also opened up between the SPD's theory and praxis, but here orthodoxy came under direct theoretical attack by the democratic revisionism of Eduard Bernstein. As one of the keenest contemporary observers of fin-de-siècle socialism noted, revisionism was "presented by Bernstein and demonstrated by" the French:

If Bernstein's theoretical criticism and political yearnings were still unclear to anyone, the French took the trouble strikingly to demonstrate the "new method." ... The French socialists have begun, not to theorize, but to act. The democratically more highly developed political conditions in France have permitted them to put "Bernsteinism into practice" immediately, with all its consequences.[1]

By the end of the century, in short, orthodoxy faced growing practical and theoretical challenges.

During the first years of the twentieth century, this challenge continued to spread as the reality of European economic and political life caused more and more socialists to question orthodox Marxism. In particular, socialist parties and the Socialist International became consumed by debates about such issues as cooperation with bourgeois parties and non-proletarian social groups, the role of reform work, the value of democracy, and how to deal with the rising tide of nationalism. What made these debates so heated and divisive was that at their core lay one simple question: Would socialism be the result of inevitable economic development and class struggle, or would it be the consequence of

---

[1] V. Lenin, "What Is to Be Done?" in Robert C. Tucker, ed., *The Lenin Anthology* (New York: W. W. Norton, 1975), 13–14.

democratic political action and cross-class cooperation? By arguing for the latter, revisionists were calling not merely for a dilution of orthodox Marxism but rather for an abandonment of its core principles – for a socialism severed from Marxism. The revisionist rejection of Marxist orthodoxy was as thorough as Marx's had been of liberalism a half a century earlier – something revisionists themselves were not eager at this time to admit, but which their opponents clearly recognized. The result was that by 1914 a gulf had opened up between revisionists and their opponents that left the international socialist movement, like many of its constituent parties, a house divided against itself.

Paris and Its Aftermath

The Socialist International's first congress of the new century convened in Paris in 1900. The main item on the agenda got right to the heart of the debate between revisionists and their opponents, namely "the conquering of state power and alliances with bourgeois parties."[2] Delegates were tasked with debating two related questions: whether to permit electoral alliances with bourgeois parties, and whether to permit socialist participation in bourgeois governments. Since almost all European socialist parties had long accepted that meaningful participation in elections required at least occasional tactical alliances with non-socialists, discussion of the first question was short. A resolution of Guesde's passed easily allowing such cooperation, although "only in exceptional circumstances and for limited times," because "electoral alliances with bourgeois parties . . . contravene a fundamental principle of the party, namely the class struggle."[3]

The second question generated more controversy, and two competing resolutions on it were placed before the congress. The first, drawn up by Kautsky, tried to maintain the essence of the orthodox position while making some concessions to evolving reality; it declared that the conquest of political power could not "take place bit by bit" and that entry into a non-socialist government should therefore not be considered "a normal way of beginning the conquest of political power." It accepted, however, that participation in a bourgeois government could be justified "in exceptionally dire circumstances," in which case the move would be acceptable as a matter of tactics rather than principle. To avoid some of the problems generated by the Millerand case, the resolution added that such a "dangerous experiment" could be allowed only if officially approved by the party and only if the socialist minister pledged to follow the party line rigorously while in office.[4] The second resolution was drawn up by Guesde and Enrico Ferri, a representative of the "revolutionary" wing of

[2] *Internationaler Sozialisten Kongress zu Paris,* September 23–27, 1900 (Berlin: Vorwärts, 1900), 16.
[3] Ibid., 17.
[4] Ibid. Also, Julius Braunthal, *History of the International 1864–1914* (New York: Praeger, 1967), 273.

the Italian socialist party (PSI). It rejected unconditionally any concession to revisionism by refusing to countenance any socialist participation in bourgeois governments. Ultimately the congress decided in favor of Kautsky's less intransigent resolution, but despite this decision very little was actually settled.

In France, for example, Guesde and Jaurès picked up their debate over the stakes and implications of ministerialism right where they had left off. In an open debate in October 1902, Guesde once again insisted that accepting alliances with non-socialist parties or allowing socialists to enter bourgeois governments meant nothing less than an abandonment of socialism's soul: "Once we let the Socialist party abandon any fragment of its class stronghold, once we let it conclude any alliance with any faction of the bourgeoisie, it will begin to roll down the slippery slope to ruin." Jaurès, on the other hand, reiterated his position that the safeguarding of democracy was more important than the maintenance of proletarian purity:

... when Republican liberty is at stake, when intellectual liberty is in jeopardy, when freedom of conscience is menaced, when ancient prejudices reviving racial antagonism and the atrocious religious quarrels of centuries gone by are being aroused – it is the duty of the Socialist working class to go forward with those sections of the middle class which are determined not to go backward. I am astonished, truly, to have to recall these elementary truths, which ought to be the inheritance and guide of all Socialists.[5]

Ultimately, the divisions between these positions proved too great and the French socialist movement split. Guesde, the POF, and other antiministerialists joined together in the Parti Socialiste de France; Jaurès and other supporters of ministerialism united in the Parti Socialiste Français. In the following years, the latter cooperated at election time with bourgeois groups, participated in the Delegation des Gauches (a steering committee designed to coordinate the actions of the parties of the left) and supported the government, while the former denounced these moves and trumpeted its doctrinal purity. So deep was the divide between these two parties that the Parti Socialiste de France ran its own candidate for Jaurès' parliamentary seat in 1902.

The Parti Socialiste Français itself remained somewhat conflicted about ministerialism in general and Millerand's increasingly cozy relationship with his bourgeois colleagues in particular. Jaurès, as always, tried to stake out a compromise position that included an insistence on the centrality of democracy as well as a recognition of its limits. As he put it, "to say that the state is the same – the same closed, impenetrable, rigid state, brazenly bourgeois – under an oligarchic regime... and under a regime of universal suffrage... is to contradict all the laws of nature." But one had also to recognize that it was not "enough to lay down the principle of democracy in order to resolve, in a sort of automatic fashion, the antagonisms of society": Since the bourgeoisie and other groups still had a structural advantage in society thanks to their economic power, the contemporary state could not be considered neutral. So socialists still

5 J. Hampden Jackson, *Jean Jaurès* (London, George Allen and Unwin, 1943), 85.

had to be wary about collaboration with non-socialist forces and participation in bourgeois governments.[6]

The Parti Socialiste Français' 1903 congress considered two resolutions dealing with the Millerand controversy, one favoring his expulsion and the other (put forward by Jaurès) censuring certain of his actions but allowing him to remain in the party. Millerand himself urged his colleagues to recognize that in passing judgment on him, they were in essence making a decision about the identity and future of their movement:

> By what inconsistency should [a socialist party] consent to canvass every mandate, and yet rigorously forbid itself to join in the Government and take, along with the highest responsibilities, the most certain power? Such an illogical course, if possible to continue, would soon ruin the credit and influence of the party weak enough and sufficiently uncertain of itself to commit it. To put the people off to the mysterious date when a sudden miracle will change the face of the world, or day by day, reform by reform, by a patient and stubborn effort to win step by step all progress – those are the two methods which we must choose between.[7]

In the end, Jaurès' resolution emerged victorious and ministerialism was allowed to continue.[8] But the anti-Millerand forces were not mollified, and the following year were able to push through his expulsion at the local level. Jaurès tried once again to bridge the divide, but this time he was unsuccessful.

At the same time that the French socialist movement was tearing itself apart debating democracy, cross-class alliances, and ministerialism, its Italian counterpart was subjecting itself to similar internecine warfare. As in France, Italian defenders of orthodoxy were a particularly crude bunch: Men such as Ferri and Achille Loria championed an extremely simplistic, scientific, and deterministic version of Marxism, one that in fact had only a tenuous connection with the writings of Marx and Engels themselves. The crudity of this doctrine spurred a counterreaction early on. For example, the man many have referred to as the "greatest theorist of Italian Marxism and among the greatest teachers of European Marxism,"[9] Antonio Labriola, argued against the extreme determinism and scientism of Ferri and others and offered in its place what one scholar

---

[6] Ibid., 167–77.

[7] Millerand, "Preface to French Reformist Socialism" (appeared in 1903 just before the congress), reprinted in R. C. K. Ensor, *Modern Socialism* (New York: Harper and Brothers, 1904), 64.

[8] In response, the Parti Socialiste de France released a resolution stating that the outcome of the congress "only confirms what we had always said: once admit the participation of a Socialist in bourgeois government and every compromise, every desertion of Socialistic standpoint, is not only possible but necessary.... The thing to note is ... that there cannot be any Socialism away from that basis of the class-war and uncompromising opposition to the bourgeois state, upon which the Socialist party of France fights." "Resolution of the Executive of the Socialist Party of France Regarding the Verdict of the French Socialist Party Congress at Bordeaux," reprinted in ibid., 185–6.

[9] Edmund Jacobitti, "Labriola, Croce, and Italian Marxism," *Journal of the History of Ideas*, 36, 2, April/June, 1975, 300–1.

has referred to as "an open orthodoxy."[10] Labriola scoffed at the notions that history would unfold in a predetermined, schematic manner; that economic forces were all-powerful; and that socialism could result from only a violent collapse of the existing order. In doing so, he helped pave the way for a whole generation of Marxist critics. Italy's most prominent intellectual during this time, Benedetto Croce, was in fact originally drawn to Marxism by Labriola's work, but after an initial infatuation, Croce concluded that Labriola's attempt to salvage Marxism was doomed to failure. Croce argued that history could never be a science and that social development could not be predicted in advance, while also rejecting Marxism's emphasis on the primacy of economics, insisting instead on the role of idealism in history and socialism. "It is clear," he wrote, "that idealism or absolute morals are a necessary postulate for socialism.... How can one explain Marx's political activity and the tone of violent indignation and bitter satire that appears on every page of *Das Kapital* without understanding [this] moral basis?"[11]

Alongside the critiques of Croce and others, Francesco Merlino became the prime advocate of a "Bernsteinian" type of revisionism in Italy. Originally an anarchist, Merlino had been forced to flee to England and, like Bernstein, had been greatly influenced by his time there. In 1897, he published a book called *Pro e control il socialismo*, in which he too attacked both historical materialism and class struggle. Merlino argued that the core of socialism was moral rather than material and that its realization would depend not on capitalism's utter collapse, but rather on a gradual, reformist transformation of the existing system.[12] Insisting that the class struggle as described by Marx had not emerged and that socialists needed to reach out to and work with a wide range of social groups, Merlino came to focus on the "people" rather than the proletariat since he was convinced that "socialism [would represent] not the victory of one class over the others, but the triumph of the general interest over the particular interests."[13]

---

[10] Leszek Kolakowski, "Antonio Labriola: An Attempt at Open Orthodoxy," in *Main Currents of Marxism*, Vol. 2: *The Golden Age* (New York: Oxford University Press, 1978). Also Richard Bellamy, *Modern Italian Social Theory* (Cambridge, MA: Polity Press, 1987), 61ff; Antonio Labriola, *Socialism and Philosophy* (St. Louis, MO: Telos Press, 1980); Paul Piccone, *Italian Marxism* (Berkeley, CA: University of California Press, 1983).

[11] Croce, quoted in Bo Gustafsson, *Marxism och Revisionism: Eduard Bernsteins Kritik av Marxismen och dess Idéhistoriska Förutsättningar* (Stockholm: Svensk Bokförlaget, 1969), 260.

[12] Ibid., esp. 272–5.

[13] David Roberts, *The Syndicalist Tradition and Italian Fascism* (Chapel Hill, NC: University of North Carolina Press, 1979), 312.

 Because of the emergence of critics such as Croce and Merlino, scholars have characterized the fin-de-siècle as a period of crisis for Italian Marxism. In fact, however, what was going on there was simply part of a larger process occurring across the European continent, something Croce, Merlino, and other Italian critics recognized. Croce, for example, admired and had extensive contacts with the French revisionist Georges Sorel (on whom more later), writing at one point that his own ideas conveyed "the very same tendency that is being developed almost contemporaneously in France through the work of Sorel." Edmun Jacobitti, "Labriola, Croce, and Italian Marxism (1895–1910)," 313. See also Bellamy, *Modern Italian Social*

At the same time that numerous intellectuals were challenging orthodoxy, practical concerns were also pushing Italian socialists into heated debates about the nature and strategy of their movement.[14] For example, although the PSI early on had proclaimed its unwillingness to engage in alliances of any kind with non-socialist parties, by 1894 this policy was being questioned, thanks to the passing of a series of anti-Socialist laws by the new Italian prime minister, Francesco Crispi. In order to bring an end to this repression, the party decided to support bourgeois liberals and democrats at elections.[15] The success of this collaboration – and a wider recognition of the need to safeguard the Italian political system from authoritarian incursions – emboldened those who wanted to continue and even expand the policy. Filippo Turati, the emerging leader of the party's moderate wing, proposed just such a course shift at the party's 1896 congress, but it was roundly rejected, leading him to remark that the Socialists "continued to act as if time stood still."[16]

During the later 1890s, the party's continued electoral success and the unwill-ingness of several regional-level parties to give up alliances with bourgeois liber-als and democrats kept the debate alive. Turati and his allies continued to push for an expansion of cross-class alliances, while Ferri and others continued to oppose them. In 1899, Italian conservatives seemed on the verge of enacting a series of reactionary constitutional revisions, leading once more to broad recog-nition among Socialists of the need for alliances with other potentially friendly parties. These marriages of convenience paid off handsomely during the 1900 elections, as the Socialists doubled their share of seats in the parliament, the representation of the overall left bloc increased significantly, and the sitting prime minister was forced to resign. The results animated both the moderates around Turati and the hardliners around Ferri, with the former viewing them as a confirmation of the desirability and viability of cross-class cooperation and an electoral appeal based on the advancement of democracy, and the latter fearing them for precisely the same reason.

The divisions emerged clearly at the party's 1900 congress, where Turati and his partner-in-arms Anna Kuliscoff urged their colleagues to recognize that

---

Theory, 69. And Bernstein, Sorel told Croce, was inspired by the Italian's attempts to "moral-ize" Marxism and inject the role of idealism into history. Gustaffson, *Marxism och Revision-ism*, chapter 5. Merlino, meanwhile, played a major role in the diffusion of Sorel's ideas in Italy, and his own work was translated into German and discussed by Bernstein in *Die Neue Zeit*.

[14] On conditions in Italy during this era, see Roger Absalom, *Italy Since 1800: A Nation in the Balance?* (New York: Longman, 1995); Martin Clark, *Modern Italy* (New York: Longman, 1984); Serge Hughes, *The Rise and Fall of Modern Italy* (New York: Minerva Press, 1967); Christopher Seton-Watson, *Italy from Liberalism to Fascism* (London: Methuen, 1967); Denis Mack Smith, *Italy: A Modern History* (Ann Arbor, MI: University of Michigan Press, 1959).

[15] Alexander De Grand, *The Italian Left in the Twentieth Century* (Indianapolis, IN: Indiana University Press, 1989), chapter 1; Spencer Di Scala, *Dilemmas of Italian Socialism: The Politics of Filippo Turati* (Amherst, MA: University of Massachusetts Press, 1980), chapter 3; Michael Hembree, "The Politics of Intransigence: Constantino Lazzari and the Italian Socialist Left, 1882–1919" (Ph.D. Dissertation, Florida State University, 1981), 130ff.

[16] Di Scala, *Dilemmas of Italian Socialism*, 34.

changing conditions made a revision of the party's views and policies imperative. Only democracy, they argued, could pave the way for socialism, and democracy could be achieved if the party was fully committed to working with other groups. Ferri argued fervently in the negative, but the recent electoral success helped swing party opinion against him. The congress therefore decided to permit alliances with democratically inclined non-socialist parties, and to encourage socialists to enter and gain control of local administrative and political institutions. Turati and the moderates, however, did not score an unequivocal victory, as the congress, reflecting the divisions among its delegates, adopted a minimum and a maximum program simultaneously. The former laid out a series of reforms that would help prepare the way for socialism, while the latter reiterated an earlier series of intransigent and revolutionary demands.[17]

Debate on these topics heated up again in 1901 when the charismatic liberal leader Giovanni Giolitti – who would dominate Italian politics during the early twentieth century – gave a speech proclaiming:

We are at the beginning of a new period in history. Whoever is not blind sees this. New popular currents are entering our political life. . . . The ascending movement of the lower classes becomes faster by the day. It is an invincible movement because it is common to all civilized countries, and because it is based on the principle of the equality of all men. No one should deceive himself into thinking that the lower classes can be prevented from acquiring their share of economic and political influence. The friends of existing institutions have one duty above all: it is persuading these lower classes, with facts, that they have more to hope from existing institutions than from any [socialist] dreams of the future.[18]

Soon afterward, Giolitti, along with a colleague, was asked to form a new ministry. Since the liberals could not command a parliamentary majority by themselves, Giolitti turned for help to other groups favoring a further liberalization of the Italian political system – including the Socialists.

After much internal debate, and over strenuous opposition from the ideological hardliners, the Socialist parliamentary deputies agreed to support the new government, which proceeded to enact a program that included respect for civil rights; reform of the judicial, administrative and fiscal systems; old-age, sickness, accident, and maternity benefits; the formation of committees to analyze the conditions and suggest legislation to help improve the situation of the working class; and an end to government strike breaking. As one scholar

---

[17] H. L. Gaultieri, *The Labor Movement in Italy* (New York: S. F. Vannii, 1946), 269; Donald Horowitz, *The Italian Labor Movement* (Cambridge, MA: Harvard University Press, 1963), 51; W. Hilton Young, *The Italian Left* (London: Longmans, Green, 1949), 56.

[18] Quoted in Salvatore Saladino, *Italy from Unification to 1919: The Growth and Decay of a Liberal Regime* (New York: Thomas Cromwell, 1970), 98. For an introduction to Giolitti (and the controversies surrounding him), see Frank Coppa, *Planning, Protectionism, and Politics in Liberal Italy: Economics and Politics in the Giolittian Age* (Washington, DC: Catholic University of America Press: 1971); G. Giolitti, *Memoirs of My Life* (London: Sydney, Chapman and Dodd, 1923); W. A. Salomone, *Italian Democracy in the Making: The Political Scene in the Giolittian Era* (Philadelphia: University of Pennsylvania Press, 1945).

remarked, "when one considers the state of Italy's social legislation before and after Giolitti, it is not an exaggeration to say that he effected something of a revolution."[19]

In October 1903, Giolitti was asked to form a new government on his own. He immediately approached the parties of the left for support and let the Social-ists know that he wanted Turati to hold office. He believed, as he wrote at the time, that Turati was "serious enough to realize that it is no longer sufficient to stand on the sidelines to applaud or jeer."[20] While this may have been true in private, Turati nonetheless feared his party was not ready for such a bold move, and so he turned Giolitti down. Even this move – which drove Giolitti into the arms of the right – was not enough to placate the anticollaborationist forces, who mounted another attack on Turati and his policies at the party's 1904 congress.

The factions at the gathering included a Turatian or "rightist" faction; a "center-right" group (rejecting support for bourgeois governments in the "present phase" of Italian politics but content to let socialists help pass specific legislation); a "center-left" group that included Ferri (wanting a strict ban on supporting bourgeois governments, but still acknowledging the value of work-ing within the existing system to achieve reforms); and the syndicalists (who declared that the class struggle precluded all forms of collaboration and favored openly stating that violence might be necessary to bring about change).[21]

With no faction able to secure a majority, the congress ended on an unclear note. Socialist deputies in the legislature continued to do as they pleased and the factions continued their battles for control. This left the movement in Italy in the same position as its counterpart in France: with socialists considering "other socialists their own worst enemies" – a state of affairs that severely limited the movement's political effectiveness.[22]

To Amsterdam and Beyond

By the early years of the twentieth century, the socialist movements in France and Italy were severely divided, with debates about cooperation with non-proletarian groups, the value of democracy, and ministerialism proving partic-ularly divisive. Similar divisions were roiling the International's most powerful party, the SPD, as well. Indeed it was debates within this party that set the stage for the most important confrontation over revisionism that occurred during the prewar period at the Socialist International's 1904 Amsterdam congress. This congress brought to a head tensions that had been building with the SPD as a result of Bernstein's revisionism as well as the increasing political pressure

---

[19] Coppa, *Planning, Protectionism, and Politics in Liberal Italy*, 164.
[20] Quoted in Di Scala, *Dilemmas of Italian Socialism*, 77.
[21] Thomas Ronald Sykes, "The Practice of Revolutionary Syndicalism" (Ph.D. Dissertation, Columbia University, 1974), 78–9.
[22] Di Scala, *Dilemmas of Italian Socialism*, 66.

that the party faced to join with other groups and press for real changes in Germany's political system.

During the first years of the new century, the SPD's continued electoral growth and in particular its stunning success in the June 1903 elections – it won 3 million votes and eighty-one seats in the Reichstag – forced many within the party and without to question its role in the existing political system. Continuing with his crusade to get his party to use its political power to effect real change, Bernstein proposed that the party leverage its 1903 victory to gain the post of vice-president of the Reichstag, which would have been a noteworthy symbol of the SPD's power but would have also enmeshed the party further in the existing system and forced it to respect a number of distasteful protocols, including showing deference to the Kaiser.

These issues dominated the party's 1903 congress in Dresden. Bebel opened the meeting by noting that many felt the party's growing power required an explicit change in its behavior.[23] "This can't go on," he insisted. "We must finally make clear not only what our party's parliamentary deputies should do, but more fundamentally where the party stands on a number of essential issues and what role, if any, revisionism will play in it."[24] He made clear his own opposition to a course shift, as well as his belief that the revisionists had already caused the party much harm by dividing it internally and dissipating its power externally.[25] Kautsky, echoing Bebel's comments, stressed that what was at stake was a question about the party's theoretical foundations. He urged his colleagues to recognize that a shift would have to "emanate from a revision of the principles upon which the party is based." The only way Bernstein's "new tactic" could be correct, he noted, was "if Marxist theory [were] false."[26]

Bernstein responded by asking his opponents to engage in a thought experiment. Put aside concerns about the actual value of the vice-presidency, he instructed them, and then consider what the party would do if all agreed the post was indeed powerful. Would they still "reject it as a result of a few formalities?" They would not, he argued, and should thus lay the practical and intellectual groundwork for such a move now.[27] He also asked his colleagues to consider the implications of Kautsky's views of the bourgeoisie: "Are the ruling classes really so uniformly hostile to the proletariat? Can we really treat them all the same?"[28] The time had come, he insisted, for the SPD to face up to reality and go forward "hand in hand" with other progressive forces. "A party that knows what it wants," he claimed, would have "nothing to fear from such an alliance."[29] But at the end of the day, the congress rejected Bernstein's arguments almost unanimously, adopting a resolution that "condemned to the

[23] August Bebel, *Protokoll des SPD-Parteitages Dresden, 1903* (Berlin: Vorwärts, 1903), 300.
[24] Ibid., 309–10, 320.
[25] Ibid., 320.
[26] Kautsky, in ibid., 382.
[27] Eduard Bernstein in ibid., 399.
[28] Ibid., 395–6.
[29] Ibid., 400.

fullest extent possible the efforts of the revisionists to change"[30] the party's policies and nature.

Across Europe, defenders of orthodoxy seized upon the SPD's Dresden resolution, hoping to use it to bludgeon revisionists into submission at the Socialist International's Amsterdam congress. The Guesdists took the lead and proposed making the Dresden resolution binding on all of the International's member parties. Jaurès took up the fight, arguing that the diversity of conditions and rapidly changing political reality made it "unwise to tie the international proletariat to tactical formulas at a moment when it stands before new questions." But Jaurès did not stop there. Recognizing that what was at stake was not merely whether or not a German resolution should be foisted on the entire socialist movement, but rather the larger issue of where socialists stood vis-à-vis democracy and cross-class alliances, Jaurès proclaimed:

If in Europe and throughout the world, the questions of peace, of political freedom and the possibility of Socialist advance are now trembling in the balance, this is not through the alleged compromises or the daring innovations of French Socialists who have allied themselves with other democratic forces to safeguard freedom, progress and world peace, but because of the political powerlessness of German Social Democracy.

While his own group had achieved a number of concrete successes – such as saving democracy, preserving freedom of thought, driving back clericalism, and repelling chauvinism, nationalism, and Caesarism – the German hardliners, Jaurès' argued, could point to few gains. "Behind the inflexibility of theoretical formulas which your excellent comrade Kautsky will supply you with to the end of his days," he acidly noted, "you conceal from your own proletariat, from the international proletariat, your inability to act."[31] Bebel responded to Jaurès' attack on the SPD and the Dresden resolution by arguing:

However much we may envy you French your republic, and wish we had one, we don't intend to get our heads smashed in for its sake. Monarchy or republic – both are class states, both are a form of state that maintains the class rule of the bourgeoisie, both are designed to protect the capitalist order of society.[32]

Ultimately Bebel prevailed: The congress made the Dresden resolution its own by a vote of twenty-five to five (with twelve abstentions). The congress also passed a resolution (aimed largely at the French) stating that

... in order that the working class may develop its full strength in the struggle against capitalism, it is necessary [that] there should be but one Socialist party in each country.... [Therefore] all comrades and all Socialist organizations have the imperative duty to seek to the utmost of their power to bring about this unity ... on the basis of the principles established by the International Conventions.[33]

[30] Ibid., 419.
[31] *Internationaler Sozialisten Kongress zu Amsterdam, 1904* (Berlin: Vorwärts, 1904), 35–40.
[32] Ibid., 40.
[33] Daniel De Leon, ed., *Flashlights of the Amsterdam Congress* (New York: Labor News Company, 1904), 102–3.

Once more, orthodoxy had seemingly triumphed, but its victory would prove pyrrhic.

In the years leading up to the Great War, the socialist movement continued to tear itself apart over the same issues that had divided it before Amsterdam. In France, for example, the Amsterdam congress did have the desired effect of pushing the various socialist groups to put aside their differences and form a unified party, the SFIO (Section Française de l'Internationale Ouvriére) whose charter described it as a party of "class struggle" that rejected participation in bourgeois governments. But despite such pronouncements and the strictures laid out at Amsterdam, the party slowly but surely moved toward accommodation with almost all revisionist positions, including cooperation with bourgeois parties (both within parliament and during elections) and supporting reform work (the most important instance of which was the party's backing of the bourgeois government's 1910 pension scheme).

In Italy, as in France, the Amsterdam resolution also had little lasting impact on the ongoing tug of war for the PSI's soul. At the party's 1906 congress – so tumultuous that its president offered to resign – the various factions eventually united around a centrist position known as "integralism." Supporters of the compromise described integralism as being "for reforms, but against reformism," and as affirming that "there is no antithesis between the concept of violence . . . and the gradual development of socialism within the bosom of bourgeois society."[34] This mishmash obviously offered little more than a cover under which all factions could claim their concerns had been met, and it fractured as soon as the party was forced to take actual stands on difficult issues. In fact, after a wave of strikes in 1907–8 and the subsequent expulsion of revolutionary syndicalists from the party, revisionists and reformists found themselves ascendant, a trend that was confirmed at the PSI's 1910 congress, where Leonida Bissolati, a leading advocate of ministerialism, gave a rousing speech warning the party that if it continued to avoid governing responsibilities, it would doom itself to "impotence."[35] Watching the revisionists and reformists gain an upper hand at the congress, Giolitti gleefully announced that "Marx had been relegated to the attic."[36]

Given this, it is perhaps ironic that Giolitti himself helped the orthodox forces get back on their feet. In 1911, he asked Bissolati to join his government and help enact an ambitious program of reforms. Bissolati himself liked the idea, but the proposal threw the party into an uproar. Even many who supported the move feared it would cause an irreparable split within the movement, and so concluded that its costs probably outweighed its benefits. As Turati

---

[34] Ferri and Oddino Morgari at the 1906 congress. Quoted in Seton-Watson, *Italy from Liberalism to Fascism*, 267. See also Salomone, *Italian Democracy in the Making*, 66–8.

[35] James Edward Miller, *From Elite to Mass Politics* (Kent, OH: Kent State University Press, 1990), 131.

[36] Quoted in Mack Smith, *Italy: A Modern History*, 257.

colorfully put it, Giolitti's program "gives the impression of a very abundant meal offered at eight in the morning when the stomach isn't ready."[37] Bissolati did indeed eventually turn Giolitti down, but the episode left a bad taste in people's mouths. The revolutionaries were enraged that the offer had even been considered seriously, and were reinvigorated by the controversy. The episode, along with Giolitti's decision soon afterward to invade Libya, threw the Italian socialists back into internecine warfare.[38]

In Germany, meanwhile, not even the combination of the Dresden and Amsterdam resolutions was able to offset the pull of cross-class cooperation and real political power or stem the drift away from orthodoxy. One challenge came in the form of a budget crisis. In 1909, Chancellor Bernhard von Bülow proposed a substantial tax increase, including an inheritance tax, to deal with a budget shortfall caused largely by increased military expenditures. The Conservatives firmly rejected the proposal, believing that the move would be a slippery slope toward soaking the rich. This presented the SPD with a difficult choice: It had long demanded direct taxation, since indirect taxation, being regressive, hit its constituency disproportionately hard. But the association of financial reform with the arms buildup made it difficult for some in the party to swallow. As Carl Schorske put it, the tax bill was a "jewel of reform in a setting of military steel."[39] Revisionists in the party argued that the masses would not understand if the party joined with the Junkers to defeat one of its own longheld goals, and that the time was ripe for the SPD to abandon its isolation and join in a progressive alliance against the Conservatives. Party radicals replied that the taxes at issue were a pittance and railed against the possibility of being associated with imperialism and the "reactionary" politics of the Wilhelmine regime.[40] Some party leaders now seemed ready to change their position on cooperation with liberals, but Kautsky – even as he was shifting his position on other issues – held firm, and once again the SPD rejected a course shift. The debate was far from over, however, since in 1910 the SPD was once again thrown for a loop when the party's Baden chapter decided to collaborate with liberals and vote for the state budget. Wilhelm Kolb, the Baden party leader, recognizing the implications of such a move, noted that the time had come for the SPD to decide "whether [it] would pursue a serious revolutionary or a serious reformist policy.... [T]he attempt of the Marxists of... [the Kautsky]

---

[37] Ibid., 141.

[38] De Grand, *The Italian Left in the Twentieth Century*, 24.

[39] Carl Schorske, *German Social Democracy 1905–1917: The Development of the Great Schism* (Cambridge, MA: Harvard University Press, 1983), 166. See also Sheri Berman, "Modernization in Historical Perspective: The Case of Imperial Germany," *World Politics*, 53, 3, April, 450–1.

[40] One problem with this argument was that in earlier years, SPD spokespeople had advocated that direct taxes finance the cost of the new fleet and had attacked the navy bills for not being so financed. At the time, the party did this purely as a propaganda move, to show up the limitations of ruling-class patriotism. This stand came back to haunt them, however, in the current debate over finance reform.

school to demonstrate the correctness of their teaching breaks down in the face of reality."[41] Other revisionists within the party seized upon the issue to point out the contradiction between "our long standing parliamentarian practice and divorced [Marxist] theory."[42] The national leadership, recognizing the threat to its own long-standing policies and authority, quickly and sharply condemned the Baden chapter. But recognizing how sensitive the issue had become, it did not want to risk a party split over the issue. So a compromise was reached: Any member who voted for a budget in the future was threatened with expulsion, but no one was actually expelled.[43]

Controversy continued alongside mounting pressure in Germany for political liberalization and a relaxation of Prussia's undemocratic voting system in particular – which increased the incentives for alliances among progressive forces. This issue came to a head in 1912, when upcoming elections held out the prospect of an immense victory for parties favoring political change.[44] To maximize chances of such a victory, the SPD would have to conclude explicit electoral agreements with bourgeois liberals. The topic elicited heated debate within the party, but by now even Kautsky's position seemed to be shifting, and the party leadership negotiated a deal with the Progressives for electoral cooperation at the national level.

The outcome of the election was a triumph for democratic forces in general and the socialists in particular: The SPD and the Progressives together captured just over 50 percent of the votes (35 percent and 16.40 percent respectively) and the SPD emerged as the single largest party in parliament, garnering twice as many votes as its closest competitor. Even with this victory, however, the SPD was unable to move forward. The electoral cooperation elicited a storm of protest internally, and because of its desire to avoid further conflict, combined with the party's fear that it might be forced to reconsider some of its long-standing principles, the party did not follow up on its triumph. This would cost the party dearly in future years, as it failed to capitalize on its strengths or chart a bold new course for Germany during its time of troubles.

What the Austrians Knew

Despite the Dresden and Amsterdam resolutions and a constant stream of condemnation from many of the Second International's most important figures, most European socialist parties found themselves drifting toward an acceptance

---

[41] Quoted in Schorske, *German Social Democracy*, 187–8. See also Hannelore Schlemmer, "Die Rolle der Sozialdemokratie in den Landtagen Badens und Württembergs und ihr Einfluss auf die Entwicklung der Gesamtpartei Zwischen 1890 und 1914" (Ph.D. Dissertation, Albert Ludwigs Universität zu Freiburg, 1953).

[42] Quote is by Eduard David in Manfred Steger, *The Quest for Evolutionary Socialism* (New York: Cambridge University Press, 1997), 196.

[43] *Handbuch der Sozialdemokratischen Parteitage von 1910–1913* (Munich: Verlag von G. Birk und Co., 1972), 50–78.

[44] Berman, "Modernization in Historical Perspective."

of cross-class alliances, the value of democracy, and even ministerialism during the first decade and a half of the twentieth century. But these were not the only areas where socialists were forced to reconsider the viability of orthodox Marxism. Perhaps the most important issue confronting European societies in this era was the growing power and appeal of nationalism. Eventually many socialists realized that this too was something they could not – and should not – ignore.

Orthodox Marxist views on nationalism at the turn of the century followed the lines set out by the master a generation earlier. Marx had famously argued that workers "had no fatherland." He claimed their primary ties were to workers across the globe, not to other social groups in their countries, and that their struggle to transform the world transcended national borders; hence the clarion call, "workers of the world unite!" Kautsky and his orthodox colleagues more or less accepted this position wholesale, enshrining in key documents such as the SPD's Erfurt program a view of nationalism as an instrument of the ruling class that held no interest for the proletariat and was doomed to fade away as material conflicts came to an end.[45]

By the end of the century, however, the continuing growth of nationalist sentiment in many countries, the rise of nationalist parties, and the growing attractions and dangers of imperialism had forced many socialists to question this dismissive stance. One critique came from democratic revisionists, such as Bernstein and Jaurès, who openly challenged the idea that the proletariat had no fatherland and the materialistic interpretation of the subject offered by Marx, Engels, Kautsky, and their ilk. As democracy spread, they argued, workers' ties to their nation, as well as their stakes in its prosperity, would naturally increase. "The working class has national commitments just as much as it has international commitments, and it thus has national interests."[46] Since Bernstein believed that reform work and democracy would pave the way for socialism and since he recognized that these things could be achieved only within the context of the nation-state, he also saw the fate of workers (and citizens more generally) as inexorably linked to that of their homeland. The greater the SPD's strength and the greater the progress Germany made toward democracy, the greater was socialism's stake in and commitment to the nation. As he once put it:

... although this proposition [that workers have no fatherland] might perhaps apply to the worker of the 1840s, deprived of rights and excluded from public life, nowadays it

[45] Horace Davis, *Nationalism and Socialism* (New York: Monthly Review Press, 1967); Michael Forman, *Nationalism and the International Labor Movement* (University Park, PA: Penn State Press, 1998); Hermann Heidegger, *Die Deutsche Sozialdemokratie und der Nationale Staat* (Göttingen: Musterschmidt Verlag, 1956); Hans Mommsen, *Arbeiterbewegung und Nationale Frage* (Göttingen; Vandenhoeck and Ruprecht, 1979).

[46] Eduard Bernstein, *The Preconditions of Socialism* (New York: Cambridge University Press, 1993), 163–4, and Roger Fletcher, *Revisionism and Empire. Socialist Imperialism in Germany, 1897–1914* (London: George Allen and Unwin, 1984), 143.

has already lost most of its truth ... and will lose even more, the more the worker ceases to be a proletarian and becomes a citizen through the influence of [the labor movement]. The worker who has equal voting rights in state and municipality, etc. and shares in the common good of the nation, whose children the community educates, whose health it protects, and whom it insures against injury, will have a fatherland without therefore ceasing to be a citizen of the world.[47]

Jaurès expressed similar views. Although Marx and Engels had asserted in the *Communist Manifesto* that "the workers have no Fatherland," their words reflected an age before democracy had endowed men with the instruments of their liberation.[48] "For me," Jaurès once noted, "I consider that nations, home-lands, are a fact [and] that at the present time they have a socialist and human value. Humanity is not, at the present time, in fact, an international proletarian organization, it is not a proletarian socialist unity; at the present time, only an imperialistic militarism would be able to realize, in crushing nations, a sort of uniformity in slavery, and as long as humanity will be represented only by nations, the latter are a necessary guarantee for human activities."[49] Only the nation "and the nation alone ... can enfranchise all citizens. Only the nation can furnish the means of free development to all."[50]

Jaurès went beyond these practical concerns, acknowledging that nations satisfied "the natural, almost physical longing of human beings to live in a community larger than the family; the whole of mankind was too large a unity to satisfy that need."[51] He respected the "community of spirit, language, memories and hopes" encompassed in national communities, even remarking on the "touching unity of the French family."[52] "Nations" he once commented, "when they have been fashioned by a long process of history, when history has created within a large group of people similarities of psychology and harmonies of thought – are organic unities; and some of the characteristics of the nation are so deeply imprinted upon individuals that the destruction of the nation would be the destruction of individualism."[53] He therefore accepted the fact that it was the duty of socialists to defend their nations from outside attack because if "France were conquered, she could no longer transmit abundantly to her sons the treasures of her language and literature ... there would also be a loss of vitality, psychological weakening, intellectual bankruptcy, and organic suffering of individuals."[54]

---

[47] Bernstein, *The Preconditions of Socialism*, 188.
[48] Harvey Goldberg, *The Life of Jean Jaurès* (Madison, WI: University of Wisconsin Press, 1962), 351–2.
[49] Jean Jaurès, *Parti Socialiste Quatrième Congrès National*, Nancy, August 1907 (Paris: Siège du Conseil National), 264.
[50] Jean Jaurès, "The Socialist Aim," in Jaurès, *Studies in Socialism* (New York: G. P. Putnam's Sons, 1906), 8.
[51] Kolakowski, *Main Currents of Marxism*, 2, 132.
[52] Harold Weinstein, *Jean Jaurès* (New York: Columbia University Press, 1936), 45.
[53] Jackson J. Hampden, *Jean Jaurès* (London: George Allen and Unwin, 1943), 131.
[54] Weinstein, *Jean Jaurès*, 124.

Perhaps most importantly, both Bernstein and Jaurès recognized nationalism's powerful emotional and psychological appeal – and the danger to the
socialist movement that could come in ceding the issue to others. Bernstein
often bemoaned "Bebel's and Kautsky's defeatist strategy of dealing with the
national question by invoking a 'meaningless' Marxist utopia in an 'international socialist future' which would make the issue of nationalism irrelevant."[55]
He feared that if the SPD continued to champion a "mushy internationalism" that it would "push the proletariat into the arms of nationalist fanatics
while also failing to attract progressive segments of the bourgeoisie."[56] Bernstein urged his colleagues to avoid "the Schylla of ethnonationalism and the
Charybdis of an amorphous internationalism," and instead champion a noble
patriotism based on citizens' "natural feelings of love for their own country
and their people."[57] He saw no contradiction between this kind of patriotism and true internationalism; in fact, he believed that they reinforced each
other.[58]

Jaurès adopted a similar position, arguing that socialists should seek not "to
destroy patriotism but to enlarge it."[59] He also similarly advocated a "true
patriotism" – one that recognized and celebrated the particular values and
heritage of one's own nation while also respecting the fact that other nations
were "equally precious portions of the same humanity."[60] Such a "true patriotism," Jaurès argued, recognized no contradiction between socialist nationalism
and internationalism and would help socialists counter the destructive progress
of right-wing nationalism. Jaurès even insisted that socialists were the "true
nationalists," because they alone had a viable plan for "bring[ing] profound
unity to the nation."[61] Alongside the concerns of democratic revisionists like
Bernstein and Jaurès, the most powerful theoretical reevaluation of nationalism came, interestingly enough, from a group of socialists who were not
fundamentally hostile to orthodoxy: the Austro-Marxists.[62] Austro-Marxism
was one of the most innovative schools of Marxist thought during the early
twentieth century. Among their many contributions, its members promoted an
"ethical" interpretation of socialism, advocated the injection of morality and
Kantian thought into the socialist world view, and engaged in pioneering analyses of the modern state. Both committed to Marxism and willing to revise it

---

[55] Steger, *The Quest for Evolutionary Socialism*, 197.

[56] Ibid., 199.

[57] Bernstein wrote a series of articles on these themes; see discussion of the articles in ibid.,
197ff.

[58] Susanne Miller, "Bernstein's Political Position, 1914–1920," in Roger Fletcher, ed., *Bernstein to
Brandt* (London: Edward Arnold, 1987), 96.

[59] Kolakowski, *Main Currents of Marxism*, 132. See also Karl Vorländer, *Kant und Marx*
(Tübingen: J. C. B. Mohr, Paul Siebeck, 1926), 105ff.

[60] Weinstein, *Jean Jaurés*, 134.

[61] Ibid., 62.

[62] Of course, Lenin and Luxemburg also grappled extensively with the issue of nationalism during
this time, but the former in particular lies outside the scope of this analysis.

when necessary, they often occupied a position somewhere in between orthodox Marxists and their challengers.[63]

It was only natural for the Austro-Marxists to be consumed by the issue of nationalism. As Victor Adler noted, "We in Austria have a little International ourselves, we are the ones who know best the difficulties which have to be overcome."[64] Because of its unique supranational composition, the Austrian socialist party "was called upon, indeed compelled, to serve as an example of socialist internationalism by preventing or healing national strife. Its mission was to present a paradigm of the international socialist order of the future."[65] But by the turn of the century, the rising tide of nationalism in both Austria-Hungary and the party itself was making this internationalism increasingly difficult to maintain.

In response, figures such as Otto Bauer and Karl Renner began to devote themselves to the study of national identities – and found themselves forced to jettison most orthodox Marxist positions. Bauer and Renner became increasingly convinced of the powerful historical role that nationalism could play, and came to view national identities as a "primary and indestructible datum"[66] that could not be ignored.[67] They found themselves forced to discard the view of nationalism as either epiphenomenal or as a tool of the ruling classes, as well as the orthodox assertion that it would fade away with the transition to socialism. In fact, they concluded, just the opposite was likely to occur: By eliminating the societal conflicts and exclusion engendered by capitalism, socialism would actually serve to strengthen nationalist consciousness.[68] As Bauer put it:

This revolution in consciousness [brought about by the transition to socialism] will be consolidated by the everyday praxis of socialist society, which gives the masses for the first time the power to determine their own destiny, to decide by free discussion and resolution their own future, and thus make the development of human culture a deliberate,

[63] Tom Bottomore and Patrick Goode, *Austro-Marxism* (Oxford, UK: Clarendon Press, 1978); Ernst Glaser, *Im Umfeld des Austromarxismus* (Vienna: Europaverlag, 1981); Peter Kuleman, *Am Beipiel des AustroMarxismus* (Hamburg: Julius Verlag, 1979); Norbert Leser, *Sozialismus Zwischen Relativismus und Dogmatismus* (Freiburg: Verlag Rombach, 1974); idem, "Austro-Marxism: A Reappraisal," *Journal of Contemporary History*, 11, 1976; idem, *Zwischen Reformismus und Bolshevismus* (Vienna: Europa Verlag, 1968); Hans-Jörg Sandkühler and Rafeal de la Vega, eds., *Austromarxismus* (Vienna: Europäische Verlag, 1970).
[64] Quoted in James Joll, *The Second International 1889–1914* (Boston: Routledge and Kegan Paul, 1974), 120.
[65] Jacob Talmon, *Myth of the Nation and Vision of Revolution* (New Brunswick, NJ: Transaction, 1991), 133.
[66] Ibid., 164.
[67] Otto Bauer, "The Concept of the Nation," in Bottomore and Goode, eds., *Austro-Marxism*, 107.
[68] Arthur Kogan, "The Social Democrats and the Conflict of the Nationalities in the Habsburg Monarchy," *Journal of Modern History*, 21, 3, September 1949; Mommsen, *Arbeiterbewegung*; Hans Mommsen, *Die Sozialdemokratie und die Nationalitätenfrage in Habsburgischen Vielvölkerstaat* (Vienna, Europa Verlag, 1963).

intentional, conscious human act.... There is no doubt that [these] development[s] will strengthen the principle of political nationality.[69]

Rather than ignoring nationalism or wishing it away, they argued, socialists needed to accommodate and direct it.

With regard to their own country, these socialists argued for a reorganization of the Habsburg Empire that would allow national communities a significant degree of control and autonomy. These ideas were incorporated into their party's own routines, as well as its 1899 Brno (Brünn) program, which advocated the establishment of a democratic federation within which national minorities would be protected and nations would have local autonomy in matters of "cultural or national significance."[70]

The implications of Bauer's and Renner's reevaluations were profound. Following their lead, the Austrian socialist party came to accept the functionality of the existing multinational Habsburg Empire and worked to improve and strengthen rather than destroy it. (As Renner put it, "Austria-Hungary served regional requirements so perfectly that it would have to be invented if it were not already in existence."[71]) The anomalous consequence of these efforts was to turn the Austrian Socialist Party (SDAP), ostensibly dedicated to revolution, into "the staunchest upholder of the indivisibility of the venerable monarchy, and as objectively the most reliable ally of the dynasty."[72]

But despite the efforts of Bauer, Renner, and other Austro-Marxists to understand and accommodate nationalism, the centrifugal tendencies of the Habsburg Empire proved increasingly difficult to contain. During the early twentieth century, nationalist sentiment and conflicts among the Empire's constituent groups grew. Governance degenerated into frustrating bargaining sessions over national and administrative matters, political life grew demoralized, parliament lost sympathy among the population, and radical nationalist parties grew – all of which made it almost impossible for the Socialists to pursue a positive agenda.[73]

To make matters worse, the socialist party itself was not immune to these trends. By the turn of the century, the Czechs in particular were chafing under what they saw as the hegemony of the German-speaking Austrians. The situation came to a boil when the Czech group threatened to leave the union federation and set up an independent organization. Unable to solve the problem at home, a decision was made to refer it to the International for arbitration. The 1910 Copenhagen congress of the International thus duly took up the question of whether the Czechs, and by extension other national groups, had the right

[69] Bauer, "Socialism and the Principle of Nationality," in Bottomore and Goode, eds., *Austro-Marxism*, III, 110.

[70] Forman, *Nationalism and the International Labor Movement*, 96.

[71] Quoted in Leser, "Austro-Marxism," 135.

[72] Talmon, *Myth of the Nation and Vision of Revolution*, 138. Also Kogan, "The Social Democrats and the Conflict of Nationalities," 206.

[73] Ibid., 206, and Mommsen, *Arbeiterbewegung*, 95.

to form their own organizations. As the Austrians had hoped and expected, the call for separate unions was duly rejected. But the rebuff did not quell nationalist sentiments, and not long after the end of the Copenhagen congress, the Czechs broke away and formed their own socialist party anyway – making painfully obvious, as one observer notes, that "Czech nationalism [was] more powerful than the international bonds of ideology."[74]

Although it remained the official ideology of most West European socialist parties and the Socialist International, orthodox Marxism was increasingly beleaguered in the years leading up to the First World War. Democratic revisionists attacked its main pillars head on while the practical realities facing socialist parties led to a reconsideration, even abandonment, of orthodox positions on issues like cross-class alliances, democracy, ministerialism, and nationalism. And as if this were not enough, orthodox Marxism had to face a challenge from yet another corner. During the fin-de-siècle, the same forces that had pushed many socialists toward democratic revisionism and many socialists parties to reorient their praxis led another group of socialists to develop yet another critique of Marxism, one greatly influenced by the anti-Enlightenment and nationalist backlashes of the era. It is to this critique and its relationship with forces on the right that we now turn.

[74] Clifton Gene Follis, "The Austrian Social Democratic Party, June 1914–November 1918" (Ph.D. Dissertation, Stanford University, 1961), 39.

4

Revolutionary Revisionism and the Merging of Nationalism and Socialism

As we saw in the last two chapters, democratic revisionism emerged in response to the inability of orthodox Marxism to explain or deal with many of the challenges of Western Europe's fin-de-siècle. Yet this was not the only revisionist challenge to emerge in response to orthodox Marxism's perceived problems during the late nineteenth and early twentieth centuries. Indeed, the most famous revisionist of this time was a figure who came not from Western Europe, but from its periphery – V. I. Lenin. Operating in a country in the early rather than later stages of capitalist development, Lenin found a doctrine that preached that socialism would develop only when economic conditions were ripe as unattractive as Eduard Bernstein and other West European socialists found it unbelievable. Having little faith in or patience with the inexorable unfolding of history, Lenin therefore also developed a strategy that was based on the primacy of politics rather than economics in the transition to socialism. Recognizing, in other words, that socialism would not come about simply because it was inevitable (or unwilling to wait around for such an eventuality to occur), Lenin concluded that it would have to be achieved as the result of human action. This realization Lenin shared with other revisionists; where he differed is in the conclusions he drew from this. Where democratic revisionists put their faith in the ability of an inspired majority to effect fundamental change through democratic means, in Lenin's revisionism historical materialism was replaced by the view that socialism could be imposed through the politico-military efforts of a revolutionary elite. Lenin believed that if left to themselves the masses would develop neither the will nor the ability to fight successfully for socialism; instead, acquiring the necessary "revolutionary consciousness" and organization was the task of a revolutionary party, and in particular of its leadership.[1]

---

[1] For example, in *What Is to Be Done?* Lenin argued that "the history of all countries shows that the working class, exclusively by its own effort, is able to develop only trade union consciousness.... The theory of socialism, however, grew out of the philosophic, historical, and economic theories elaborated by educated representatives of the propertied classes, by

In short, in the Leninist revision of Marxism historical materialism and class struggle were replaced by the primacy of politics and revolutionary vanguards.[2] Indeed it was precisely Lenin's revisionism – his rejection of the economic determinism of orthodox Marxism and his emphasis on the possibilities of informed and determined political action – that inspired generations of socialists to come.[3] From the Chinese insistence that "armed with the great thought of Mao Tse-tung" a minoritarian revolutionary party could become the motive force of historical change, to Che Guevara's claim that "it is not always necessary to wait for all the conditions for a revolution to exist; the insurrectional focal point can create them,"[4] to Georg Lukács' proclamation that "Lenin succeeded in refuting the 'laws' of capitalist development and injected a sense of urgent political action in Marxism,"[5] twentieth century activists found in Lenin's revisionism justification for their belief that communism could be brought to any country, regardless of economic circumstance.[6]

Although its most important impact was not in Western Europe but in parts of the world that like Russia were struggling to speed up their transition to modernity, Lenin and the movement he inspired exerted a profound influence on West European politics and will therefore reappear in later parts of this story. However, alongside the democratic revisionism of Bernstein and the communism of Lenin, a third strand of revisionism appeared at this time, one that would indeed form the basis of a movement that would come to power in Western Europe in the decades to come.

intellectuals." Therefore, the revolution will require a "strong and centralized organization of revolutionaries" who can provide the "conscious element" necessary to direct the "spontaneous element." Lenin, *What Is to Be Done?* Reprinted in Robert Tucker, ed., *The Lenin Anthology* (New York: W. W. Norton, 1975), 24.

[2] Perry Anderson, *In the Tracks of Historical Materialism* (Chicago: University of Chicago Press, 1983); Alfred G. Meyer, *Leninism* (New York: Prager, 1972); Joseph M. Schwartz. *The Permanence of the Political: A Democratic Critique of the Radical Impulse to Transcend Politics* (Princeton, NJ: Princeton University Press, 1995); Ellen Wood, *Democracy Against Capitalism* (New York: Cambridge University Press, 1995), 6ff.

[3] That Lenin insisted on his fidelty to Marx and Engels does not in any way detract from his status as a revisionist: According to the criteria laid out in this book, both his theory and praxis place him in this category. See footnotes 4 and 5 as well as Eric Hobsbawm, "Preface," in Georges Haupt, *Aspects of International Socialism, 1871–1914* (Cambridge, UK: Cambridge University Press, 1986), xvi, and Chantal Mouffe, *Gramsci and Marxist Theory* (London: Routledge and Kegan Paul, 1979), 176. For another interesting view of how Lenin fits into the larger scheme of Marxist theorizing (and indirectly to the categories laid out in this book), see Stephen Hanson, *Time and Revolution: Marxism and the Design of Soviet Institutions* (Chapel Hill, NC: University of North Carolina Press, 1997).

[4] A. James Gregor, *Contemporary Radical Ideologies* (New York: Random House, 1968), 99–100.

[5] Quoted in Carl Boggs, *The Socialist Tradition: From Crisis to Decline* (New York: Routledge, 1995), 45.

[6] See also famously Antonio Gramsci, "The Revolution Against Das Kapital," in Gramsci, *Selections from the Prison Notebooks* (New York: International Publishers, 1987), xxxi–xxxii, and more recently François Furet, *The Passing of an Illusion* (Chicago: University of Chicago Press, 1999), 31–2.

Western Europe's fin-de-siècle was a period of rapid and disorienting change. A wave of globalization was sweeping the world, transforming European societies and generating immense social dislocation, fragmentation, and conflict. Between 1870 and 1900, Europe's population grew more than 30 percent, life expectancy and literacy rose dramatically, and the industrial and service sectors boomed while agriculture continued its steady decline.[7] These changes contributed to unprecedented migration, both internally (thanks to massive urbanization) and externally (as staggering numbers abandoned the "old" world for the "new").[8] Rapid social change weakened old elites and long-standing social and economic relationships and created an "extraordinary number of *deracines*.... that is, persons uprooted from ancestral soil and local allegiances,"[9] who had trouble adjusting to the dynamics of modern society. Amid the turmoil, not just workers, but artisans, farmers, and other marginal groups struggled to adjust to the ruthless competitive pressures of the capitalist system and the anomie and atomization of modern society. The result was a backlash, of which the new nationalist movements were a prime example and major beneficiary.[10]

Nationalists argued that only a revival of national communities could provide the sense of solidarity, belonging, and collective purpose that Europe's divided and disoriented societies so desperately needed. Many of them came to see socialism as a necessary component of their larger political program, but this was a socialism divorced from Marxism – based on a deep suspicion of capitalism and liberalism and a firm belief that something had to be done for those most discomfited by the new modern world order, but vehemently rejecting historical materialism and class struggle. At the same time that some on the right were calling for a non-Marxian socialism, dissident socialists on the left were gaining an appreciation for the revolutionary potential of nationalism. They saw it as an opportunity – a way to forge the motivated cadres and troops that workers and existing socialist parties seemed unable to deliver. These revisionist socialists were also influenced by the larger anti-Enlightenment backlash of the fin-de-siècle; unlike their democratic revisionist counterparts, they had nothing but disdain for liberalism and all it represented. They therefore rejected the democratic path of Bernstein and believed that socialism would emerge only

---

[7] B. R. Mitchell, *European Historical Statistics 1750–1970* (New York: Columbia University Press, 1978).

[8] For example, during the first decade of the twentieth century, approximately 5.5 million Italians left their homeland while in Sweden an astounding 20 percent of the population emigrated between 1860 and 1910. Maurice Neufeld, *Italy: School for Awakening Countries* (Ithaca, NY: Cayuga Press, 1961), 521, and Franklin Scott, *Sweden: The Nation's History* (Minneapolis, MN: University of Minnesota Press, 1977), 369–70.

[9] J. H. Carlton Hayes, *A Generation of Materialism, 1871–1900* (New York: Harper and Brothers, 1941), 254.

[10] These movements were considered "new" because the nationalism of the late nineteenth century was very different from earlier nationalism, which had been associated with liberalism, democracy, and humanism. See the discussion in this chapter.

from "active combat which would destroy the existing state of things."[11] This strand of revisionism has thus been called "revolutionary," and during the late nineteenth and early twentieth centuries, figures in this group came to believe that they might share a true community of interest with the growing nationalist movements on the right.[12] For these and other reasons, the fin-de-siècle witnessed the birth of a "national" socialism, a trend both midwifed and epitomized by Georges Sorel.

Sorel and Revolutionary Revisionism

Although largely forgotten today, Sorel was once considered by many to be "the greatest revolutionary in twentieth century political philosophy."[13] According to one popular (but possibly apocryphal) story, in the same week in the 1920s the director of the Bibliothèque Nationale in Paris was approached by the ambassadors of both Soviet Russia and Fascist Italy with offers to repair Sorel's tombstone. During the turmoil of the first third of the twentieth century, many would have agreed with Wyndham Lewis's characterization of Sorel as "the key to all contemporary political thinking."[14]

Sorel's path to prominence was a complicated one. Born in provincial France in 1847 and employed for many years as an engineer, it was not until he was in his forties that he moved to Paris and devoted himself full-time to intellectual pursuits. He soon established himself as "one of the leading theoreticians of Marxism in France"[15] and developed an association with the mainstream, orthodox wing of the movement. By the turn of the century, however, he was already questioning some of orthodoxy's basic premises.

As with Bernstein and other revisionists, Sorel's doubts were rooted in a realization of the gap between orthodox Marxism and the demands of contemporary politics. At first he hoped to be able to update Marxism for his own time, and focused his criticism on supposed distortions of Marx's work propagated by figures such as Engels, Lafargue, and Guesde. As time went on, however, he decided that many of orthodoxy's problems originated with Marx himself.

As did many of his contemporaries, he came to recognize that many of Marx's predictions about capitalism were simply not coming to pass. "Marx had written *Capital*," Sorel observed, "on the basis of observations made in England. But in the thirty years following its publication many great changes

[11] Georges Sorel, *Reflections on Violence* (London: Collier Macmillan, 1950), 50.
[12] Zeev Sternhell, *Neither Right Nor Left* (Princeton, NJ: Princeton University, 1986), and idem with Mario Sznajder and Maia Asheri, *The Birth of Fascist Ideology* (Princeton, NJ: Princeton University Press, 1994).
[13] Hans Barth, *Masse und Mythos* (Hamburg: Rowolt Taschenbuch Verlag, 1959), 10.
[14] J. L. Talmon, "The Legacy of Georges Sorel," *Encounter*, 34, February 1970.
[15] J. R. Jennings, ed., *Georges Sorel: The Character and Development of His Thought* (New York: St. Martin's Press, 1985), 38.

took place in English industry, politics and in English life generally."[16] Indeed, Sorel noted, "experience shows us that the capitalist system is changing rather rapidly before our eyes. Orthodox [Marxists] make extraordinary efforts of imagination in order to not see what is clear to everyone; they have abandoned the terrain of social science to pass into utopia."[17] If capitalism had become more complex and differentiated since Marx's time, Sorel argued, then it was unlikely to collapse soon. He was in fact impressed by capitalism's immense productive powers and came to believe that the "primacy of production was essential to the operation of socialism."[18] Instead of calling for the socialization of private property and other measures that would hinder economic development, Sorel limited his opposition to capitalism "to the political, intellectual, and moral aspects of the liberal and bourgeois system; he [did not question] the foundations, principles and competitive mechanisms of the capitalist economy."[19]

Like the democratic revisionists, Sorel came to believe that historical materialism was not only wrong, but that it was also robbing the socialist movement of its vitality. As he noted, "belief in inevitable progress means paralysis of the will to power and creation":[20]

Orthodox Marxists had such confidence in their theories that they end in quietism. Among Marxists there is a widespread opinion that social evolution is like a natural process which fulfills itself independently of every human effort, and before which individuals can do nothing but fold their arms and wait until the fruit is ripe enough to harvest.... The words which Marx used to express the analogy between the economy and nature have contributed in large measure to developing the fatalist illusion, above all through the use of the term "necessary."[21]

Any movement that described history in terms of rigid laws thus doomed itself to failure: "It is impossible to speak of determinism for nothing is determined."[22] Many Marxist theoreticians were, to Sorel's chagrin, unwilling to confront the problems he identified and to admit that socialist doctrine needed to change with the times. "Time after time," he lamented, "the theorists of socialism have been embarrassed by contemporary history. They had constructed magnificent formulas, clear cut and symmetrical, but they could not make them fit the facts.

[16] Sorel, "The Decomposition of Marxism," in Irving Louis Horowitz, ed., *Radicalism and the Revolt Against Reason* (London: Routledge and Kegan Paul, 1901), 215.
[17] Sorel, "Is there a Utopia in Marxism?" in John L. Stanely, ed., *From Georges Sorel* (New Brunswick, NJ: Transaction, 1987), 135.
[18] Jack J. Roth, *The Cult of Violence: Sorel and the Sorelians* (Berkeley, CA: University of California Press, 1980), 58.
[19] Sternhell, *The Birth of Fascist Ideology*, 90.
[20] Quoted in Roger Henry Soltau, *French Political Thought in the Nineteenth Century* (New York: Russell and Russell, 1959), 447–8.
[21] Georges Sorel, "Necessity and Fatalism in Marxism," reprinted in Stanley, ed., *From Georges Sorel*, 111, 124.
[22] Ibid., 57, and Soltau, *French Political Thought*, 461.

Rather than abandon their theories, they preferred to declare that the most important facts were anomalies, which science must ignore if it is to obtain a real understanding of the whole."[23]

In the revisionist controversy discussed earlier, Sorel firmly supported Bernstein, noting that his efforts had "produced an effect analogous to that of a Protestant sermon amidst a Catholic population."[24] "When Bernstein, perceiving the enormous contradiction between the language of [socialism] and the true nature of its activity," Sorel wrote, "urged his German comrades to have the courage to appear what they were in reality, and to revise a doctrine that had become mendacious, there was a universal outburst of indignation at his audacity."[25] This was unfortunate, Sorel felt, since what Bernstein wanted was for "socialists to throw their doctrines overboard in order to observe, understand and, above all, play a truly efficacious role in the world."[26] Bernstein's revisionism was thus a sign of hope for the socialist movement:

With Bernstein, one likes to think that Marxism constitutes a . . . doctrine still full of the future, that it suffices to free it from badly made commentaries and to develop it, while taking recent occurrences into account. With admirable good faith and great ability, [Bernstein] pursues the task of rejuvenating Marxism: from superannuated formulas or false impressions, he calls it back to the very spirit of Marx; we are talking about a *return to the spirit of Marxism*. With Kautsky, it is the complete opposite; Marxism appears as a very old thing, a compilation of disparate theses that the disciples keep from exposing too much. For them it is above all a matter of defending words, appearances and petrified formulas. . . . If [the socialist movement] were compromised of men sufficiently *emancipated from superstition*, undoubtedly Bernstein would have the great majority grouped around him. His book would be received as a deliverance. . . . *The triumph of Kautsky would signify the definitive ruination of Marxism.*[27]

Sorel agreed with Bernstein's conclusion that what was needed was an activist and voluntarist alternative to orthodoxy's economic determinism and political passivity. He too realized that if socialism was not, in fact, inevitable, then it would have to emerge as the result of directed human action. Indeed, perhaps even more than his democratic revisionist counterparts, Sorel was possessed by the idea of man as "creator," "fulfilled only when he creates, and not when he passively receives or drifts with the current."[28] For Sorel, history was as an act of creation that could be "forced" forward by "heroic acts of will."[29] If they

[23] Sorel, *Reflections on Violence*, 63. See also idem, "The Decomposition of Marxism."

[24] Idem, "Polemics on the Interpretation of Marxism: Bernstein and Kautsky," in Stanley, ed., *From Georges Sorel*, 150.

[25] Idem, *Reflections on Violence*, 64.

[26] Idem, "Polemics on the Interpretation of Marxism: Bernstein and Kautsky," in Stanley, ed., *From Georges Sorel*, 150. See also idem, "The Decomposition of Marxism."

[27] Idem, "Polemics on the Interpretation of Marxism," 174–5. Emphasis in the original.

[28] Isaiah Berlin, "Georges Sorel," *Times Literary Supplement*, 3644, December 31, 1971, 1617.

[29] John Stanley, introduction to Georges Sorel, *The Illusions of Progress* (Berkeley, CA: University of California Press, 1969), xxxv.

wanted to motivate great collective efforts, he concluded, socialists "must be convinced that the work to which they are devoting themselves is a serious, formidable, and sublime work; it is only on this condition that they will be able to bear the innumerable sacrifices."[30] And so, like Bernstein, Sorel too called for a rediscovery of the moral content of Marxism:

We know that [socialists] generally have a great disdain for ethical considerations. They treat morality with as much contempt as the Voltarians treated religion (which is no worse for wear because of it). When Bernstein writes: "The degree of development attained now gives to ideological factors and more particularly to ethical factors a freer field than ever before," Kautsky responds, "There is no place in historical materialism for a morality that is independent of economic forces and superior to them." It is like dreaming to read such an audacious declaration![31]

Yet despite similar criticisms of orthodoxy and comparable emphases on the primacy of politics, Sorel and Bernstein came up with very different suggested courses of action as a result of their very different readings of the fin-de-siècle world. When he surveyed Western Europe, Bernstein saw many reasons for optimism. He believed the reigning bourgeois liberal order was flawed but such was his respect for its genuine achievements that he believed socialism's task was not to destroy the order it created but rather to improve it. He once wrote, for example: "It is indeed true that the great liberal movement of recent times has in the first instance, benefited the capitalist bourgeoisie, and that the parties which took the name of Liberal, were, or became in time, nothing but straightforward defenders of capitalism.... But with respect to liberalism as a historical movement, socialism is its legitimate heir, not only chronologically, but also intellectually."[32] He thus believed socialists could and should work within the reigning liberal order to effect change, and viewed democracy as the most logical instrument for this task.

Sorel, on the other hand, was convinced of the utter decay, decadence and corruption of the contemporary world, and, like many other intellectuals of the day, he wanted not to reform it but to destroy it. (He once argued that Bernstein might have too, had he lived in France rather than Germany and thus been more directly exposed to a revolutionary tradition.[33]) For him, nineteenth bourgeois liberalism was itself the source of Europe's contemporary malaise and societal disorder,[34] and he had nothing but disdain for democracy,

---

[30] Sorel, *Reflections on Violence*, 139.

[31] Idem, "Polemics on the Interpretation of Marxism," 157–8.

[32] Eduard Bernstein, *The Preconditions of Socialism*, Henry Tudor, ed. (New York: Cambridge University Press, 1993), 147. On Bernstein's relationship to liberalism, see Roger Fletcher, *Revisionism and Empire* (London: George Allen and Unwin, 1984); Peter Gay, *The Dilemma of Democratic Socialism* (New York: Columbia University Press, 1952); Manfred Steger, *The Quest for Evolutionary Socialism* (New York: Cambridge University Press, 1997).

[33] Sorel, *Reflections on Violence*, 141, 214.

[34] Horowitz, *Radicalism and the Revolt Against Reason*; Jennings, *Georges Sorel*; Roth, *The Cult of Violence*; Sternhell, *The Birth of Fascist Ideology*; idem, *Neither Right nor Left*.

which he believed inevitably robbed socialists of their revolutionary fervor.[35] "Experience has quickly shown," Sorel claimed, "that . . . in entering into middle class institutions, revolutionaries have been transformed. . . . All . . . agree that there is very little difference between a middle class representative and a representative of the proletariat."[36] Socialism, accordingly, should stand as "an irreconcilable adversary" of the contemporary order, "threatening it with moral catastrophe."[37]

Sorel believed that bringing this catastrophe about would require a constant and probably "violent" struggle.[38] At first, he thought the revolutionary ardor necessary for such a struggle could come from a reemphasis on Marxism's moral roots. As time passed, however, and he became increasingly disillusioned with Marxism, he began to look elsewhere for something capable of motivating radical action; he eventually settled on the motivating power of myths. For Sorel, myths were "not descriptions of things, but expressions of a determination to act . . . [they] lead men to prepare themselves for a combat which will destroy the existing state of things [rather than directing] men's minds towards reforms which can be brought about by patching up the existing system."[39] By galvanizing the masses, myths would "permit the social and economic reality of the beginning of the century to be surmounted."[40] And while myths could inspire, to maintain revolutionary ardor it would also be necessary to keep the proletariat separate from bourgeois society. "All our efforts," Sorel wrote, "should aim at preventing bourgeois ideas from poisoning the class which is arising; that is why we can never do enough to break every link between the people and [all forms] of bourgeois deceit and decadence."[41] He saw conflict as a way to "restore the separation of the classes, just when they seemed on the point of intermingling in the democratic marsh."[42]

However, by the first decade of the twentieth century, Sorel had begun to lose faith in the revolutionary potential of the proletariat. To begin with, the economic and social developments that Marx had predicted would create a powerful, revolutionary working class and inevitable class conflict were not coming to pass: The proletariat was not growing ever larger, other classes were not disappearing, and societies were in general becoming more socially differentiated

---

[35] Jacob L. Talmon, *Myth of the Nation and Vision of Revolution* (New Brunswick, NJ: Transaction, 1981), esp. 456ff.

[36] Ibid., 55.

[37] Quoted in Jeremy Jennings, *Syndicalism in France* (New York: St. Martin's Press, 1990), 57. See also Talmon, "The Legacy of Georges Sorel."

[38] There is some confusion about precisely what Sorel was calling for here. Sometimes the term "violence" in his work does not necessarily seem to refer to action that results in bloodshed, but rather simply to direct, intense effort.

[39] Sorel, "Letter to Daniel Halevy," in idem, *Reflections on Violence*, 50.

[40] Sternhell, *The Birth of Fascist Ideology*, 59. See also Michael Tager, "Myths and Politics in the Works of Sorel and Barthes," *Journal of the History of Ideas*, 47, 4, October–December 1986.

[41] Talmon, *Myth of the Nation and Vision of Revolution*, 458, 462.

[42] Sorel, *Reflections on Violence*, 92.

and complex.[43] In fact, he believed that the reigning bourgeois, liberal order had managed to "domesticate" the proletariat and deradicalize workers' movements. The result of these observations was that Sorel, like his democratic revisionist counterparts, abandoned his exclusive focus on the working class. But whereas the abandonment of a workers-only strategy led democratic revisionists to emphasize possibilities of cross-class cooperation and compromise, it led Sorel to embrace the revolutionary possibilities of a revitalized mass nationalism and to encourage the fusion of antidemocratic forces of the left with those of the right. Over the first decades of the new century, such ideas would spark the beginnings of something new and very dangerous.

Italy

Although Sorel was French, his ideas had their greatest impact in Italy. Some of his most important writings originally appeared in Italian, and he was widely read and discussed in Italian society. As one observer notes, "Every publication of his was widely commented upon by writers of the most diverse views. Every newspaper and weekly in Italy, whatever its political orientation, went to great lengths to secure an interview with the celebrated author of *Reflections on Violence* [Sorel's 1908 manifesto]."[44] Indeed, the Italian translation of *Reflections* was introduced by Benedetto Croce, the country's most well-known and influential intellectual. Sorel's greatest influence, however, was on the extremes of the Italian political spectrum, where he helped the syndicalist and nationalist movements realize how much they had in common – thus laying the intellectual foundations for what would become known as fascism.

Until 1908, syndicalism had been a significant faction within the Italian labor movement in general and the PSI in particular. Like democratic revisionists, syndicalists rejected orthodox Marxism's determinism and passivity, but they disdained political organizations and advocated direct revolutionary attacks on the existing order rather than a peaceful and evolutionary strategy of democratic transformation. At first, they assigned this revolutionary role to the proletariat. As time passed, however, many of them decided that the proletariat had become, as one observer noted, "saturated with 'democratic prejudices' and 'petit bourgeois in spirit,'" and thus unable to "develop the type of superior morality which creates the hero – the man who considers himself a warrior with a vow of sacrifice."[45] Such views brought many syndicalists into conflict with the leadership of the PSI, and in the aftermath of a massive strike wave in 1907–8, PSI leaders declared revolutionary syndicalism with its rejection of

[43] Jennings, *Georges Sorel*, 86; Larry Portis, *Georges Sorel* (London: Pluto Press, 1980), 55ff; John Stanley, *The Sociology of Virtue: The Political and Social Theories of Georges Sorel* (Berkeley, CA: University of California Press, 1981), esp. 114ff.

[44] Talmon, *Myth of the Nation and Vision of Revolution*, 475.

[45] Thomas R. Sykes, "The Practice of Revolutionary Syndicalism in Italy" (Ph.D. Dissertation, Columbia University Press, 1974), 132.

political organization and emphasis on violence and direct action incompatible with the party's doctrines and expelled all its adherents.

The expulsion of revolutionary syndicalists did not, however, put an end to the party's internal debates. As noted in Chapter 3, the PSI's 1908 and 1910 congresses were victories for its moderate democratic revisionist wing, but when this led Giovanni Giolitti to proclaim that "Marx had finally been relegated to the attic," the party's internal battles reignited. The invasion of Libya soon afterward stopped the PSI's drift toward revisionism and accommodation in its tracks.

At the party's 1911 congress, opponents of democratic revisionism played the war card. Giolitti's Libya policy, they argued, showed what could be expected from cooperation with the bourgeois order – a charge which divided the democratic revisionists themselves. Some argued that it was possible, and indeed desirable, to continue supporting the government's reform program while making clear the party's opposition to the war. But others came to feel that the war might actually benefit the nation and its workers, and so rejected a move back into opposition and the political wilderness. One prominent proponent of this latter position was Ivanoe Bonomi, one of the party's leading revisionists, who had for years mounted spirited attacks on orthodox Marxism's rigidity, sterility, and determinism. Bonomi championed the active participation of socialists in the parliamentary and electoral systems, which he believed implied support for ministerialism, and he favored loyalty to the government on the war issue for both substantive and political reasons. By supporting Giolitti, Bonomi argued, the PSI would show that "there is a national solidarity that is not opposed to, but rather complements, class solidarity."[46] Bissolati felt the same way, arguing that socialists should support Giolitti's Libyan policies in order to "keep the nation from being strangled in the Mediterranean and to prevent, as well, the dangerous nationalist movement from exercising a monopoly on Italian patriotism."[47] With the party's factions split both among and within themselves, the outcome of the congress was inconclusive.[48]

Then, on March 14, 1912, an anarchist made an unsuccessful attempt to assassinate the King. In response, a group from the Chamber of Deputies went to the Palace to congratulate the monarch on his survival. Three socialists – Bissolati, Bonomi, and Angiolo Cabrini – were part of the delegation, a final affront that gave the anti-accommodationists the ammunition they needed. When the party assembled that July for its congress at Reggio Emilia, they were ready to attack. A young and previously little-known activist named Benito

[46] Maurice Neufeld, *Italy: School for Awakening Countries. The Italian Labor Movement in Its Political, Social, and Economic Setting from 1800 to 1960* (Ithaca, NY: Cayuga Press, 1961), 240.
[47] Ibid.
[48] Alexander De Grand, *The Italian Left in the Twentieth Century* (Indianapolis, IN: Indiana University Press, 1989), 24; James Edward Miller, *From Elite to Mass Politics* (Kent, OH: Kent State University Press, 1990), 151; Charles Yarrow, "The Ideological Origins of Italian Fascism" (Ph.D. Thesis: Yale University, 1938), 117.

Mussolini gave an impassioned speech, electrifying the assembled delegates with his calls for the expulsion of the deputies who had visited the King. Bonomi responded by reminding the gathering that

The case you are asked to judge is not a question of the crisis of a few individual consciences, but rather the crisis of two conceptions: Revolutionary and Reformist... Expulsion is not... a disciplinary action against a few dissidents, but... the separation of two methods, two conceptions, two modes of interpreting socialism.... While we Reformists of the right have an open view of society and of the party, you men of the left are the champions of dogma.... We believe that the rising force of the proletariat makes this the period to reform; you hold after Libya, no reform is possible. In a few words, you restrict yourself to opposition, we enlarge ourselves in action.[49]

But attempts to broker a compromise failed, and the result was the expulsion of Bonomi and the others, who immediately left the congress and founded a new party, the Italian Socialist Reformist Party (Partito Socialista Riformista Italiano, or PSRI).[50]

Mussolini emerged from the congress as "hero of Reggio"[51] and, more importantly, as the champion of a new type of socialism; his followers, including such future stars as Antonio Gramsci, dubbed themselves "Mussoliniani." Opposed to the passivity and sterility of orthodox traditionalists, but also repulsed by the gradualism and accommodationism of democratic revisionism, Mussolini called for a new type of socialism, one that was active and truly revolutionary – and he found in Sorel and his syndicalist supporters the basic elements of the new ideology that he was groping toward.

The patriotic frenzy unleashed by the invasion of Libya had convinced many syndicalists that "national sentiment was capable of generating the selfless enthusiasm and sacrificial disposition among sectors of the population that syndicalists had expected exclusively among proletarians."[52] Many also saw the material benefits of conquest as too attractive for a poor nation like Italy (and its workers) to pass up.[53] And many valued the war's "moral" and "pedagogical" impact, as training for the sort of grand activist endeavor that revolution would necessarily involve. Many syndicalists were thus increasingly impressed by Sorel and his sophisticated theoretical treatement of revolutionary revisionism, which struck similar notes.

Mussolini felt the same way. Reading and corresponding with many of the leading syndicalists and revolutionary revisionists of the day, he adopted their ideas as his own and identified Sorel as one of his key inspirations. ("It is to

[49] Miller, *From Elite to Mass Politics*, 160.
[50] The new party took with it some deputies and led the confederation of labor to declare itself autonomous. It fell apart, however, during the war.
[51] Mirella Mingardo, *Mussolini Turati e Fortchiari. La Formazione della Sinistra Socialista a Milano 1912–1918* (Genova: Graphos, 1992), 44.
[52] A. James Gregor, *Phoenix: Fascism in Our Time* (New Brunswick, NJ: Transaction, 1999), 42.
[53] Charles Lloyd Betrand, "Revolutionary Syndicalism in Italy, 1912–22" (Ph.D. Dissertation, University of Wisconsin, 1969), 53, and Sternhell, *The Birth of Fascist Ideology*, 166.

Sorel that I owe the most," he was later to claim.[54]) As he explained, "socialism, committed as it was to economic determinism, subjected man to inscrutable and little understood laws, to which he was required to submit. Syndicalism restores to history the effective will of man, who is both passive and active in turn – man who can leave the imprint of his influence on the things and institutions which surround him."[55] Although it would be wrong to ignore Mussolini's (intellectual and political) opportunism, it is fair to say, along with one of his leading biographers, that "The most important influence upon Mussolini's development, all the relationships and influences of the successive years notwithstanding, was that exercised by revolutionary syndicalism."[56]

Mussolini's new status after the congress at Reggio Emilia was reflected in his appointment as editor of the PSI's paper *Avanti!* It soon became clear, however, that his goals were too radical to be contained within the framework of party institutions. So, in November 1913, he decided to found a journal of his own, *Utopia*. It would enable him, he said, to "present my own opinion, my vision of the world, without worrying about whether it conforms to the predominant opinion of the party."[57] And reveal his evolving vision it did. Mussolini intended to use the journal to effect a "revolutionary revision of socialism" and believed that this would require an appeal to those outside the traditional left. Revolutionary revisionists and syndicalists were prominent contributors to *Utopia*'s pages, but so were other figures with little or no previous connection to the socialist movement. He appealed to "Young People" in general, and referred to not "the proletariat" but "the people" and "the nation."[58]

At the same time that Mussolini and other socialist dissidents were undergoing an ideological and political reorientation, Italian nationalists were also undergoing an evolution of their own. As was the case in other parts of Europe, Italian nationalists had been energized by fin-de-siècle conditions. Their ranks swelled with those disappointed not only by Giolitti's reformist policies but also by the perceived inadequacies of the Risorgimento – namely, Italy's continued status as the weakest of Europe's great powers and the inability of the reigning order to deal with many of the country's most pressing problems.[59]

[54] In an interview in 1926. See Roth, *The Cult of Violence*, 224, and Eugen Weber, *Varieties of Fascism: Doctrines of Revolution in the Twentieth Century* (Malabar, FL: Krieger, 1964), 32.

[55] Quoted A. James Gregor, *Young Mussolini and the Intellectual Origins of Fascism* (Berkeley, CA: University of California Press, 1979), 51.

[56] Renzo De Felice, *Mussolini il Rivuluzionario* (Turin: Einaudi, 1965), 40, and Gregor, *Young Mussolini*, 29. However, Mussolini later became disillusioned when Sorel turned toward monarchism. See, for example, Roth, *The Cult of Violence*, 136ff.

[57] Quoted in Sternhell, *The Birth of Fascist Ideology*, 209.

[58] Ibid., 207–8.

[59] Ronald Cunsolo, *Italian Nationalism* (Malabar, FL: Krieger, 1990); Alexander De Grand, *The Italian Nationalist Association and the Rise of Fascism in Italy* (Lincoln, NE: University of Nebraska Press, 1978); Armand Patrucco, *The Critics of the Italian Parliamentary System, 1860–1915* (Dusseldorf: Bertelsmann Universitätsverlag, 1973); John A. Thayer, *Italy and the*

One of the first places that the nationalist movement's ideology was elaborated was in a small journal called *Il Regno* (the Kingdom), founded in 1903 by Enrico Corradini. *Il Regno* was concerned with national integration and rejuvenation, and "with passion and little bombast its program called for the end of democracy, a reassertion of the principle of authority, and the fulfillment of Italy's imperialist destiny."[60] In its opening number, Corradini proclaimed that its "voice will be lifted to re-erect the statues of the higher human and national values before the very eyes of those who are awakening to a new life."[61] *Il Regno* proved to be short-lived, but as a "first indication of a right wing interest in Sorel,"[62] it created a stir nonetheless, and attracted a wide range of contributors, including a number of revolutionary revisionists and syndicalists.

In the following years, Corradini's exposure to Sorel combined with his concern with national integration led him to advocate an accommodation between nationalism and some form of socialism. Corradini characterized nationalism and socialism as the "two great facts of the modern world," which although "commonly held to be contradictory, were instead very similar."[63] Both, he argued, "were manifestations of a rebirth of stern moral values" and had heroic and activist spirits.[64] He was particularly interested in syndicalism, which he argued was, like nationalism, a "school...for mass organization, mass mobilization, and mass heroism"[65] and argued that both also had "a common love of conquest."[66] Nationalist enthusiasm for war, he claimed, paralleled, and had similar goals to, syndicalism's emphasis on the general strike. As one observer noted, Corradini "breathed the spirit of the *Réflections*. Sorel wrote to Croce that the 'remarkably intelligent' Corradini understood 'exceedingly well the value of my ideas.'"[67]

As part of his effort to bring nationalists and syndicalists together, Corradini reinterpreted the class struggle, substituting conflict between capitalists and the proletariat with the struggle between rich and poor nations. All domestic groups, and especially workers, thus had a stake in Italy's success, since in a poor country such as Italy, "the proletariat could significantly improve its lot not through domestic class struggle against the bourgeoisie, but through collaboration with other classes." If Italy as a whole were to remain poor, the workers would remain poor too; only increased production and international expansion would allow the country to take proper care of all its sons and

---

Great War: Politics and Culture, 1870–1915 (Madison, WI: University of Wisconsin Press, 1964).

[60] Roth, *The Cult of Violence*, 92.

[61] Article reprinted in Cunsolo, *Italian Nationalism*, 212–13.

[62] Roth, *The Cult of Violence*, 92.

[63] Corradini, "Nazionalismo e socialismo" (1914), quoted in Norberto Bobbio, *An Ideological Profile of Twentieth Century Italy* (Princeton, NJ: Princeton University Press, 1995), 53.

[64] Betrand, "Revolutionary Syndicalism," 117, and Sternhell, *The Birth of Fascist Ideology*, 164.

[65] Cunsolo, *Italian Nationalism*, 104.

[66] Roth, *The Cult of Violence*, 92.

[67] Ibid., 92.

daughters.[68] Corradini thus transformed Italy into a "proletarian nation" – one engaged in a desperate struggle against the old and plutocratic powers for its fair share of international wealth and glory.

Others too were bringing together Sorelian, socialist, and nationalist themes for Italian audiences. Giuseppe Prezzolini, one of *Il Regno*'s chief contributors, founded the review *La Voce* in 1908. With contributions from a diverse group of intellectuals interested in the theme of "national renewal," many of whom were influenced by Sorel, it became a major cultural force. The *Pagine Libere*, meanwhile, founded in 1906 by the syndicalist Angelo O. Olivetti, "propagated a proletarian nationalism and 'national syndicalism.'" It was a strong advocate of the war in Libya, which it characterized as the "'revolt' of proletarian Italy against her bourgeois oppressors,"[69] and attracted contributions from both syndicalists and nationalists, including such (future) luminaries as Mussolini, Luigi Federzoni, and Edmondo Rossoni. And the journal *Lupa*, founded in 1910 by the revolutionary syndicalist Paolo Orano, championed Sorel's revolutionary revisionism.

Corradini's own growing popularity and a continuing upsurge in nationalist sentiment led him to decide that the time was ripe for a formal nationalist organization, and in December 1910 the opening congress of the Italian Nationalist Association (Associazione Nazionalista Italiana) was held. The assembled delegates included syndicalists, socialists, republicans, and conservative liberals. In the keynote address, Corradini expanded on the themes of populist nationalism, national syndicalism, and Italy as a proletarian nation. To begin dealing with Italy's problems, he argued, Italians had to recognize that their interests lay not in competition against each other but in a struggle against others outside their borders. "For years and years," Corradini declared, "the socialists . . . have been preaching to the workers that it was in their interest to show solidarity with the workers of Cochin-China or Paraguay and to dissociate themselves completely from their employers and the Italian nation. We must drum it into the workers' heads that it is in their best interests to maintain solidarity with their employers and, above all, with their own country and to hell with solidarity with their comrades in Paraguay or Cochin-China." He continued: "Just as socialism taught the proletariat the value of the class struggle, we must teach Italy the value of the international struggle." And by so doing, the nationalists would become a force for national unity and rejuvenation – "our national socialism."[70]

[68] David Roberts, *The Syndicalist Tradition and Italian Fascism* (Chapel Hill, NC: University of North Carolina Press, 1979), 118.

[69] Ibid., 73, 133.

[70] Enrico Corridini, "The Principles of Nationalism" (Report to the First National Congress in Florence on December 3, 1910). Reprinted in Adrian Lyttelton, ed., *Italian Fascisms* (New York: Harper and Row, 1973), 146–8. Also Eugen Weber, "Introduction," in Hans Rogger and Eugen Weber, eds., *The European Right: A Historical Profile* (Berkeley, CA: University of California Press, 1965), 7.

In the years after its founding, the Nationalist Association continued to refine its ideology and goals. Its third congress, held in May 1914, brought Alfredo Rocco to the forefront of the movement. In his youth briefly a social-ist sympathizer, Rocco was a well-respected professor of commercial law who had become the nationalists' chief economics spokesperson. He berated social-ists for not recognizing that Italy was a "poor country in a constant struggle against the richer nations of Europe. Distribution of poverty would gain the worker little."[71] Nationalism was superior to socialism, he argued, because it recognized the overarching need to promote both national production and unity; it aimed "to achieve ... a strengthening of society from within through the creation of national awareness and strong national discipline; it wishes in addition an increase in internal wealth by intensifying economic production; it wants improved economic and moral status for the working classes because this higher status is necessary to strengthen social cohesion, to increase the wealth of the nation and ensure that the nation is properly prepared for war."[72] Rocco attacked socialists for their lack of social solidarity and their neglect of Italy's developmental needs, and he also fervently opposed economic and political lib-eralism. He objected that the "materialism and fatalism"[73] of the former was a luxury that a poor nation like Italy could not afford; the latter he believed served merely to weaken and divide the nation. (One result of these attacks was to push many liberals out of the nationalist movement.) His vision of national-ism, in contrast, advocated a "mixed syndicalism" – which, by bringing together workers and industrialists, would help "achieve [the] political stability, spiri-tual oneness, economic unity and social harmony"[74] that Italy so desperately needed.

In the years leading up to the First World War, nationalism thus wreaked havoc on the Italian socialist movement and the Italian political scene more generally. A growing number of figures on both the revolutionary left and the nationalist right recognized that their movements had important similarities. The former, disillusioned with orthodox Marxism and its institutions and con-stituencies, appreciated the mobilizing and revolutionary potential of nation-alism. The latter, disillusioned with the failures of the post-Risorgimento order and the inability of traditional bourgeois political parties to do anything about them, appreciated syndicalism's and revolutionary revisionism's voluntarist and revolutionary spirit and its potential to broaden nationalism's appeal to Italy's workers. Sorel's ideas facilitated this embryonic rapprochement by offering a doctrine through which these groups could find common ground. The result was that in the years before the First World War, "Sorelianism" began to lose

---

[71] De Grand, *The Italian Nationalist Association*, 50.
[72] Alfredo Rocco, "The Critical Objections to Nationalism," reprinted in Lyttelton, *Italian Fascisms*, quote on 245.
[73] Yarro, "The Ideological Origins of Italian Fascism," 55.
[74] Cunsolo, *Italian Nationalism*, 113.

its clear association with left or right in Italy and instead became associated with a "national" version of socialism that attracted adherents from across the political spectrum. Thus in the years leading up to the First World War, the intellectual, if not yet the organizational, lines between nationalism and socialism had begun to break down in Italy.[75]

France

In France, as in Italy and much of the rest of Europe, a tentative accommodation between nationalism and socialism began to emerge during the fin-de-siècle. As noted in the last chapter, Jaurès (and other democratic revisionists) had long defended the French nation and the principle of nationality, but a growing interest in the nation could also be found among French syndicalist intellectuals as well – many of whom "looked to Sorel as their maître."[76] Among this group, Hubert Lagardelle and Édouard Berth[77] were probably the most influential. The former edited a review called *Le Mouvement Socialiste,* which became a critical organ for revolutionary revisionism and exerted considerable influence over the development of French and European syndicalism. Sorel published much of his own work in the review, for example, including, in 1905–6, the series of articles that would become *Reflections on Violence.* The latter, meanwhile, was Sorel's "closest and staunchest friend."[78] Berth had been an early critic of Guesde and orthodoxy more generally,[79] and was particularly dismissive of the passivity and fatalism associated with much of the contemporary socialist movement.[80] Berth also diverged from the mainstream left in his views of capitalism, which he criticized trenchantly but primarily on ethical rather than material grounds. He objected, for example, to the "egoism, conflict, brutality and ugliness"[81] generated by capitalism and believed that socialism was best understood as a "revolt of the spirit against a world in which man had been reduced to the status of an automaton, a world in which man was threatened by 'a monstrous moral and metaphysical materialism.'"[82]

---

75 Roth, *The Cult of Violence,* 128. Also Roberts, *The Syndicalist Tradition and Italian Fascism,* esp. chapter 5, and Yarrow, "The Ideological Origins of Italian Fascism."

76 Roth, *The Cult of Violence,* 34. In fact, nationalism proved to be less of a problem for French socialists than it did for others. The French Revolution's association with democracy and liberation had given rise to a republican patriotism, and so nationalism in France retained a long-term association with the left. French socialists thus generally did not see a stark trade-off between internationalism and love of country the way many other socialists did.

77 Jennings, *Syndicalism in France,* 71. On Langardelle and Berth, see also Jules Levey, "The Sorelian Syndicalists: Édouard Berth, Georges Valois, and Hubert Lagardelle" (Ph.D. Dissertation, Columbia University, 1967); Roth, *The Cult of Violence;* Sternhell, *Neither Right nor Left.*

78 According to Pierre Andreu. See Jennings, *Syndicalism in France,* 72.

79 Ibid., 77, 80.

80 Ibid., 77.

81 Ibid., 73.

82 Ibid., 74, 195.

However, unlike the case in Italy, most French syndicalists mellowed with time; indeed, especially after the failure of a general strike in 1906, most (including Lagardelle) moved toward an accommodation with parliamentarism and gradualism. Others (including Berth) refused, however, to make their peace with the existing order and began to see in France's growing nationalist movement a potential alternative outlet for their revolutionary aspirations. This development was facilitated by changes that had been brewing there, in particular the growing interest expressed by nationalists in traditionally socialist and Sorelian themes.

The "new" nationalism in France began with the Boulangist movement of the late 1880s and early 1890s. Although the movement is normally considered to be of the right (because of its nationalism and authoritarianism), many Boulangists referred to themselves as socialists and championed policies traditionally associated with the left. They supported an extensive program of social reforms and cooperated with socialists in parliament; indeed, notes one observer, "the only issue which ... distinguish[ed] the Boulangist from the socialists was nationalism."[83] In addition to championing many policies and themes most often associated with socialism, Boulangists also went after some of the left's natural constituencies. Boulangists' calls for national unity and class collaboration and their insistence that they were the true champions of France's "disinherited" and "little people"[84] found support across the political spectrum.

The Boulangist episode proved relatively brief, but it had a lasting impact. It marked the birth of a new type of right-wing movement in France, one that appropriated themes, appeals, and policies traditionally associated with the left. Indeed, after its collapse, many of its members drifted back to the socialist camp.[85] Unlike traditional conservative and rightist groups, moreover, Boulangism was committed to attracting a cross-class, mass constituency, and was thus "a forerunner of all future mass political movements"[86] on the right that aimed at capturing the support of broad swathes of society in order to destroy the foundations of French democracy.[87] It also brought to the fore a man who would play a critical role in later events: Maurice Barrès.

Barrès was a leading member of a cohort of fin-de-siècle European intellectuals antagonistic to the Enlightenment, and his influence was profound.

---

[83] Ibid., 94.

[84] Michael Curtis, *Three Against the Third Republic: Sorel, Barrès and Maurras* (Princeton, NJ: Princeton University Press, 1959), esp. chapter 2; Patrick H. Hutton, "Popular Boulangism and the Advent of Mass Politics in France, 1866–90," *Journal of Contemporary History*, 11, 1976; René Rémond, *The Right Wing in France: From 1815 to de Gaulle* (Philadelphia: University of Pennsylvania Press, 1969), esp. chapter 6.

[85] C. Stewart Doty, *From Cultural Rebellion to Counterrevolution* (Athens, OH: Ohio University Press, 1976), and George Mosse, "The French Right and the Working Classes," *The Journal of Contemporary History*, 7, 3–4, July–October, 1972.

[86] Curtis, *Three Against the Third Republic*, 33.

[87] See also Zeev Sternhell, "Paul Deroulede and the Origins of Modern French Nationalism," *Journal of Contemporary History*, 6, 4, 1971, 68.

His great passion was nationalism: The most important task facing the country, he felt, was restoring France to greatness. Like many intellectuals of the day, Barrès viewed modernity, and capitalism in particular, as a hindrance to this goal. By dividing the nation into "winners" and "losers," by placing self-interest above communal interest, and by giving the market and private interests control over France's destiny, capitalism threatened the national unity and social cohesion that France so desperately needed. To succeed, Barrès believed, nationalism needed to find some way to reintegrate the "casualties of modern society" back into the national community. This would require a forthright commitment to solving the "social question" and support for some type of socialism.[88]

Through the 1890s, accordingly, Barrès claimed to be a socialist (he even ran on a worker's platform in 1893 and 1896) while rejecting the materialist orthodoxy of Guesde. He supported almost all the same social programs and reforms as the socialists did and claimed to recognize the desirability of "social revolution." In 1890, he wrote that "Boulangism is a Socialist program, a general movement against the omnipotence of capital, in favor of national reconciliation and love of the disinherited."[89] Barrès' success in pushing Boulangism to coopt many of the left's traditional themes was widely recognized. As one contemporary newspaper put it, "today the National party is composed only of socialists."[90] But, of course, as a nationalist, Barrès did not accept the entire socialist agenda; he objected in particular to its insistence on class conflict and doctrinaire internationalism. What was needed instead was a new type of socialism, one shorn of its class conflict and antinational stances. He called this new doctrine "socialist nationalism" and himself a "national socialist."[91]

The Dreyfus Affair picked up where Boulangism left off. As one observer remarked, "Boulangism drew up nationalism's birth certificate, the Dreyfus Affair its baptismal record."[92] By highlighting and sharpening the divisions in French society and increasing the number of those who saw the Dreyfusards as a threat to "traditional" French values and institutions, the affair helped create a potential mass constituency for an antidemocratic nationalist movement. And noting the outcome of the case, many nationalists recognized that achieving their goals would require more determined proselytizing, organizing,

---

[88] Curtis, *Three Against the Third Republic*, and George F. Putnam, "The Meaning of Barrèsisme," *Western Political Quarterly*, June 1954.

[89] Curtis, *Three Against the Third Republic*, 49–50.

[90] Doty, *From Cultural Rebellion to Counterrevolution*, 76–7.

[91] The term "socialist nationalism" was apparently first used when Barrès stood as the nationalist candidate for Nancy in 1898. R. D. Anderson, *France 1870–1914: Politics and Society* (Boston: Routledge and Kegan Paul, 1977), 107; Zeev Sternhell, "Fascist Ideology," in Walter Laqueur, *Fascism: A Reader's Guide* (Berkeley, CA: University of California Press, 1976), 326; "Nationalism, Socialism, and National Socialism," *French Historical Studies*, 2, 3, Spring 1982, 276; idem, *Varieties of Fascism*, 12.

[92] Rémond, *The Right Wing in France*, 60.

and political activity. Out of this recognition emerged a man and an organization that would play critical roles in subsequent French political life: Charles Maurras and the Action Français.

The Dreyfus Affair catapulted Maurras to the top of the French nationalist movement. An ardent nationalist, Maurras was propelled by a hatred for the Third Republic and an obsession with restoring France to its natural glory. He claimed not to be able to find a single "example in history of a positive and creative action initiated by a majority"[93] and firmly believed that political order required dedicated leadership. As he bluntly put it, "The mob always follows determined minorities."[94] These views led him to support a restoration of the monarchy. Yet despite his authoritarian and monarchist convictions, Maurras was not merely an old-fashioned conservative. Like Barrès, he expressed sympathy for a particular type of socialism, one that would bring back national unity. And again like Barrès, Maurras held modernity and capitalism to blame for the breakdown of social cohesion and believed that counteracting contemporary ills required a determined effort to bring workers and other marginal groups back into the national community. He thus supported explicit outreach to workers and an extensive program of social reforms. Socialism, he noted, "delivered of its democratic and cosmopolitan elements can fit nationalism like a well made glove fits a beautiful hand."[95]

Over the following years, Maurras continued to develop his vision for the nationalist movement as the chief ideologue of an organization called the Action Français. Under the leadership of Maurras and Léon Daudet, the Action Français attacked democracy and the Republic, called for a return of the monarchy, and advocated an "integral nationalism" that would strengthen France and purify it of "foreign elements." Although clearly a movement of the right, the Action Français continued the Boulangist tendency to voice both socialist and nationalist themes. As one of its most prominent observers noted, "it combined and reconciled the popular radicalism of nationalism with the reactionary elitism of the royalists."[96] It held laissez-faire capitalism to blame for the social divisions plaguing contemporary society and took an active interest in the "social question," championing an extensive program of social reforms designed to reintegrate workers into the national community.

Some members of Action Français became attracted to the ideas of Georges Sorel – an attraction that was reciprocated as the years went by. In 1908, the Action Français published an interview with Sorel that introduced him as "'the brilliant and profound theoretician of antidemocratic socialism' who, though he believed a monarchist restoration improbable, had 'no serious objection to

---

[93] Ibid., 73.

[94] Roland Stromberg, *European Intellectual History Since 1789* (Englewood, NJ: Prentice Hall, 1966), 236.

[95] Sternhell, "Fascist Ideology," 326; Weber, *Varieties of Fascism*, 131.

[96] Eugen Weber, *Action Français: Royalism and Reaction in Twentieth Century France* (Palo Alto, CA: Stanford University Press, 1962), 52. Also Stephen Wilson, "History and Traditionalism: Maurras and the Action Français," *Journal of the History of Ideas*, 29, 3, July–September 1968.

it.'"[97] Sorel returned the compliment, evincing a growing interest in Maurras' integral nationalism and the potential for a rapprochement between left- and right-wing antidemocrats; by 1910, he was openly collaborating with the group's members.

One consequence was the founding in 1911 of the Cercle Proudhon, an organization that looked to both Sorel and Maurras for guidance. (It referred to them as the "two masters of French and European regeneration."[98]) The Cercle was characterized by its denunciations of democracy as well as its merging of socialist and nationalist themes. The first issue of the Cercle's publication *Les Cahiers du Cercle Proudhon* declared, "Democracy is the greatest mistake of the last century,' ... in economics and politics [it] permitted the establishment of the capitalist system which destroys in the state that which democratic ideas dissolve in the spirit namely the nation, the family, morals, by substituting the law of gold for the laws of blood."[99] Sorel's friend Berth was one of the Cercle's most prominent promoters, as was Georges Valois from the Action Français.[100]

Valois would emerge in the years to come as a critical figure on the new "national and social" right. He had begun his career on the left and was heavily influenced by Sorel. But by the early 1900s, his disillusionment with the moderation and parliamentary inclinations of the workers' movement had led him to abandon it for the Action Français. He became one of the organization's foremost experts on labor and economic matters and a fervent advocate of a rapprochement between left- and right-wing antidemocrats.[101] Valois was committed to increasing the "social" component of nationalism and to bringing the working class into the movement. Nationalism, he once declared, "when reduced to its essentials, demanded that the nation be placed ahead of all other considerations. Socialism was nothing more than the demand for social justice."[102] Both nationalism and socialism were determined critics of capitalism, Valois argued, although (like a growing number of his revolutionary revisionist and nationalist colleagues) he focused more on capitalism's "excesses" and negative social consequences than on the inherent nature of the system itself. As he once wrote:

It can be conceived that the capitalist principles ... are pernicious to any human group when applied outside of the [economic] domain, considering that they have been established solely in order to insure the highest possible yield on capital, the heads of the firms are led, as much because of the force of these principles as because of their natural egoism (happy in other conditions), to destroy all the institutions that limit, in view of a superior interest – the national interest – the immediate possibilities of the yield of

[97] Roth, *The Cult of Violence*, 90–1.
[98] Ibid., 123.
[99] Ernst Nolte, *The Three Faces of Fascism: Action Français, Italian Fascism, National Socialism* (New York: Holt, Rinehart, and Winston, 1966), 71; Sternhell, "Fascist Ideology," 333.
[100] Georges Valois was actually the pen name that A. G. Gressent took when he turned away from the left.
[101] Levey, "The Sorelian Syndicalists," 98ff.
[102] Quoted in ibid., 210.

capital and of the exploitation of the soil. Thus religious life is diminished, the working life degraded, the family destroyed, the foreign worker brought in, the natural resources are exploited without restraint, the political institutions are transformed into organs of coercion in order to increase the excessive output of capital. In everything the national interest is gravely compromised.[103]

Through his efforts in the Cercle Proudhon and after, Valois helped further the idea that nationalism and socialism complemented and reinforced one another – an idea that would find increasing resonance in France after the war.

Germany

As in Italy and France, during the fin-de-siècle a growing number of nationalists in Germany began calling for a new type of socialism – one opposed to Marxism but harshly critical of capitalism and focused on overcoming the conflicts and divisions that plagued modern societies. Also as in France and Italy, at the same time that figures on the right were working towards a synthesis of nationalism and socialism, some figures on the left were moving in the same direction.

As the standard-bearer of orthodox Marxism and the Socialist International's most important party, the SPD had long opposed German nationalism, and the party's initial estrangement from the Wilhelmine political system and demonization by conservatives solidified its antipathy. But during the early twentieth century, this hostility began to soften. Especially after the party's setback in the 1907 election, the SPD was buffeted by calls for a reassessment of its stance. Neither Sorel nor syndicalism was a force to reckon with in Germany as in Italy and France, but otherwise the debates about nationalism within the German socialist movement had much in common with those taking place in other parts of Western Europe. It was revisionists who led the charge, and once again they fell more or less into two broad categories. As noted in the previous chapter, democratic revisionists, typified by Bernstein, insisted that the working class had national as well as international commitments and worried that the movement was ignoring the powerful appeal of nationalism at its peril. But even more influential in this regard was another faction of the party centered on Joseph Bloch's *Sozialistische Monatshefte*. Although not explicitly Sorelian, this group bore a distinct resemblance to revolutionary revisionists in other parts of Western Europe.

Under Bloch's leadership, the *Sozialistische Monatshefte* became the party's most popular and influential journal and the main forum for German revisionism. The full panoply of revisionist critiques were aired in its pages, with the determinism and passivity of the party's orthodox Marxism coming in for particular disapproval and calls for the SPD to break out of its "proletarian ghetto" a regular theme (especially after 1907). Because most contributors to the *Monatshefte* shared so many revisionist positions – a rejection of orthodox

---

[103] Quoted in Mazgaj, "The Social Revolution or the King," 438.

Marxism, a dedication to expanding the SPD's appeal, a commitment to active reform work, an embrace of German culture and patriotism – they are misleadingly placed in the general "revisionist" category. But while Bernstein adamantly rejected the ethnic or primordial nationalism of the day and retained a strong commitment to liberal ideals and policies, Bloch and many other members of the *Monatshefte* group agitated for reconciliation between socialism and *Deutschtum* (German-ness) and denounced the liberal "canker."[104]

Antiliberalism in particular was a central feature of Bloch's thinking. He had "no time for Enlightenment progressivism, disdained 'humanitarian chimeras,'" and denounced liberal economic policies.[105] He argued that free trade was bad for Germany and its workers, and he was a vociferous advocate of protectionism – which carried as an added benefit, he felt, the ability to bind together different socioeconomic groups. Bloch's support for protectionism was part of his broader backing for almost all aspects of German *Weltpolitik*, including imperialism. (Indeed, Bloch took positions that would have made many conservatives and nationalists proud, such as support for a "continental Europe under German domination."[106]) He favored a strong German state and a unified national community, seeing no contradiction between such positions and socialism, since he defined the latter as merely seeking "the highest attainment of all" and as having at its essence "service to the common weal."[107] And he also believed that the *Volksgemeinschaft* (or what he often referred to as "the solidarity of classes") would be "at least as important as its complement, the class struggle" to the construction of socialism.[108] For Bloch:

...the national idea was more than the sum total of the collective economic interests of the nation. It also had cultural and spiritual dimensions, which transcended class and fostered a sense of national community among all classes. If the *Volkskraft*, or vitality of a people, was as potent of that of the Germans, socialists would be dogmatic fools to pretend that only the class struggle mattered to the worker.[109]

The group's most influential spokesperson, meanwhile, was Karl Leuthner. Like Bloch, Leuthner disdained Enlightenment progressivism and liberalism, commenting on the latter that "there [had] possibly never existed an intellectual current that [was] so bereft of healthy political insight as the Manchester liberal world view." He believed that there was little hope for either socialist or German progress until "liberal economic and political doctrines had been eradicated"[110] and advocated the virtues of *Deutschtum*. Leuthner too was a

[104] This is how Roger Fletcher describes Bloch's views of liberalism. See Fletcher, *Revisionism and Empire*, 55, 93.
[105] Fletcher, *Revisionism and Empire*, 52 and chapter 2 in general.
[106] Ibid., 61. Not surprisingly, Bloch was a dedicated Anglophobe – yet another way in which he differed from the Anglophilic Bernstein.
[107] Fletcher, *Revolution and Empire*, 48, 52.
[108] Ibid., 58.
[109] Quoted in ibid., 58.
[110] Ibid., 83.

proponent of a strong state, which, once infused with the power of popular sovereignty, would "bring state and nation into harmony on the basis of the *Volksgemeinschaft*."[111] To help this process along, he believed that the SPD needed to expand its appeal and pursue cross-class alliances, which would be facilitated by the adoption of "national" rhetoric and policies. As he argued, to be "politically effective the German labor movement could not do otherwise than transform itself into a mass or people's party and place the national or general interest above class interests."[112] Finally, Leuthner was a proponent of military expansion, imperialism, and protectionism.

With this "national" reorientation of socialism, Bloch, Leuthner, and other contributors to the *Monatshefte* hoped to achieve a number of goals. They aimed at strengthening the German state and the country's international position. They hoped to broaden the appeal of the SPD. And they hoped that a national reorientation on the part of the SPD would bridge the gap between the workers and the rest of the nation. As one observer noted, Bloch and the *Monatshefte* group's ultimate goal was the "integration of the German working class into the existing social order with the aid of a *Sammlung* or common front founded on an illiberal and anti-Marxist nationalism [that aimed at] the pursuit of a German superpower position of truly global and epoch-making dimensions."[113]

It is difficult to judge the precise impact of the *Monatshefte* group. Although the SPD never suffered the kind of high-profile defections or explicit flirting with the nationalist movement by its members as did the Italian and the French socialist movements, there does seem to have been an increasing willingness within the SPD during these years to consider the kind of "national" socialist positions advocated by Bloch, Leuthner, and others. As some observers have noted:

...at the various post-1907 party conferences, nationalist revisionists staged impassioned hymns to the "virtues of fatherland," receiving louder applause from the delegates than Karl Liebknecht's plea to renew the party's efforts toward providing the working class with a "proper education in the tradition of proletarian internationalism." It would take years for Kautsky to admit that his cherished theoretical mission of imparting "correct Marxist principles" to the party had been severely jeopardized by nationalist-revisionist forces and the SPD was actually going backwards.[114]

---

[111] Ibid., 84.

[112] Ibid., 86.

[113] Ibid., 183. In addition, these socialists hoped that by actively supporting Germany's international aspirations, and its military endeavors in particular, the party would be able to gain benefits for its supporters. As Wolfgang Heine had put it: "We give military credits to the government; the government thereupon grants us new liberties.... The policy of 'compensation' has worked... for the Catholic Centre, why not for" us? Quoted in John Snell, *The Democratic Movement in Germany 1789–1914* (Chapel Hill, NC: University of North Carolina Press, 1976), 297.

[114] Steger, *The Quest for Evolutionary Socialism*, 194. Also Stanley Pierson, *Marxist Intellectuals and the Working-Class Mentality in Germany, 1887–1912* (Cambridge, MA: Harvard University Press, 1993), 234.

Many have seen the party's decision to support the German war effort in 1914 as evidence that nationalist and revisionist forces had influenced the SPD to a much greater degree than Kautsky and other prewar SPD leaders had been willing to admit.

Turning to the other half of the political spectrum, because of the rapidity of Germany's economic transformation (it industrialized much more quickly and completely than either France or Italy during the late nineteenth century) and the social strains emanating from this process as well as national uni-fication, critiques of modern liberal capitalist society and calls for national unity found even more fertile ground in Germany than in Italy or France. As one observer notes, the degree to which German intellectuals "attacked the progress of modernity" in general and liberalism and capitalism in particular was unprecedented and turned what was elsewhere a troubling but still con-tained current into a "decisive intellectual and political force."[115] Germanic nationalism also was far more prone than its counterparts to define national identity in racial rather than linguistic, cultural, or historical terms, and to paint Jews as a central threat. Anti-Semitism thus came to play a more central role in German and Austrian nationalism than it did in many of its European counterparts.[116]

The intellectual backlash against modernity and the embrace of radical nationalism in fin-de-siècle Germany was widespread, but there were two fig-ures whose contributions were particularly important and representative: Paul de Lagarde and Julius Langbehn. As one observer notes, "If the *Volkish* move-ment can be said to have had a founder, it was a cranky scholar [named] Paul de Lagarde; if the founder, in turn, had a prophet, that role was filled by Julius Langbehn."[117]

Obsessed by a belief that even after Bismarck's successes Germany was a weak and divided nation, Lagarde became one of the most prolific and popular critics of the Wilhelmine Reich.[118] According to Lagarde, there was little right about the country: Its culture and educational systems were in disarray, its morality was in decline, and its people were disunited and discontented. He saw it as his mission to correct these problems, a task that required "bringing to his people [a] vision of a Germany reborn." This meant reuniting a society

---

[115] Friz Stern, *The Politics of Cultural Despair: A Study in the Rise of the Germanic Ideology* (Berkeley, CA: University of California Press, 1961), xi, xxiii.

[116] There is debate on this issue, however. Anti-Semitism was certainly widespread and strongly attached to nationalism in France. However, the forces defending the reigning order were more powerful and the nationalist movement weaker in France than in Germany, thus diminishing the political force of anti-Semitism in the former. For comparative studies of anti-Semitism, see Jacob Katz, *From Prejudice to Destruction* (Cambridge, MA: Harvard University Press, 1982); Peter Pulzer, *The Rise of Political Anti-Semitism in Germany and Austria* (London: Peter Halban, 1988); Meyer Weinberg, *Because They Were Jews* (New York: Greenwood Press, 1986); Robert Wistrich, *Anti-Semitism: The Longest Hatred* (New York: New York University Press, 1990).

[117] George L. Mosse, *The Crisis of German Ideology. Intellectual Origins of the Third Reich* (New York: Grosset and Dunlap, 1964), 31.

[118] Stern, *The Politics of Cultural Despair*, 16.

torn apart by modernity and capitalism, evils whose "parasitic carriers" (that is, liberals and Jews), Lagarde asserted, "should be extirpated." In addition to purging German society of its "foreign" and "destructive" elements, his plan for the country's regeneration included the cultivation of a "new religion" capable of uniting and mobilizing disparate interests and the replacement of *Parlamentarismus* by a new type of political order centered on a *Führer* who would represent all Germans and spur them to pursue their country's national destiny.[119]

Lagarde's obsession with national unity and the degenerative effects of modernity were further developed and popularized by Langbehn, particularly in his extremely influential 1890 book *Rembrandt als Erzieher*.[120] Langbehn claimed that the "ultimate cause of German decay was modernity itself, that complex of new and violent forces that had destroyed the traditional society and the traditional faith. But the immediate cause was the Jews."[121] Like Lagarde, Langbehn favored removing Jews from positions of public authority and influence. He also believed that national unity required paying special attention to those groups marginalized by the reigning liberal, capitalist order, such as workers. In order to lure them back into the national community, he advocated "nationalizing" the SPD – "that is, transforming it into a nationalistic-socialistic movement" – and creating a pseudocorporatist system that would help regulate and harmonize relations among different social groups.[122] And he also believed that national unity required replacing *Parlamentarismus* and democracy with a new type of political system centered on a strong national *Führer* who could represent and mobilize the German *Volk*.

The ideas developed and disseminated by men such as Lagarde and Langbehn grew in popularity during the early twentieth century. One particularly important advocate of them was Werner Sombart, one of the "most renowned social scientists of his day."[123] Sombart's contemporary fame came largely from his influential analyses of modern capitalism (in fact, the term "capitalism" was taken from his 1902 book *Der Moderne Kapitalismus*), a subject that became something of an obsession in Germany in the years preceding the First World War. (As Friedrich Naumann, whose own calls for a national socialist movement reflected concerns similar to those of Sombart, noted in 1911: "Just as the French have their theme, namely 'What was the great Revolution?' so our national destiny has given us our theme for a long time to come, namely 'What

[119] Ibid., 3.
[120] In the book's first year, sixty thousand copies were printed and more than forty printings of the book appeared in the first two years after its publication. By the end of the Second World War, at least 150,000 copies had been sold. Even after Langbehn's death, new editions of the book continued to appear. Ibid., 155.
[121] Ibid., 139–40. Langbehn identified assimilated Jews in particular as the problem. Orthodox Jews, who retained their own separate identity and religion, he saw as less of a threat.
[122] Stern, *The Politics of Cultural Despair*, 146.
[123] Jerry Z. Muller, *The Mind and the Market: Capitalism in Modern European Thought* (New York: Alfred Knopf, 2002), 253.

is capitalism?'"[124]) Even more than Lagarde or Langbehn, Sombart blamed his country's current misfortune on the baneful effects of capitalism. Social conflict, materialism, the destruction of national cultures, the undermining of national unity – all of these problems could be laid at capitalism's door. And Jews, he felt, were not only largely responsible for capitalism's rise, but also embodied its most offensive features – egoism, self-interest, and abstraction.[125] As a result, as one scholar notes, in Sombart's work the triumph of capitalism was portrayed as the "replacement of a concrete, particularist, Christian *Gemeinschaft* by an abstract universalistic, judaized *Gesellschaft*"[126] – giving all those discontented with and alienated from the reigning order someone to blame.

In addition to deepening the link between anticapitalism and anti-Semitism, Sombart played an important role in developing the idea of a particularly "German" or "national" form of socialism. Sombart's socialism had little in common with its Marxist brethren; indeed, Sombart was a vehement critic of Marxism, finding particularly offensive its emphasis on the primacy of economics. He argued instead that economics had to be subordinated to political and social factors, with the economy serving the needs of the *Gemeinschaft*, and public interests trumping private ones. As time passed, he and others began to believe that this goal could be achieved without destroying capitalism, by simply controlling it and purging it of its extreme and "Jewish" elements.

These sorts of ideas had a profound effect on German political life during the late nineteenth and early twentieth centuries. An immense number of civil society organizations developed around this time in response to the perceived failures of the Wilhelmine system and disillusionment with aspects of modern life.[127] On one end of the spectrum were explicitly apolitical organizations such as the Wandervogel, whose goal it was to counter "the sense of frustration, alienation, and loneliness which mass industrial society induced" in German youth by creating a sense of solidarity and nationalist commitment among them.[128] Endless hiking trips through the countryside would expose the young Wandervogel to the virtues of the "real" Germany (that is, rural areas viewed as untainted by capitalism and modernity) and the simple *Volk* (most often peasants who were viewed as still enjoying the benefits of a pre-industrial *Volksgemeinschaft*). The movement embodied the combination of romantic anticapitalism and nationalist longing for community so typical of the era.

---

[124] Ibid., 229.
[125] Ibid., 253–4.
[126] Muller, *The Mind and the Market*, 254. Also Jeffrey Herf, *Reactionary Modernism* (New York: Cambridge University Press, 1984), chapter 6.
[127] On the proliferation of such organizations and their implications for German political development, see Sheri Berman, "Civil Society and the Collapse of the Weimar Republic," *World Politics*, 49, 3, April 1997.
[128] Peter Stachura, *The German Youth Movement 1900–1945: An Interpretive and Documentary History* (New York: St. Martin's Press, 1981), 17.

On the other end of the spectrum were nationalist associations best known for their insistence that German expansionism was necessary for the survival and health of the German *Volk*. Eager to expand the appeal of nationalism to all social groups, nationalist associations often referred to themselves as *Volksvereine* (people's organizations), explicitly attacking many of the Reich's reigning political institutions for dividing the *Volk* and alienating key groups from the national community. The constitution of the Pan German League, for example, stated, "The League strives to quicken the Germanic-national... sentiment of all Germans in particular to awaken and foster the sense of racial and cultural kinship of all sections of the German people."[129]

For the nationalists, of course, "the German people" did not include Jews, and the growing power of anti-Semitism was reflected in the appearance of a number of explicitly anti-Semitic groups and parties preaching an extreme form of racialist nationalism and an extreme hostility to liberalism and capitalism, both blamed on the Jews. In fact, as one observer notes, "such was the enmity towards capitalism that we find in anti-Semitic programs proposals which look very much like pure Socialism – for instance, the nationalization of railways, insurance, banking, or advertising. Indeed a great many anti-Semites proclaimed themselves Socialists." One of the anti-Semitic movement's founders, Wilhelm Marr, proclaimed that "anti-Semitism is a Socialist movement, only in nobler and purer forms than" the SPD.[130] (Or, as August Bebel once put it, "Anti-Semitism is the socialism of fools.") In order to highlight their commitment to social reform, many anti-Semitic groups put the word "social" in their name (for example, Christian Social, German Social Reform, and National-Social). Over time, however, the anti-Semites developed a subtler picture of capitalism and the market, differentiating, for example, between *raffendes* (grasping) and *schaffendes* (creative) capital, the former associated with Jews and the latter with "true Germans."[131]

These groups generally adopted explicitly populist stances, appealing directly to the "people" or the "masses" and opening their leadership ranks to talent and effort. They were also often very good at making use of modern methods of political organizing and propaganda to expand their appeal and support base. As a result, their ideas spread throughout civil society associations and the German right during the decades ahead, even if many explicitly anti-Semitic organizations went into decline around the turn of the century. As one scholar of the movement notes "the decline of the overtly anti-Semitic organizations after 1900 is deceptive. In Germany the various parties quarreled and vegetated; at the same time anti-Semitism was more openly accepted than before by several other parties, an increasing number of political and economic interest

[129] Stern, *The Politics of Cultural Despair*, 169. On the nationalist associations in general, see Geoff Eley, *Reshaping the German Right: Radical Nationalism and Political Change After Bismarck* (Ann Arbor, MI: University of Michigan Press, 1991).
[130] Pulzer, *The Rise of Political Anti-Semitism*, 44–5.
[131] Ibid., 42–3.

groups, and many nonpolitical bodies, such as students' corps or athletic or mountaineering clubs." [132]

Across the border in Austria, meanwhile, a political party that placed anti-Semitism at the center of its appeal and program was becoming an extremely powerful political force, and would seize the imagination of a wandering young aspiring artist who was drifting through Vienna at the time. The modern anti-Semitic movement in Austria owes much to Georg Ritter von Schönerer, an ardent German nationalist who brought together anti-Semitism, anticapitalism, and populism in a potent (and by now familiar) mix. Schönerer's 1882 Linz program, in addition to advocating closer to ties between Austria and Germany, called for the defense of civil liberties, the installation of a progressive income tax, improved and expanded social policies, protection of the peasants and "honest labor," and nationalization of the railways and insurance industries. As one observer notes, the program contained a "mixture of nationalism with semi-socialism" and racial anti-Semitism. Its economic proposals contained a "well-developed statement of the antithesis between 'honest' and 'harmful' capital and a denunciation of the professions notably associated with Jews." [133] In 1885, the program added a plank advocating "the removal of Jewish influence from all sections of public life." Although Schönerer ultimately failed to create a mass movement, he succeeded in expanding the appeal of anti-Semitism and "almost single-handedly created a German national rightist movement and [gave] it the fundamental character and ideology it would have for at least a generation after his death. He was the first representative of the radical Right in Austrian political life." [134]

Many pieces of Schönerer's ideology were picked up by Karl Lueger. Although he began as a democrat and even a sympathizer of the left, Lueger, always careful to see the way the winds were blowing, by the end of the 1880s recognized that anti-Semitism was increasingly a force to be reckoned with in Austrian political life. He thus skillfully integrated it and Catholicism (another rising force) into a larger political package, and in 1889 the Christian Social Party was born – the type of dynamic, modern mass movement that had previously eluded anti-Semites and the right more generally. [135] Lueger persuasively argued that his was a party of the "people," but for Lueger that really meant the middle class. Particularly important for Lueger were those lower-middle-class and artisan groups suffering under capitalism. As in other parts of Europe, these groups proved particularly vulnerable to anti-Semitism, and they were ripe for the picking because they had essentially been abandoned by the two

---

[132] Pulzer, *The Rise of Political Anti-Semitism in Germany and Austria*, 185.

[133] Ibid., 145.

[134] Ernst Nolte, "Austria," in Rogger and Weber, eds., *The European Right*, 321.

[135] The analysis of the Christian Socials draws most heavily on John Boyer's classic studies of the movement, *Political Radicalism in Late Imperial Vienna: Origins of the Christian Social Movement 1848–1897* (Chicago: University of Chicago Press, 1981) and *Culture and Political Crisis in Vienna: Christian Socialism in Power, 1897–1918* (Chicago: University of Chicago Press, 1995).

other main forces in Austrian political life, the liberals and the socialists. The Christian Socials thus exploited the discontent and alienation of these groups to integrate them into a "single, multi-interest coalition by forcing...traditional intra-Bürger tensions into subordinate roles. Given the hostility of the [Austrian Socialists] to the master artisans and the property owners, the success of the anti-Semites' tactic was insured, at least in the short term."[136]

Since the Christian Socials wanted to create a mass constituency, they strongly supported universal suffrage – a reform that once finally enacted in 1906 pushed the party to accelerate its own modernization and professionalization. They also developed "a new style of high-tension, issue politics in which dramatic social and economic problems were used as mobilization devices both to manipulate public sentiment and, if necessary, to create it."[137] From early in his political career, Lueger had recognized the mobilizing effect of economic grievances, and so the party stressed that it was committed to improving people's lives. Once in power, moreover, the Christian Socials actively pursued a reform program, known as "municipal socialism," which included improved public services; the building of parks and recreation areas; municipal control of gas works, street railways, and electrical works; and the founding of a city mortgage bank.[138] In general, these programs were well run and gave the party "an immediate, large-scale object on which to focus public attention as proof of the party's 'revolution' in municipal government, and its propaganda value was therefore enormous."[139]

Although the Christian Socials often touted their policies as "anticapitalist," they never threatened the property or livelihoods of their bourgeois constituents; what they did instead was try to protect them from the harshest winds of the market and economic change. They reserved their most fervent condemnation not for the owners of private property per se or even capitalists more generally, but rather for those who could be portrayed as unfairly exploiting the system and living off the labor of others – in their view, the Jews. In the end, this proved to be a powerful political formula. The party came in first in every political contest it entered from 1895 until Leuger's death in 1910, and after 1895 Lueger himself became the undisputed master of Vienna. When he died, the main Socialist newspaper remarked that "he had managed to achieve in Vienna what had proven almost impossible elsewhere in Central Europe: 'to organize the *Kleinbürgertum* politically and to constitute them as an independent party.' Lueger was perhaps the first bourgeois politician to 'take the masses into account, who moved the masses who sank the roots of his power deep in the ground.'"[140]

[136] Boyer, *Political Radicalism in Late Imperial Vienna*, 402–3.
[137] Ibid., 415.
[138] Boyer, *Culture and Political Crisis in Vienna*, 7ff.
[139] Ibid., 8.
[140] Ibid., 237–8.

That the Christian Socials' success made a deep impression on the young Adolf Hitler is indisputable. But Lueger differered from Hitler in critical ways: He maintained a general respect for the rule of law, and his "Jew baiting" was "primarily a political act" rather than a reflection of insane racialist thinking. Nonetheless, Lueger's mixture of nationalism, socialism, and populism provided a model that a future generation built upon with the most horrific of results. This is "a burden that Austrian Christian Socialism shall forever have to bear."[141]

[141] Ibid., 26.

5

From Revisionism to Social Democracy

By the first years of the twentieth century, democratic revisionists had developed a powerful critique of the international socialist movement's reigning Marxist orthodoxy and laid the foundations for an ideological alternative. But it would take the vast changes unleashed by the First World War for democratic revisionism to blossom into a movement of its own. The key steps in this transformation were the open rejection of the twin pillars of orthodox Marxism – class struggle and historical materialism – and the embrace of their antitheses – cross-class cooperation and the primacy of politics.

The first pillar suffered a critical blow with the outbreak of the war. Socialist parties across the continent abandoned their suspicion of bourgeois parties and institutions and threw their support behind the states they had hitherto pledged to destroy. Even the German SPD, the International's largest party and the standard-bearer of Marxist orthodoxy, pledged itself to the defense of the *Vaterland* and quickly voted to authorize war credits.[1] As the Russian Menshevik leader Paul Axelrod reported, "the news [that the SPD had voted to support the war] was a terrible, stunning blow. It appeared as if an earthquake had overcome the international proletariat. The tremendous authority of [the SPD] disappeared with one stroke."[2] In France, the Socialists not only joined with other groups in a *union sacrèe* to defend the *patrie* but, putting aside years of controversy, also sent two of their most prominent members – Jules Guesde and Marcel Sembet – to join the government.

The doctrine of class struggle came under even more pressure in the postwar era, as the democratic wave that spread across much of Europe confronted socialists with unprecedented opportunities for participation in

---

[1] It is important to note, however, that they did this at least partially under the false impression that Germany was in danger of attack by Czarist Russia.

[2] Julius Braunthal, *History of the International 1914–1943* (London: Thomas Nelson and Sons, 1967), 7.

bourgeois governments. Given a chance to help form or even lead democratic administrations, many were forced to recognize the uncomfortable truth that workers alone could never deliver an electoral majority and that cooperation with non-proletarians was the price of political power. The war also revealed the immense mobilizing power of nationalism and bred a generation that valued community, solidarity, and struggle. Populist right-wing movements across the continent were riding these trends, and many socialists worried that clinging to orthodox Marxism's emphasis on class conflict would prevent them from responding to the needs of ordinary citizens and thus cause them to lose ground to competitors.

The second pillar, historical materialism, was also dealt a critical blow by the war and its aftermath. The pivotal position occupied by socialist parties during the interwar years made it increasingly difficult to avoid the question of how political power could contribute to socialist transformation, and the subsequent onset of the Great Depression made preaching submission to economic forces tantamount to political suicide. Indeed, by the early 1930s, the protest against liberalism and capitalism that had been growing since the end of the nineteenth century reached fever pitch, with the legions of the disaffected ready to be claimed by any political movement willing to press for change. Because of their emphasis on letting economic forces be the drivers of history, orthodox Marxist parties here too ceded ground to activist groups on the right.

Hence by the end of the interwar years many socialists found themselves firmly convinced that orthodox Marxism was theoretically exhausted and politically irrelevant and that the time had come to embrace a whole new vision for the left – one that would supplant rather than tinker with orthodoxy. So they turned to the themes set out by revisionism's pioneers a generation earlier: the value of cross-class cooperation and the primacy of politics. Now they could acknowledge these principles for the radical departures they in fact were and translate them into a distinctive and viable policy agenda, one based on communitarian, even nationalist appeals and a "people's party" approach together with a commitment to using states to control or reshape capitalism. The result was the final severance of socialism from Marxism and the emergence of what can correctly be called social democracy.

To Participate or Not to Participate

With the end of the First World War, socialist parties found themselves in positions of power that would have been unimaginable before 1914. In some countries (such as Germany, Austria, and Sweden), socialists helped lead the transition to democracy and were the main political support for the new regime. In other countries (such as Italy and France), where democracy came before 1914, the interwar years nonetheless provided socialists with new opportunities to join with other groups and potentially even help form governments.

Despite these changes, many socialist parties remained wedded to prewar traditionalist, orthodox positions. In Germany, for example, the SPD could not shake its ambivalence about democracy, even as the old regime was collapsing around it. As pressure was building for political change, the SPD held a congress in Würzburg in 1917[3] where a number of speakers expressed their frustration with the party's dithering. Thus Friedrich Stampfer argued that the party

> could no longer limit itself to the politics of rejection, of protest, because we have become too strong and must now push a politics of positive demands.... When a young boy [comes] crying, and says he has been beaten up unfairly, then you comfort him. But when the boy becomes bigger and stronger and the same thing happens – and he can do nothing more than complain about the injustice done to him –...then one becomes annoyed.... It is the same with the party. As long as it was small and weak, its emphasis... could be on protest, it could go out... and say "we have fought in the Reichstag, we have rejected this and that [and] it has not helped".... But when the voters ask what have you achieved... then a party of our strength... cannot say "nothing"![4]

Similarly, Otto Stollten pleaded with his colleagues not to "shy away from accepting [political] responsibility." A large party that can influence things

> ... has the duty not to shut itself out, but rather to use every opportunity to gain for the working class whatever possible. We cannot have it all, since we do not have a majority. Our politics must, therefore, be one of compromises, and the party must be prepared to make compromises, so that something can be achieved for the workers. This is the essence of politics. This [kind of policy] has long been practiced, but always pulled back by the revolutionary demonstration politics.[5]

This ambivalence did not fully dissipate with the war's end and the transition to democracy. Despite having the most to gain from the new republic and being its leading political force, the SPD justified its decision to join Germany's first fully democratic government by declaring, "Only in order to protect our country and its economy against collapse have representatives of our party made the sacrifice of entering the government."[6]

As the interwar years progressed, it became increasingly clear to all how much the Weimar Republic's fortunes were tied up with those of the SPD. As Heinrich August Winkler once noted, "writing the history of the [SPD] in the years from 1918 to 1933 is, to a large degree, writing the history of the

---

[3] During the war, the party had not been able to meet normally, so this meeting gave vent to a discussion and anlaysis of party activities from 1914 onward.

[4] *Protokoll über die Verhandlungen des Parteitages der Sozialdemokratischen Partei Deutschlands* (Berlin: J. H. W. Dietz, 1973), 362, also 376–7.

[5] Ibid., 377.

[6] On November 9, the Kaiser finally abdicated, the office of Chancellor was transferred to the SPD's Friedrich Ebert, and his colleague Philipp Scheidemann proclaimed the founding of the German Republic from the balcony of the Reichstag. Susanne Miller, *Die Bürde der Macht. Die deutsche Sozialdemokratie 1918–1920* (Düsseldorf: Droste Verlag, 1978), 35.

Weimar Republic."[7] Despite this, the party remained unable to accept fully the compromises necessary for defending democracy. This was reflected clearly in its views of class struggle. Although the SPD did join with other parties to form governments and manage, at least in the initial stages of the Republic, to attract groups outside the traditional working class (especially white-collar workers and civil servants), the party could not shake its commitment to class struggle and proletarian purity. Growing numbers recognized that this was not only foolish from an electoral perspective; it was also detrimental for democracy to have its largest party officially indifferent to broader societal interests. When the party decided to revise its program in the early 1920s, Bernstein and others urged the party to recognize changed times and make an explicit commitment to a *Volkspartei* (people's party) strategy and declare itself the party of the "working people" – a term explicitly designed to include groups outside the traditional proletariat – and drop the doom-and-gloom scenario of historical materialism.[8] Yet this shift was ultimately rejected, with the party accepting a draft designed by Kautsky that returned the SPD to the rhetoric of economic determinism and class struggle. The result was that by the mid-1920s the SPD offered a program that "corresponded more with the self-image of a notorious opposition party in a pre-parliamentary state, like that of the German Empire, than with what the [SPD] actually [was] – the official party par excellence of the Weimar Republic."[9]

To justify this equivocation toward bourgeois parties and institutions, Kautsky turned to the theory of the "the balance of class forces" (*Gleichgewicht der Klassenkräfte*),[10] which proved attractive during these years to a wide range of socialist intellectuals searching for a way of reconciling their Marxism with the changed reality of the postwar era. The most powerful and original proponent of this theory was Otto Bauer, probably the most influential intellectual in the Austrian SDAP – a party that during the interwar years made its name trying desperately to walk the fine line between "reformism and Bolshevism."[11] Bauer argued that with the transition to democracy, an equilibrium had developed between society's social groups. The bourgeoisie, while still dominant,

---

[7] Heinrich August Winkler, *Von der Revolution zur Stabilisierung: Arbeiter und Arbeiterbewegung in der Weimarer Republik, 1918–1924* (Berlin: J. H. W. Dietz, 1984), 11.

[8] Heinrich August Winkler, "Eduard Bernstein as Critic of Weimar Social Democracy," in Roger Fletcher, ed., *Bernstein to Brandt* (London: Edward Arnold, 1987).

[9] Ibid. Part of the reason for this shift back was that in 1922, the democratic elements of the USPD (the independent socialist party that split from the SPD during the war to protest its support for the war effort) rejoined the SPD, and the old radicals from the USPD strongly opposed any weakening of the party's traditional stance.

[10] Wolfgang Luthardt, *Sozialdemokratische Verfassungstheorie in der Weimarer Republik* (Opladen: Westdeutscher Verlag, 1986), 3; Richard Saage, *Rückkehr zum starken Staat?* (Frankfurt: Suhrkamp Verlag, 1983), 108; idem, "Parlamentarische Demokratie, Staatsfunktionen und Das Gleichgewicht der Klassenkräfte," in idem, ed., *Solidargemeinschft und Klassenkampf* (Frankfurt: Suhrkamp Verlag, 1986).

[11] This was a characterization used by Bauer in particular. Norbert Leser, *Zwischen Reformismus und Bolshevismus. Der Austromarxismus als Theorie und Praxis* (Vienna: Europa Verlag, 1968).

could no longer rule alone nor in any manner it pleased, and interwar democratic regimes, as a result, were not "dictatorships, [or] the unlimited rule of the
capitalist class"[12] (as Marx had posited). Democracy was thus a clear improvement over prewar semi-authoritarianism. Still, it was hardly synonymous with
socialism. And since the prime determinant of further development toward
socialism remained "the development of capitalism," the degree to which
socialists should sacrifice or compromise for democracy remained somewhat
limited.[13]

The consequences of this view were profound. To begin with, the conviction
that economic forces rather than (democratic) political action held the key to
socialism led to a "submissive surrender to the inescapable logic of events."[14]
(Many thus likened Bauer to Hamlet, highlighting his tragic inability to make
hard decisions.) On a practical level, the "balance of class forces" theory led
to a preference for opposition rather than governance. As Bauer once put it,
"the government of a bourgeois state, as long as it remains a bourgeois state,
falls naturally to the bourgeois class."[15] Furthermore, although this theory did
rule out coalitions entirely, it led naturally to a view of them as "emergency
measures" and ones that should occur only when socialists were the dominant
partners.

This desire to avoid the "Charybdis" of revisionism and the "Scylla" of
communism was characteristic of many socialists and socialist parties during
the interwar years. In France, the would-be reconciler was Léon Blum, who
devoted himself to trying to find some way to maintain socialist unity in the
face of a significant communist threat. In the years after the First World War,
he brokered a series of compromises designed to placate the party's left and
right wings, but by 1920 it had become clear that the center could not hold. At
the SFIO's congress that year, Blum tried to broker an agreement that would
pledge the party to defend democracy while rejecting ministerialism, but radicals within the party were unwilling to compromise and voted to join Lenin's
Third International. This split the party in two: Those favoring affiliation with
the Comintern formed the French Communist Party (PCF), while the others
turned back to reconstruct a rump SFIO.

The schism eliminated the hard left from the mainstream party, but left the
latter divided, as before the war, into warring orthodox and revisionist camps.
The former was stronger, and insisted that the SFIO reaffirm "its fidelity to

---

[12] Otto *Bauer, Austrian Revolution* (London: Leonard Parsons, 1925); Leser, *Zwischen Reformismus und Bolshevismus*, 119; Anson Rabinbach, *The Crisis of Austrian Socialism* (Chicago:
University of Chicago Press, 1983), 40ff.

[13] See, for example, the SDAP's important Linz party program. Rabinbach, *The Crisis of Austrian
Socialism*, 119.

[14] Norbert Leser, "Austro-Marxism: A Reappraisal," *Journal of Contemporary History*, 11, 1976,
146; Leser, *Zwischen Reformismus und Bolshevismus*, 136, 429; Rabinbach, *The Crisis of Austrian Socialism*, 123ff; idem, "Ernst Fischer and the Left Opposition in Austrian Social Democracy" (Ph.D. Dissertation, University of Wisconsin, 1973), 67.

[15] Leser, *Zwischen Reformismus und Bolshevismus*, 350.

traditional prewar orthodoxy." The result was an official declaration that, "In its goal, its ideal, its methods, the Socialist party, while seeking the fulfillment of immediate reforms demanded by the working class, is not a party of reform but a party of class struggle and revolution. . . . Neither Left blocs nor ministerialism, condemned both in theory and practice, will find in its ranks the slightest chance of success."[16] The party thus tried to return to its prewar compromise of publicly declaring its suspicion of everything "bourgeois" while simultaneously pursuing improvements for workers within the existing system. But now even more than before, such a course proved untenable.

When the SFIO, under pressure from its left wing, shunned alliances with the Radicals (an important left-liberal party) in the 1919 elections, the results were predictable: Although the socialists' total share of the vote rose somewhat, they lost a significant number of seats, while the parties of the center and the right, which had joined together in the Bloc National, won an almost two-thirds parliamentary majority. In the next election, the SFIO, stung by defeat, reversed course and cooperated with the Radicals. The result was a resounding victory. The Radical leader Edouard Herriot promptly offered the Socialists some cabinet positions, writing to Blum that "the Socialists and Radicals have together campaigned against the coalition of high finance and slander. The evident will of the country is that this collaboration continue in the councils of government."[17] But resistance to ministerialism among the SFIO's traditionalists remained high, and the offer was turned down. The result was a succession of short-lived cabinets, which increased everyone's frustration and left the country's growing financial and economic problems unaddressed. Not surprisingly, the public returned a solid majority for the center and right in the 1928 elections. The conservative Raymond Poincarè returned to power – this time with the support of a Radical Party that had given up on its erstwhile Socialist partner.

The SFIO's reformers argued that by refusing to consider participating in the government, the party was handing the country over to conservatives. But their orthodox, Guesdist opponents were unmoved. Blum tried once again to broker a compromise, claiming a distinction between the "exercise" and the "conquest" of power. The latter, he argued, remained the party's ultimate goal, but did not preclude the former, which characterized everyday life within a parliamentary system. Even a special party congress that adopted Blum's line as official policy only papered over the basic conflict, as was thrown into clear relief in 1929 when the left Radical Edouard Daladier asked Socialists to join his cabinet. A large majority of the SFIO's parliamentary group wanted to accept the offer. But again the leadership rejected it, since Socialists would not be in control. As a result, Daladier failed to form a government and had to hand over power to a man whom the left loathed, André Tardieu.

---

[16] Robert Mead, "The Stuggle for Power: Reformism in the French Socialist Party, 1919–1939" (Ph.D. Dissertation, Columbia University, 1952), 61ff.
[17] Joel Colton, *Léon Blum: Humanist in Politics* (New York: Alfred Knopf, 1966), 66.

By the end of the 1920s, the SFIO had reached an impasse. Unwilling to join the revolutionary fantasies of the communists or to embrace explicitly bourgeois parties and institutions, the party found itself sitting on the sidelines unsure of what to do.[18] It was, as one socialist put it, plagued by "the paradox of a doctrine without practice combined with a practice without a doctrine."[19]

The Italian Story

The same story, meanwhile, had been playing out in Italy, only at a quicker pace and with a more tragic outcome. As in France and Germany, the Italian Socialists emerged from the First World War as the strongest political party. Yet not even the political, social, and economic turmoil of the immediate postwar era could shake the intransigence of the PSI, which had been radicalized by the Russian Revolution and made clear its disdain for bourgeois institutions; if anything, turmoil strengthened the hand of those who looked forward to the reigning order's collapse.

The party's 1919 congress revealed a movement split, as elsewhere, into three main factions. An extreme left led by Amadeo Bordiga supported the Bolsheviks, insisted that revolution was "right and around the corner," and rejected all compromises.[20] On the right, Filippo Turati led a group committed to democratic socialism. He urged his colleagues to recognize that "in the present Italian situation, dictatorship of the proletariat cannot be anything other than the dictatorship of some men on top of, and eventually against, the vast majority of the proletariat," and predicted that continuing the party's revolutionary rhetoric would one day lead

...our appeal to violence [to be] taken up by our enemies, one hundred times better armed than we, and then goodbye for a long time to Parliamentary action, goodbye to economic organizations, goodbye to Socialist party.... To speak ... of violence continually and then always postpone it until tomorrow is ... the most absurd thing in this world. It only serves to arm, to rouse, to justify the violence of the adversary, a thousand times stronger than ours.... This is the ultimate stupidity to which a party can come, and involves a true renunciation of any revolution.[21]

[18] One reason that the SFIO was probably able to maintain its somewhat ambiguous relationship to bourgeois parties and institutions for so long was the very strength of French democracy and the at least implicit belief that even if socialists refused responsibility for the Republic, parties of the center and center-left would defend it. Thus, at least until the 1930s, socialists were never forced to confront the possibility that their unwillingness to participate might actually mean the end of the Republic. This was a luxury that their German and, in a different way, Italian colleagues never had.

[19] Julian Jackson, *The Politics of Depression in France 1932–1936* (New York: Cambridge University Press, 1985), 36.

[20] Alexander De Grand, *In Stalin's Shadow* (Dekalb, IL: Northern Illinois University Press, 1986), and Albert Lindemann, *The "Red Years": European Socialism Versus Bolshevism* (Berkeley, CA: University of California Press, 1974), 59–60.

[21] Daniel L. Horowitz: *The Italian Labor Movement* (Cambridge, MA: Harvard University Press, 1963), 134–5.

In between stood the party's dominant faction, the Maximalists. Like the extreme left, they supported the Russian Revolution, but they were less enamored of insurrectionism and were unwilling to rule out all compromises with the existing order. As Maximalist leader Giacinto Serrati put it, "We deny voluntarism, both anarchical and reformist.... We Marxists interpret history and do not make it, and we operate in the times, according to the logic of events and things." He would later famously add that socialists needed to understand one another on the meaning – apparently voluntaristic – of the verb "to make":

To make the revolution does not so much mean to incite to the violent determinant act...as it does to prepare the elements that will enable us to profit from this inevitable act as a party and to draw from it all the Socialist consequences permitted by the times and the circumstances. Making the revolution means – in my opinion – profiting from the elements that the situation naturally puts at our disposition in order to turn events to our ends. In other words, it is not we who make the revolution...it is we who, conscious of this new force created under the desired conditions, intend to make use of it to bend it to the ends of our doctrine.[22]

The Maximalists' dominance was reflected in the resolutions that the congress passed, which split the difference between the reformists and the revolutionaries. The party proclaimed its support for the "dictatorship of the proletariat," condemned the national parliament and local governments as "bourgeois" institutions, and declared "the proletariat must resort to the use of force to defend itself against bourgeois violence, to conquer power, and to consolidate revolutionary conquests." At the same time, the party also permitted participation in elections (although not governments), something that it justified by claiming that victory at the polls would only "hasten the destruction of parliament and 'the organs of bourgeois domination.'"[23]

The 1919 national elections put this compromise to the test. They confirmed the PSI as Italy's largest party, one that, together with the new Catholic Popular Party, could even command a majority in parliament. But the Catholics disliked the Socialists, and the PSI had already made clear that it wanted nothing to do with "bourgeois" parties and was uninterested in governing. So the PSI sat on its hands while urging its supporters to take solace in the fact that the revolution was on its way.[24] As Mussolini (who had by this time left the party to build his own revolutionary movement – see Chapter 6) perceptively noted:

The marvelous victory at the polls has simply shown up the inefficiency and weakness of the socialists. They are impotent alike as reformers and revolutionaries. They take...action...[n]either [in] the parliament [n]or the streets. The sight of a party wearing itself out on the morrow of a great victory in a vain search for something to apply

[22] Norberto Bobbio, *Ideological Profile of Twentieth-Century Italy* (Princeton, NJ: Princeton University Press, 1995), 110.
[23] Ibid.; Christopher Seton-Watson, *Italy from Liberalism to Fascism* (London: Butler and Tanner, 1967), 548; Denis Mack Smith, *Italy: A Modern History* (Ann Arbor, MI: University of Michigan Press, 1959), 328.
[24] Horowitz, *The Italian Labor Movement*, 139–42.

its strength to, and willing to attempt neither reform nor revolution, amuses us. This is our vengeance and it has come sooner than we hoped![25]

In the following months, economic and social conditions continued to deteriorate, while a weak and ultimately short-lived government could do little of consequence. Unemployment reached 2 million; inflation continued to rise; food riots erupted; strikes exploded in both the industrial and agricultural sectors; and peasants, who had been promised land during the war by a government eager to sustain morale, began seizing it in parts of the country.[26] In Turin, a stronghold of an extreme left-wing socialist faction headed by Antonio Gramsci, a factory council movement sprang up.[27] These were independent organizations of workers, seen by Gramsci's group as proto-Soviets preparing for the not-too-distant day when the proletariat would control the economy itself. The council movement spread throughout 1920, generating massive strikes, factory occupations, and lockouts. "By the end of the year almost 1.3 million workers had participated in the struggle and many had begun to insist that they, and not the owners and managers, were in charge of their industries."[28] As one commentator noted, to many "this seemed to be nothing short of the revolution itself."[29]

The Italian left was divided over how to respond to this movement. The PSI claimed that the situation was revolutionary, but union leaders argued that pushing beyond issues directly related to worker control in industry would lead to disaster. At one point, the union leader Ludovico D'Aragona offered the socialists leadership of the movement, telling them, "You think that this is the time to begin a revolutionary action, well, then, you assume the responsibility. We who do not feel able to assume this responsibility of pushing the proletariat to suicide, we tell you that we retire and submit our resignations."[30] Ultimately workers voted to limit the movement's aims. Although defeated, the PSI leadership was also somewhat relieved: Having long proclaimed their advocacy of revolution but having never prepared for it, the PSI leaders had no plan for what to do next. As one observer notes: "After the [vote] the leaders [of the PSI] breathed a sign of relief. Relieved of all responsibility, they could now scream themselves hoarse about the 'treason' of the [unions]. Thus they

---

[25] A. Rossi, *The Rise of Italian Fascism 1918–1922* (London: Methuen, 1938), 53.

[26] Anthony Cardoza, *Agrarian Elites and Italian Fascism: The Province of Bologna, 1901–1926* (Princeton, NJ: Princeton University Press, 1982), chapter six; Martin Clark, *Modern Italy 1871–1982* (New York: Longman, 1984), 206ff; Alexander De Grand, *Italian Fascism* (Lincoln, NE: University of Nebraska Press, 1982), 24.

[27] Richard Bellamy and Darrow Schecter, *Gramsci and the Italian State* (Manchester, UK: Manchester University Press, 1993); John M. Cammett, *Antonio Gramsci and the Origins of Italian Communism* (Stanford, CA: Stanford University Press, 1967); Gwyn A. Williams, *Proletarian Order: Antonio Gramsci, Factory Councils and the Origins of Italian Communism, 1911–1921* (London: Pluto Press, 1975).

[28] Maurice Neufeld: *Italy: School for Awakening Countries* (Ithaca, NY: Cayuga Press, 1961), 379.

[29] Horowitz, *The Italian Labor Movement*, 149.

[30] Ibid., 151.

had something to offer the masses whom they had abandoned at the crucial moment, and were able at the same time to save face."[31] Still, after having been continuously told that revolution was imminent, many workers felt robbed of their victory and betrayed by their leaders. The PSI's verbal commitment to revolution combined with its inability or unwillingness to "make" one fed resentment against the Maximalist leadership and deepened divisions within the party.

If workers were upset, employers and the middle classes were downright horrified. The council movement's threats to property and management prerogatives, combined with an impressive showing by the socialists during local elections in 1920, seemed to confirm their worst fears. During the crisis, the government had chosen not to intervene, with its leader Giolitti calculating that the council movement would soon burn itself out and that the use of troops would only play "into the hands of the revolutionaries."[32] He was right, but his refusal to endorse a hard line led many to believe that the existing regime could not or would not defend their interests. The young Fascist movement took advantage of these fears, and by the end of 1920 it was beginning to move out from urban to rural areas and make increasing use of terror.

At this critical juncture in Italian history, the socialists were more concerned with their own internecine battles than with the growing chaos in the country at large. When the PSI applied to join the Communist International, Moscow informed the party that in order to join, it would have to expel all its "reformists" (that is, Turati and his supporters), end its relationship with the labor unions, and change its name to "Communist." At the party's 1921 congress, the leftists favored accepting these conditions, but the Maximalists, while claiming to be committed to Moscow's objectives, were reluctant to launch such a purge. When the congress voted to support the Maximalists' position and reject the deal, Bordiga, Gramsci, and their allies walked out and formed the Italian Communist Party.[33]

At this point, Turati and the reformists, concerned about political turmoil and the growing strength of the Fascists, argued that the PSI should join a coalition with other parties committed to democracy. But the Maximalists refused. Serrati, for example, taunted those who thought that they could "help settle the bourgeois crisis and pick up some trifling advantages" by participating in the existing system. "Let all who wish to work for the revolution come with us," he proclaimed, "and all who wish to thwart it go with the bourgeoisie."[34]

[31] Ibid., 151–2; Rossi, *The Rise of Italian Fascism*, 70.
[32] Giovanni Giolitti, *Memoirs of My Life* (London: Chapman and Dodd, 1923), 437–8.
[33] Cammett, *Antonio Gramsci and the Origins of Italian Communism*, 133ff; Alastair Davidson, *The Theory and Practice of Italian Communism*, Vol. 1 (London: Merlin Press, 1982) 97ff; Spencer Di Scala, *Italy from Revolution to Republic* (Boulder, CO: Westview Press, 1998), 218; Horowitz, *The Italian Labor Movement*, 157–9.
[34] Angelo Tasca, *The Rise of Italian Fascism* (Methuen: London, 1938), 244.

As the Fascists continued their forward march (they won thirty-five seats in the 1921 parliamentary elections, up from zero two years earlier), the PSI leadership persisted in resisting calls from its ranks to support the government and help it counter Italy's economic crisis, social conflict, and rising tide of violence. Even when Giolitti was forced to resign and Bonomi, the old prewar Socialist reformist, presented a new cabinet for parliamentary approval, the PSI insisted on opposition.[35]

The situation continued to deteriorate after the elections when the Fascists formed an alliance with the nationalists. The national government and local authorities offered no response, which facilitated Fascist takeovers of prefectures, police headquarters, and other institutions across the Italian countryside. The PSI's right wing was growing increasingly alarmed by these trends, and in June 1922 a majority of the party's parliamentary group voted to support a government that was committed to guaranteeing basic liberties. The labor unions voiced their support of the decision, pleading for the PSI to change its official course. But once again the leadership refused, this time responding to the breach of discipline by expelling Turati and other "collaborationists" from the party. So, in early October, the reformers founded their own party, the Unitary Socialist Party (PSU), and pledged cooperation to save the democratic order. It was too little too late[36]: On October 27, the sitting government resigned, and on October 29, the King invited Mussolini to Rome to form a cabinet. Fascism had come to power in Italy.

Not surprisingly, after Mussolini's rise, the PSI (and the Maximalists in particular) came in for harsh criticism. For socialism to ever regain its footing, critics argued, it would have to recognize that a better future would not simply drop into its hands, but would have to be fought for and won. The most famous such call from the communist left came from Gramsci. He had little patience for the determinism and economism of orthodox Marxism, and fervently attacked the "'worse the better' school of Marxism for the naïve view that economic crises would automatically give rise to progressive political change."[37] True revolutionaries were those who took history into their own hands. And like others who turned away from orthodox Marxism, Gramsci insisted that the battle for the future would be fought not only in the economic sphere, but the political, cultural, and ideological realms as well. Such views help to explain his early infatuation with Mussolini and his support of Lenin and the Bolshevik revolution.

The most famous and influential democratic revisionist critic of the PSI Maximalists was Carlo Rosselli. Like Gramsci, Rosselli devoted his life to providing an alternative to the economistic and deterministic Marxism that he believed

[35] Horowitz, *The Italian Labor Movement*, 167.

[36] Alexander De Grand, *The Italian Left in the Twentieth Century* (Indianapolis, IN: Indiana University Press, 1989), 51, and Horowitz, *The Italian Labor Movement*.

[37] Bellamy and Schecter, *Gramsci and the Italian State*, 90.

had destroyed the socialist movement, but unlike his more famous countryman, he believed in both democracy and liberalism. Indeed, his most important work was entitled *Liberal Socialism*[38] and it drew on all of the classic themes of democratic revisionism to construct a new vision for the left.

Rosselli's critiques of the socialist movement were withering. "The great weakness of contemporary socialists," he wrote, "lies precisely in their steadfast resistance to the evolution of reality; in the way they always refer to outdated factual situations even when they are trying to illustrate their ideal form of society; in their use of old, worn-out arguments that have very little to do with the reality of modern economic life."[39] This unwillingness to adjust to changing circumstances, he argued, was largely a consequence of orthodox Marxism. Historical materialism, he argued, had proved its usefulness in guiding the actual socialist movement to be "virtually zero."[40] The goal must therefore be to extricate socialism from Marxism's economistic and deterministic fantasies: "The whole of revisionism of both the Right and Left" – of Bernstein in Germany, Jaurès and Sorel in France, and Labriola in Italy – "can in fact be summed up as the effort to make room in the Marxist system for the will and the optimism of the workers' movement."[41]

Rosselli's recognition that workers and others had to be inspired to struggle for a better world led him to an appreciation of Sorel's emphasis on myths and mysticism, but he also believed that "the spirit could be awakened" by calls for justice, liberty, and the collective good. Rosselli's commitment to such values – and his experience with the dictatorships of the interwar years – led him to admire many aspects of liberalism. And like Bernstein, he wanted to "join" together the best of liberalism and socialism and saw the latter as in many ways the successor to the former:

Socialism is nothing more than the logical development taken to its extreme consequences of the principle of liberty. Socialism, when understood in its fundamental sense and judged by its results – as the concrete movement for the emancipation of the proletariat – is liberalism in action; it means the liberty that comes into the life of poor people. Socialism says: the abstract recognition of liberty of conscience and political freedoms for all, though it may represent an essential moment in the development of political theory, is a thing of very limited value when the majority of men, forced to live as a result of circumstances of birth and environment in moral and material poverty, are left without the possibility of appreciating its significance and taking any actual advantage of it. Liberty without the accompaniment and support of a minimum of economic autonomy, without emancipation from the grip of pressing material necessity, does not exist for the individual; it is a mere phantasm.[42]

---

[38] Carlo Rosselli, *Socialismo Liberale*, published in English as *Liberal Socialism* (Princeton, NJ: Princeton University Press, 1994).
[39] Ibid., 68.
[40] Ibid., 28.
[41] Ibid., 23.
[42] Ibid., 86.

Rosselli therefore proposed separating the economic and political arms of liberalism – "liberating" liberalism, so to speak, from its attachment to the free market. The time had passed "when bourgeois politics and liberal free market politics were one and the same.... With its dogmatic attachment to the principles of economic libertarianism ... it has managed to shackle the dynamic spirit of liberalism to the transitory pattern of a particular social system."[43] Liberalism had become enervated, he argued, had turned into a system benefiting the well-off. Socialism's task was to bring liberalism's revolutionary potential to all:

In the name of liberty, and for the purpose of ensuring its effective possession by all men and not just a privileged minority, socialists postulate the end of bourgeois privilege and the effective extension of the liberties of the bourgeoisie to all. In the name of liberty they ask for a more equal distribution of wealth and the automatic guarantee for every person of a life worth living.... They want social life to be guided not by the egoistic criterion of personal utility, but by the social criterion, the criterion of the collective good.... The socialist movement is, in consequence, the objective heir of liberalism: it carries this dynamic idea of liberty forward through the vicissitudes of history towards its actualization. Liberalism and socialism, rather than opposing one another in the manner depicted in outdated polemics, are connected by an inner bond. Liberalism is the ideal force of inspiration, and socialism is the practical force of realization.[44]

Rosselli argued that the time had come for revisionists to recognize that "the logical conclusion to which [their movement] leads is the splitting off of socialism from Marxism."[45] To cement this trend, Rosselli insisted that alongside a new theoretical foundation, socialists also needed new practical policies. He favored, for example, abandoning socialism's traditional emphasis on class struggle and proletarian purity and instead focusing on the collective good. He also urged socialists to break "the absurd monopoly on patriotism held by the so-called national parties." Echoing sentiments voiced by Bernstein, Jaurès, and other revisionists a generation before, Rosselli argued that:

The initial denial of national values by the precursors of socialism was a natural reaction to the profound inferiority and oppression inflicted on the masses.... Today, when the masses in the most advanced countries have been granted full parity in political rights and have come to possess extremely powerful means to make themselves and their own material and ideal concerns felt in the life of the state, the outdated internationalism that denies or even reviles the national homeland is nonsense, a mistake, just another ball and chain shackled to socialist parties by the Marxist fetish.[46]

Alongside this broadened, even communitarian appeal, Rosselli believed socialists needed to work actively to control capitalism. "It is probable,"

---

[43] Ibid., 87.
[44] Ibid., 86–7.
[45] Ibid., 57. See also Stanislao G. Pugliese, *Carlo Rosselli. Socialist Heretic and Antifascist Exile* (Cambridge, MA: Harvard University Press, 1999), 106.
[46] Rosselli, *Liberal Socialism*, 122–3.

he wrote, "that capitalism will have to renounce its hegemony and submit increasingly to limitations and interventions on the part of public authorities and that various forms of regulated economy, in which the principle of satisfying wants will prevail over the profit motive, will appear."[47]

Against the backdrop of socialism's collapse in Italy, in short, Rosselli began developing a new vision and program for the left, one based on a belief that socialism would emerge only through the active, collective efforts of human beings motivated by a belief in a higher good. And unlike his prewar counterparts, Rosselli's loyalty to the mainstream socialist movement had frayed beyond repair, leading to his recognition that the time had come for an explicit break with Marxism. As the left in other European nations stumbled in the years after the Italian Republic's collapse, Rosselli's criticisms and conclusions would be echoed by a growing number of socialists across the continent.

Standing at the Sickbed of Capitalism

Unfortunately the Italian socialists were not the only ones to stand by while democracy collapsed. Ten years later, their powerful German counterparts found themselves facing a tragically similar situation. Although the SPD was much more engaged than the PSI in the life of its republic, the former never fully accepted its role in either "bourgeois" democracy or the compromises which that role would entail. Indeed, even when it became painfully clear to all that German democracy was in trouble, the SPD remained wedded to many traditional, orthodox positions that dramatically hindered its ability to respond to the admittedly daunting challenges it faced.

By the early 1930s, the SPD found itself flanked on the right by a rapidly growing Nazi Party and on the left by Communists. In the 1928 elections, the Nazis had polled 2.6 percent and the Communists 10.6 percent; two years later, with the country ravaged by the Great Depression, those figures rose to 18.3 percent and 13.1 percent, respectively. In response, the SPD declared that its most important task was to defend the Republic and supported the new conservative chancellor, Heinrich Brüning, as the lesser evil.[48] But while perhaps the lesser evil, Brüning was no friend to the SPD or its interests. For example, despite the devastating economic downturn, during his time in office Brüning chipped away at what remained of Germany's social support system. The SPD responded by attacking the chancellor's "antisocial" policies, but since the SPD accepted the need to cut state expenditure, it did not have much of an alternative to offer. (In fact, Brüning's memoirs make clear that he often

---

[47] Ibid., 125.

[48] Eberhard Kolb, "Die Sozialdemokratische Strategie in der Ära des Präsidialkabinetts Brüning: Strategie ohne Alternative?," in Ursula Büttner, ed., *Das Unrechtsregime: Internationale Forschung über den Nationalsozialismus*, Vol. 1 (Hamburg: Christians, 1986), and Heinrich August Winkler, *Der Weg in die Katastrophe: Arbeiter und Arbeiterbewegung in der Weimarer Republik, 1930–1933* (Berlin: J. H. W. Dietz, 1987), chapter 2, section 3.

turned to members of the SPD for support; the party's chief economist, Rudolf Hilferding, was a confidant.[49])

Over time, however, the inconsistencies in the SPD's position became increasingly problematic. And not surprisingly, the SPD's support of Brüning and failure to put forward any distinctive plans of its own for dealing with the Depression elicited storms of protest. At the party's 1931 congress, one typical complaint was: "On the one hand we claim that Brüning's policies can only make the crisis worse and increase our misery, but on the other hand we must tolerate his government.... If we do not find a way out of this vicious circle then I am very skeptical about the future."[50] In the meeting's most electrifying speech, Fritz Tarnow, a leading figure in both the unions and the SPD, concisely summed up the SPD's dilemma:

Are we standing at the sickbed of capitalism not only as doctors who want to heal the patient, but also as prospective heirs who can't wait for the end and would gladly help the process along with a little poison?... We are damned, I think, to be doctors who seriously want to cure, and yet we have to maintain the feeling that we are heirs who wish to receive the entire legacy of the capitalist system today rather than tomorrow. This double role, doctor and heir, is a damned difficult task.

Tarnow urged his colleagues to recognize that: "it is not so much the patient that is causing us such trouble but rather the masses standing behind him.... If we recognize this and find a medicine – even if we are not convinced that it will fully cure the patient – we should ... [nonetheless] give the medicine and not be so concerned that we also in fact wish for the patient's demise."[51]

In the remaining sessions of the congress, many speakers embraced Tarnow's frontal assault on the party's immobilism. Others, however, rejected the idea that the Republic – and the party – could reform its way out of the crisis. Eventually the congress ignored Tarnow's call for change and decided to stay the course.

The sterility of the SPD's position also soured the party's relationship to organized labor. By 1930, the German unions had begun shifting from supporting a policy of paying off reparations in full to a belief that reparations were simply too great a burden on an already weakened economy.[52] They also decided that fighting unemployment had become the top priority. In 1931, accordingly, the

[49] Heinrich Brüning, *Memoiren 1918–1934* (Stuttgart: Deutsche, 1970), for example 105, 115–16, 118, 133, 315, 501–2, and also Gottfried Reinhold Treviranus, *Das Ende von Weimar* (Düsseldorf: Droste, 1968), 156–61.

[50] *Protokoll über die Verhandlungen des Sozialdemokratischer Parteitages*, 31 Mai bis 5 Juni in Leipzig 1931 (Berlin: J. H. W. Dietz, 1974), 60.

[51] Ibid., 45–6.

[52] Thomas Hahn, "Arbeiterbewegung und Gewerkschaften: eine Untersuchung der Strategiebildung der Freien Gewerkschaften auf dem Arbeitsmarkt" (Ph.D. Dissertation, Free University of Berlin, 1977); Peter Jahn with Detlev Brunner, *Die Gewerkschaften in der Endphase der Republik* (Köln: Bund, 1988); Michael Schneider, "Konjunkturpolitische Vorstellungen der Gewerkschaften in den Letzten Jahren der Weimarer Republik," in Hans Mommsen, Dietmar Petzina, and Bernd Weisbrod, eds., *Industrielles System und Politische Entwicklung in*

unions began to consider seriously various job-creation proposals, the most important of which was the WTB plan.[53]

The plan was the brainchild of Wladimir S. Woytinsky, a Russian émigré who headed a major union organization's statistical bureau.[54] During the late 1920s, Woytinsky had begun mulling active state intervention in the economic cycle, and in a series of articles he began to build the framework for a full-fledged assault on the Depression. By 1931, he had come to the conclusion that Germany's only way out of the crisis was through stimulating the domestic economy,[55] and he joined with Tarnow and Fritz Baade (an SPD member of parliament) to come up with a proto-Keynesian strategy based on domestic stimulus.[56] The WTB plan (it took its name from the initials of its sponsors) called for about 2 billion marks to be spent on work creation. The work generated by these programs would be "socially useful," pay competitive wages, and supposedly help create the basis for a self-perpetuating recovery. Deficit financing would be necessary at first.[57]

Woytinsky argued that the time had come for Social Democrats to surrender their faith in historical development and the "mystical powers of the market" and recognize that improvement would depend on active intervention in the economy. He also touted the WTB plan's political and ideological merit: By using the levers of power to help improve the lives of the masses, by helping to tame the anarchy of the market, and by showing the way to a more organized and just economy, the WTB plan could finally provide the SPD (and the unions) with a concrete step toward a new economic and social order.[58] The labor movement, he suggested, should begin a frontal assault on deflation and the radical right under the banner "the struggle against the crisis."[59]

der Weimarer Republik (Dusseldorf: Athenäum, 1977); Gerhard Schulze, Ilse Mauer, and Udo Wengst, eds., *Politik und Wirtschaft in der Krise, 1930–1932* (Düsseldorf: Droste, 1980).

53 The most complete discussion of union debates over work creation is Michael Schneider, *Die Arbeitsbeschaffungprogramme des ADGB* (Bonn: Neue Gesellschaft, 1975).

54 Woytinsky's life was fascinating. After the rise of the Nazis, Woytinsky fled Germany for the United States, where he contributed to the New Deal. In his autobiography *Stormy Passage* (New York: Vanguard Press, 1961), one gets an engrossing account of some of the most important events of the twentieth century. See also Emma Woytinsky, ed., *So Much Alive: The Life and Work of W. S. Woytinsky* (New York: Vanguard Press, 1962).

55 He had previously hoped for international action to stem the crisis.

56 Tarnow had, for example, in 1928 published *Warum Arm Sein?* (Why Be Poor?) (Berlin: Verlagsanstalt des ADGB, 1928). See also R. Wagenführ and W. Voss, "Trade Unions and the World Economic Crisis," in Hermann van der Wee, ed., *The Great Depression Revisited* (The Hague: Martinus Nijhoff, 1972).

57 Wladimir Woytinsky, "Arbeitsbeschaffung und Keine Inflationsgefahr," *Die Arbeit*, 3, March 1932, and "Der WTB Plan der Arbeitsbeschaffung," reprinted in G. Bombach, H. J. Ramser, M. Timmermann, and W. Wittmann, eds., *Der Keynesianismus: Die Beschäftigungspolitische Diskussion vor Keynes in Deutschland* (Berlin: Springer, 1976), 172–5.

58 Woytinsky, "Sozialistische Wirtschaftspolitik Heißt Heute Arbeitsbeschaffung," *Leipziger Volkszeitung*, 68, March 21, 1932.

59 "Thesen zum Kampf Gegen die Wirtschaftskrise," in Michael Schneider, *Das Arbeitsbescaffungsprogramm des ADGB* (Bonn: Neue Gesellschaft, 1975), 230.

The union movement embraced the WTB plan and began planning a large-scale press campaign to popularize the program and a special "crisis" congress to put pressure on the government for a course shift.[60] The unions also echoed Woytinsky's emphasis on the political value of the plan. The newspaper of the German metalworkers' union, for example, warned: "Our people have been waiting for months for advice and direction.... It is [getting] late.... We must come forward with a work creation program, regardless of any scientific differences of opinion, otherwise the quacks [i.e., the Nazis] will find increasing support for their views. We can't wait until our theoreticians are united; the issue at hand must...be solved."[61]

Despite increasing pressure from inside and outside his own government, Brüning stuck to his course, forcing the SPD into a very difficult position.[62] Never having developed a strategy for working within the capitalist system to achieve its goals, the party was divided over how to respond to the unions' suggestion. Some on the right argued for work creation, but many of these same "reformers" scorned the idea of deficit financing. Many on the left, meanwhile, argued that the time was ripe for a full-fledged "socialist" strategy.[63]

Amid this confusion, the party's most important economic theoretician, Rudolf Hilferding, emerged as a key figure in the debate, mounting a full-scale campaign against the plan.[64] He began his attacks by stressing that the WTB plan was "un-Marxist" and threatened the "very foundations of our

[60] Gerard Braunthal, *Socialist Labor and Politics in Weimar Germany: The General Federation of German Trade Unions* (Hamden, CT: Archon, 1978), 62–5; Ursula Hüllbüsch, "Die Deutschen Gewerkschaften in der Weltwirtschaftskrise," in Walter Conze, ed., *Die Staats-und Wirtschaftskrise des Deutschen Reichs, 1929–1933* (Stuttgart: Ernst Klett, 1967); Wolfgang Zollitsch, "Einzelgewerkschaften und Arbeitsbeschaffung: Zum Handlungsspielraum der Arbeiterbewegung in der Spätphase der Weimarer Republik," *Geschichte und Gesellschaft*, 8, 1982.

[61] "Raus aus dem Engpaß," *Deutsche Metallarbeiter Zeitung*, 9, February 27, 1932.

[62] To alleviate demands for a change, he did, however, appoint a commission led by former Labor Minister Heinrich Braun to study means of dealing with unemployment. The commission recommended work creation, but Brüning's cabinet remained divided over financing measures. See Robert Gates, "The Economic Policies of the German Free Trade Unions and the German Social Democratic Party, 1930–33" (Ph.D. Dissertation, University of Oregon, 1970), 186–7; Rainer Schaefer, *Die SPD in der Ära Brüning: Tolierung oder Mobilisierung* (Frankfurt: Campus Forschung, 1990); Winkler, *Der Weg in die Katastrophe*, 436ff. To follow the internal government discussions on economic policy during Brüning's tenure, see Gerhard Schulz et al., eds., *Politik und Wirtschaft in der Krise* and *Akten der Reichskanzlei. Das Kabinett Brüning I: 30 März bis Oktober 1931* (Boppard am Rhein: Harald Boldt, 1982), and idem, *Das Kabinett Brüning II: 10 Oktober 1931 bis 1 Juni 1932* (Boppard am Rhein: Harald Boldt, 1988).

[63] Donna Harsch, *German Social Democracy and the Rise of Fascism* (Chapel Hill, NC: University of North Carolina Press, 1993); Thomas Meyer, "Elemente einer Gesamttheorie des demokratischen Sozialismus und Hindernisse ihrer Durchsetzung in der Weimarer Republik," in Horst Heimann and Thomas Meyer, eds., *Reformsozialismus und Sozialdemokratie* (Berlin: Verlag J. H. W. Dietz, 1982); Schaefer, *SPD in der Ära Brüning*, 380–92; Winkler, *Der Weg in die Katastrophe*, 431–511.

[64] Reflecting this, Hilferding appears in Woytinsky's memoirs as the evil villain of German Social Democracy and the main cause of the WTB plan's defeat. See Woytinsky, *Stormy Passage*, esp. 468–71.

program."[65] The only solution to economic difficulties, he claimed, was to wait for the business cycle to run its course; an "offensive economic policy" had no place because the ultimate arbiter of developments was the "logic of capitalism."[66]

But even Hilferding privately recognized that his position doomed the SPD to continued sterility. In a letter to Karl Kautsky, he wrote: "[W]orst of all in this situation is that we can't say anything concrete to the people about how and by what means we would end the crisis. Capitalism has been shaken far beyond our expectations but...a socialist solution is not at hand and that makes the situation unbelievably difficult and allows the Communists and Nazis to continue to grow."[67] Still, to counteract the plan's appeal, Hilferding worked on a counterproposal, the "Umbau der Wirtschaft" (Reorganization of the Economy) program,[68] which had as its centerpiece a declaration that the time was ripe for building a socialist planned economy. It called for the creation of large-scale economic planning; the nationalization of banks, insurance, and key industries; state control of monopolies; the expropriation of large estates; a shortened workweek; work sharing; and a limited work-creation program financed through increased taxes and a forced loan.[69] In February 1932, as the crisis deepened, the SPD introduced two bills in the Reichstag based on these ideas.

At the labor movement's "crisis" congress in April, advocates of the WTB plan emphasized the increasing desperation of the masses and pointed out that both the Nazis and the Communists were trumpeting work-creation programs. But recognizing that there was little chance that the SPD would support the WTB plan and that an open split in the labor movement at that time would be disastrous, the unions decided to continue pushing the goal of work-creation under the banner of "Umbau der Wirtschaft."

[65] Robert Gates, "German Socialism and the Crisis of 1929–1933," *Central European History*, 7, 1974, 351, and Woytinsky, *Stormy Passage*.

[66] See, for example, his talk at the fourth congress of the Allgemeinen freien Angestelltenbundes (AfA), and Cora Stephan, "Wirtschaftsdemokratie und Umbau der Wirtschaft," in Luthardt, ed., *Sozialdemokratische Arbeiterbewegung*, Vol. 1, 283–7.

[67] Quoted in William Smaldone, "Rudolf Hilferding: The Tragedy of a German Social Democrat" (Ph.D. Dissertation, University of Binghamton, 1989), 436.

[68] Gates, "The Economic Policies," 221–2; Michel Held, *Sozialdemokratie und Keynesianismus: Von der Weltwirtschaftskrise bis zum Godesberger Programm* (Frankfurt: Campus Verlag, 1982); Franz Ritter, *Theorie und Praxis des Demokratischen Sozialismus in der Weimarer Republik* (Frankfurt: Campus, 1981).

[69] "Das Gespenst der Arbeitslosigkeit und die Vorschläge der SPD zu Ihrer Überwindung" (SPD Pamphlet, January 15, 1931); "Umbau der Wirtschaft-Sicherstellung der Existenz der Notleidenden," *Sozialdemokratische Partei-Korrespondenz*, 27, August–September 1932; Georg Decker, "Zwischen Kapitalismus und Sozialismus. Eine Betrachtung zum Wirtschaftsprogramm des AfA-Bundes," *Die Gesellschaft*, 9, May 1932; "Der Umbau der Wirtschaft," *Gewerkschafts-Zeitung*, 2, July 1932. Also Eberhard Heupel, *Reformismus und Krise: Zur Theorie und Praxis von SPD, ADGB, und AfA-Bund in der Weltwirtschaftskrise 1929–1932/3* (Frankfurt: Campus, 1981).

In the run-up to elections that July, it became clear that, next to the forceful and direct nature of the Nazis' platform, the SPD's program "contained no thoughts capable of stimulating the imagination of the masses. Abstract phrases conjured up abstract goals. One could not find in it ways out of the [problem of] mass unemployment."[70] Whatever potential it might have had, moreover, was not exploited due to a half-hearted effort by the party organization to get the message out to the masses. In general, the lack of any overarching economic or political strategy rendered the SPD's campaign incoherent. Not surprisingly, then, the elections were a disaster for the SPD, with the party losing its position as the largest party in the Reichstag for the first time since 1912. The Nazis, meanwhile, took over this position (gaining 37.3 percent of the vote in comparison to the SPD's 21.6 percent), and the Communists increased their share to 14.3 percent.[71]

In the months that followed, the new von Papen government attacked what remained of Weimar democracy. The SPD agreed to discuss the WTB plan yet again, and a closed meeting of forty union and party representatives took place in a room in the Reichstag.[72] After the unions' arguments for work creation and deficit spending were presented, Hilferding declared that such proposals called into question "the very foundations of our program ... Marx's theory of labor value. Our program rests on the conviction that labor, and labor alone, creates value. ... Depressions result from the anarchy of the capitalist system. Either they come to an end or they must lead to the collapse of this system. If [Woytinsky and others like him] think they can mitigate a depression by public works, they are merely showing that they are not Marxists."[73] Woytinsky responded to this charge with the following argument:

The flood of unemployment is rising, [and] the people are at the end of their patience. The workers, holding us responsible for their misery, are deserting the party to join the Communists and Nazis. We are losing ground. There is no time to waste. Something must be done before it is too late. Our plan has nothing to do with any particular value theory. Any party can execute it. And it will be executed. The only question is whether we take the initiative or leave it to our enemies.[74]

But ultimately the SPD's entrenched orthodox traditions proved too great an obstacle and all but one of the SPD representatives at the meeting sided with

---

[70] Winkler, *Der Weg in die Katastrophe*, 638. Also idem, "Choosing the Lesser Evil: The German Social Democrats and the Fall of the Weimar Republic," *Journal of Contemporary History*, 25, 1990, esp. 220–1.

[71] See Chapter 6.

[72] The exact date of this meeting is difficult to determine. Woytinsky's memoirs seem to place it sometime in August, and this is accepted by Donna Harsch. Robert Gates, however, seems to indicate that it took place much earlier, in February. I follow Woytinsky's memoirs here, because even though his chronology is somewhat confused, he provides the most complete record of the meeting. Regardless of when the meeting took place, however, it reveals the factors motivating SPD decision makers.

[73] Woytinsky, *Stormy Passage*, 471.

[74] Ibid., 471–2.

Hilferding over Woytinsky. The party thus went into yet another round of elections that November without a compelling practical program for dealing with the crisis – and once again did less well than it had hoped. Despite the fact that for the first time in many years the National Socialist German Workers' Party (NSDAP) also seemed to be suffering (losing 2 million votes and thirty-four seats), behind-the-scenes maneuvering, helped along by the inability of other parties to mount a convincing challenge to the Nazis, led President Paul von Hindenburg to name Hitler chancellor on January 30, 1933. Democracy had come to an end in Germany.

De Man's Plan

The Fascist takeover in Italy may have spurred soul searching and recrimination on the left, but the collapse of the SPD and the rise of Hitler to power a decade later sent shock waves throughout the international socialist movement. For many revisionists, events in Germany confirmed their long-standing fears about the dangers of orthodoxy and their conviction that without a change of course, soon socialism itself, not to mention European democracy, would be doomed. Probably the most important figure making this point was the Belgian socialist Hendrik de Man. Although largely forgotten today, de Man was an absolutely critical figure in the interwar socialist movement. Particularly influential was his 1926 volume *The Psychology of Socialism*, which established him as the movement's most vital critic of orthodox Marxism. (One reflection of the book's impact is that soon after its publication in German it was translated into French, Dutch, Spanish, English, Swedish, Czech, Italian, Danish, and Yiddish.) During the 1920s and 1930s, de Man published a series of books and articles in a wide range of languages[75] culminating in his highly influential *Plan du Travail* (discussed in more detail later in this section), critiquing orthodox Marxism and laying the foundations of an entirely new, non-Marxist vision for the left. De Man provides a crucial link between the turn-of-the-century revisionism of Bernstein and Sorel and the social democratic and national socialist projects of the interwar era.[76]

De Man's revisionist odyssey was critically shaped by his experiences during the Great War, which, as he put it, caused him to reevaluate "my whole method of thinking, my attitude towards society and the world."[77] The war proved to him that Marx's picture of social development was not reliable: Society was not dividing into ever-more-hostile groups of capitalists and proletarians, and

---

[75] During his life, de Man lived and worked in Germany, Holland, Belgium, France, and the United States, and he spoke these countries' languages and had direct connections with their labor movements. For a bibliography of de Man's works, see Peter Dodge, *Beyond Marxism: The Faith and Works of Hendrik de Man* (The Hague: Martinus Nijhoff, 1966).

[76] He also provides a crucial link between social democracy and fascism/National Socialism. During the late 1930s, he actually became a German sympathizer. See Chapter 6.

[77] Hendrik de Man, *The Remaking of a Mind* (New York: Charles Scribner and Sons, 1919), 78.

the latter were not becoming a majority of society.[78] Interests, moreover, could not be derived solely from relationships to the means of production: Workers proved to be motivated by much more than their class position, and their needs and demands often overlapped with those of other social groups.[79] The war also confirmed for de Man the power of nationalism, showing it capable of motivating great sacrifice, heroism, and loyalty. This was not, de Man argued, the result of folly or false consciousness, as many socialists believed, but rather at least partially the result of the impressive political and economic gains workers and others had made within their national states. "National sentiment," he wrote, "is an integral part of the emotional content of the socialism of each country. It grows in strength in proportion as the lot of the working masses of any country is more closely connected with the lot of that country itself; in proportion as the masses have won themselves a larger place in the community of national civilization."[80]

Such realizations led de Man to recognize that socialists needed to rethink entirely their traditional appeals and relationships to social groups. In particular, he urged socialists to focus on cross-class cooperation, and adapt to the reality of nationalism. As he once put it, socialists had to complement "the doctrine of class solidarity [with] that of social solidarity, and the appeal to the common interest of all, or nearly all, [should] be made the dominant motive of a movement that, being essentially democratic, aims at rallying to its side the majority of the people."[81]

Alongside his disillusionment with class struggle, de Man also rejected historical materialism and more particularly the picture of capitalism painted by orthodoxy. De Man recognized that contemporary capitalism was a "phenomenon whose characteristics were profoundly different from those foreseen by Marx."[82] Socialists should no longer expect it to be prone to the type of cataclysmic collapse predicted by Marx and his orthodox progeny, and should admit that it had displayed remarkable productive capacities. It had, after all, placed at humanity's disposal

… an accumulation of material wealth sufficient to bestow comfort and the possibility of happiness on all; it has created machinery by which the human effort necessary to maintain and augment this wealth can be indefinitely reduced so as to leave more time for the pursuit of higher purposes.… [S]ocialism should, therefore, be more than an antithesis to capitalism. It should be, and I think will be, a synthesis making the incentive of competition and the constant increase of human productivity which we owe

[78] E.g., Hendrik de Man, *Gegen den Strom* (Stuttgart: Deutsche Verlagsanstalt, 1953), 189, and idem, *Die Sozialistische* Idee (Jena: Eugen Diederichs Verlag, 1933), esp. 308ff.

[79] Dodge, *Beyond Marxism*, 178, and esp. Hendrik de Man, *Die Intellektuellen und der Sozialismus* (Jena: Eugen Diedrichs Verlag, 1926).

[80] Henry De Man, *The Psychology of Socialism* (New York: Arno Press, 1974), 325; also idem, *Gegen den Strom*, 189.

[81] Ibid., 286.

[82] Dodge, *Beyond Marxism*, 80.

to capitalism, serve the ideals of freedom, equality of rights and chances and universal solidarity, which we owe to democracy. Only thus can the reconciliation of the two equally vital, but still antagonistic principles of individual liberty and social unity be effected.[83]

De Man's loss of faith in the main pillars of orthodox Marxism led him to believe that if socialism were to survive, it needed to develop a whole new vision and program. As with all revisionists, de Man was convinced that this project had to be based first and foremost on a belief in the primacy of politics – that is, a conviction that a better world could only be the work of socialists themselves. As he put it, "The future is something which we have to create."[84] And since the creators would have to be inspired to devote themselves to the cause, he sought to tap the great motivating power of morality and idealism. "The thoughtful members of a younger generation" he argued, "are yearning for ... faith" that orthodox Marxism could not provide. Where a Bernstein or a Jaurès was confident that Enlightenment rationalism would be enough to draw recruits, de Man – showing himself to be following in the footsteps of Sorel and the revolutionary revisionists – emphasized the "irrational" wellsprings of human behavior. He stressed the need to appeal to emotions rather than logic and the role that manipulation and leadership would have to play in the struggle for a new world.[85]

Like Rosselli and other interwar dissidents, finally, de Man was comfortable acknowledging that the time for updating and improving Marx had passed:

I am no longer a Marxist, [he wrote,] not because this or that Marxist affirmation seems false to me, but because, since I emancipated myself from the Marxist way of thinking, I feel myself nearer to the understanding of socialism as a manifestation ... of an eternal aspiration towards a social order in conformity with our moral sense.... Socialism is a passion.... One who is fighting for the establishment of a better social system does not need scientific proof that the coming of this system is inevitable. It suffices that his conscience should tell him to work for its coming.... [86]

In addition to breaking with prewar revisionists in his explicit denunciations of Marxism and his clear intentions to put a non-Marxist socialism in its place, de Man also criticized prewar revisionists for not spending enough time thinking about how the reforms they advocated could contribute to the long-term goals of the movement. Taken individually, and separate from any overarching strategy, reforms would not have a transformative impact. Socialists needed to think more about how their own efforts – and in particular their use of political

[83] De Man, *The Remaking of a Mind*, 282–4.
[84] Idem, *The Psychology of Socialism*, 473.
[85] James Burnett, "The Development of the Political Theory of 'Neo-Socialism'" (Master's Thesis, New York University, 1963), esp. 25ff, and De Man, *Die Intellektuellen und der Sozialismus*.
[86] Ibid., 491, 497–8.

power – could reshape contemporary economies and societies.[87] To this end, in 1933 he offered the *Plan du Travail*.[88]

Although now remembered primarily as a depression-fighting strategy, the Plan was in fact intended as much more – as the embodiment of de Man's new vision for the socialist movement. The time had come, de Man argued, for socialists to recognize that they were involved in a race against the crisis itself:

> ...we can no longer afford to wait. We must have a policy based on the positive will to achieve. Away with the blessed and fatalistic optimism...which held the belief that time itself worked necessarily on the Socialist side.... It is indispensable to recognize now that hard experience has plainly proved that economic evolution works on the side of Socialism only in proportion as Socialism works on the side of economic evolution. From a doctrinal point of view also the Determinist epoch is over. There is no room left today for any doctrine that is not based on positive free will, or that fails to replace vague desires by exact determinations that can be rapidly converted into realities.[89]

To that end, the Plan involved both short-term measures to fight the Depression and long-term suggestions for economic and social transformation. For the former, de Man advocated stimulating demand and credit through public works, the creation of national credit institutes, and the socialization of some banks. He also called for nationalizing those sectors of the economy deemed "unproductive" or working against the public interest (for example, monopolies) while leaving other sectors, as well as the basic market framework, untouched.[90] He hoped that these measures would finally provide socialists with an opportunity to go to the masses and say, "Here are the things we are going to do to reach our goals within a short period of time as soon as a majority gives us the power."[91]

On the long-term side of the ledger, de Man laid out a strategy for the transformation of capitalism. From this perspective, the Plan was "not reformist but revolutionary, because it aims at bringing about, here and now, fundamental changes in the economic structure of society and not merely secondary changes in the distribution of wealth under Capitalism."[92] De Man believed that the state could alter the basic dynamics of the capitalist system, and he thus focused his attention on coming up with ways in which the state could use its powers to ensure that economy developed in a "healthy" and "socially just" manner.[93]

There are several things worth emphasizing about the Plan's transformative strategy. The first is that it was based on a conviction that "the essential

---

[87] De Man, *The Plan Du Travail* (London: Victor Gollancz, 1935).

[88] The outlines of the Plan and in particular the ideas upon which it was based had appeared earlier.

[89] Ibid., 33.

[90] Erik Hansen, "Hendrik de Man and the Crisis in European Socialism, 1926–36" (Ph.D. Dissertation, Cornell University, 1968), 194ff , and idem, "Hendrik de Man and the Theoretical Foundations of Economic Planning," *European Studies Review*, 8, 1978, 248ff.

[91] De Man, *Gegen den Strom*, 211.

[92] De Man, *The Plan du Travail*, 7, and idem, *Die Sozialistische Idee*, 326ff.

[93] Hansen, "Hendrik de Man and the Theoretical Foundations of Economic Planning," 249–50.

thing [was] not the taking over of ownership but that of *control.*"[94] Socialists no longer needed to insist on (unpopular, unrealistic, and undemocratic)
nationalizations and expropriations because the state could direct economic
development though less direct and obtrusive means. Second and relatedly,
the Plan separated socialism from its long-standing rhetorical insistence on the
destruction of capitalism. Indeed, de Man emphasized that "the struggle [was]
not against capitalism overall, but against particular forms of hypercapital-
ism...[and] those tendencies in the capitalist system which are the common
antagonists of the working classes, both proletarian and non-proletarians –
that is to say, against monopolistic capitalism and above all against financial
capitalism."[95] Accordingly, a vibrant private sector would continue to exist in
de Man's socialist future; in fact, he even insisted it would be "expanded and
strengthened" to ensure ever-increasing productivity and wealth.[96]

De Man understood that the 1930s were a time of both danger and opportunity; the force that captured the rising resentment against the existing order
and widespread longing for change would reap great political rewards. He
also recognized that for the first time in history, "anti-capitalistic resentment
[was] being turned against the socialist movement." Not just workers but also
farmers and sections of the old and new middle classes (such as artisans and
white-collar workers, respectively) were being hard hit by the Depression. To
defeat the radical right, socialists would have to recognize and respond to the
concerns of these groups.[97] The Plan, accordingly, was designed to allow socialists "to capture and ally with the working class, forces which will otherwise
appear in the field as its bitterest enemies": the fascists.[98]

As noted previously, de Man's ideas and writings had proved an inspiration
to socialist dissidents across Europe, and his Plan was particularly influential
among those struggling to find some path between the Scylla of communism
and the Charybdis of fascism and national socialism. Socialists in Switzerland,
Holland, and Belgium adopted some version of de Man's Plan, but its most
important impact was probably in France, where the socialist movement was
suffering from precisely the type of deadlock and malaise that de Man had set
out to counteract.

Although the Depression hit France later and with less force than other
countries, it was clearly suffering by the early 1930s. In addition to economic
problems and domestic political unease, the rise of the Nazis next door made
all democratic forces aware that France was entering a new and dangerous era.
Such trends helped convince many socialists that the time had come once again
to shift course. So the socialists decided to cooperate with the Radicals in the

[94] Dodge, *Beyond Marxism,* 139. Emphasis added. See also de Man, *Gegen den Strom,* 211.
[95] Idem, *Gegen den Strom,* 211 and idem, *The Plan du Travail,* 25.
[96] De Man, *Gegen den Strom,* 211. Also, Peter Dodge, "Voluntaristic Socialism," *International Review of Social History,* 3, 1958.
[97] Quoted in Dodge, "Voluntaristic Socialism," 409.
[98] Ibid, 11. Also, Hendrik de Man, *Sozialismus und National Fascismus* (Potsdam: Alfred Protter, 1931).

1932 elections – a strategy that paid off with a big victory for the parties of the left and a potential parliamentary majority. The Socialists, however, were still unwilling to take the next step, and so rebuffed the Radical Daladier's offer to join the government.

Still, when Daladier presented his budget in February 1933, a majority of the SFIO's deputies voted for it. An SFIO congress condemned the deputies' actions, but the deputies argued that France's troubled domestic situation and the threatening international environment made keeping the Radical government in power an absolute priority. When an important government bill came up for a vote in October, the deputies decided to support that too.[99] This was, however, more than party leaders were willing to countenance, and they repudiated the move and expelled the offending deputies – thereby allowing the government to fall.

The expelled parliamentarians joined together to form a new party, the Parti Socialiste de France: Union Jean-Jaurès (PSF). The new party was led by a group of "neosocialist" intellectuals who had long criticized the party's passivity and insistence on class struggle and were impressed with the rising tide of nationalism and the growing dynamism of the radical right. Their most prominent member, Marcel Déat, believed that the time had come to drop the socialist movement's exclusive focus on the proletariat and embrace the communitarianism that was increasingly common during this period.

Déat believed that an accommodation between socialism and nationalism was not only politically necessary but also desirable, arguing for an appeal that would bring together "all of the anti-capitalist forces [that] spill widely beyond the working class."[100] As one of his colleagues, Adrien Marquet, put it, "until 1914 I believed with a complete and sincere faith that in relying solely on the notion of class ... one could overthrow the capitalist regime. But on August 2, 1914 the notion of class collapsed before the concept of the Nation." Socialism, in this view, needed a new foundation for its identity, one that could "be found only in the national instinct. It is only [with] this that we will be able to ... win the popular masses and transform the regime."[101]

The neosocialists also chafed at the SFIO's unwillingness to use the levers of political power. As Déat once put it, socialists could either "give up any attempt to penetrate the cadres of bourgeois society and prepare a violent, total, desperate revolution or ... be present everywhere and do battle everywhere,

<hr />

[99] This was a particularly tricky vote since Daladier's bill would have reduced the salaries and pensions of civil servants. The deputies feared, however, that with Germany having just left the Disarmament Conference and the League of Nations, and the general frustration with parliamentary instability building, avoiding the collapse of the government was the lesser of two evils.

[100] Jackson, *The Politics of Depression*, 142. Also, Mathew Elbow, *French Corporative Theory, 1789–1948* (New York: Columbia University Press, 1953), 36–7, 134–7.

[101] Karl Harr, Jr., *The Genesis and Effects of the Popular Front in France* (Latham, MD: University Press of America, 1987), 58.

including in the government."[102] He and his colleagues of course favored the latter, and, echoing Bernstein's famous dictum, argued that what was really important was that socialists always be engaged in "movement" – in a constant struggle to change the lives of the masses and to inspire the energy to move forward.[103] This struggle was to take place under the auspices of a "new" kind of state. Déat insisted, "the [democratic] state belongs neither to the bourgeoisie nor the proletariat," and could instead "exercise authority on behalf of the general interests of the community."[104] This gave socialists every incentive to gain control of it and use it to "domesticate capitalism."

The PSF's manifesto declared that it had separated from the mainstream party "because our desire for a doctrinal rejuvenation of socialism, so indispensable to socialism in these difficult days, so that it can take into its hands the destinies of national collectivity – as Jean Jaurès wanted it to – was opposed by an obstinate refusal to act [immobilism]."[105] To signal its new vision, it adopted the motto "Order, Authority, Nation."[106] Such statements horrified the old SFIO. Blum, for example, claimed to be frightened by the PSF, and said "there were moments" when he felt as though he were listening to the "program of a 'national socialist' party.... I must warn you against the danger that in our opposition to fascism we come to adopt its methods and even its ideology."[107] But Déat replied that it was in fact Blum's "Oriental passivity" that was helping the fascists most, and that if socialists insisted on waiting "for power to fall into [their] hands like a ripe fruit... then events will outstrip [them] and [they] would be swept away."[108] The time had come, Déat proclaimed, for socialists to show that they truly wanted and were able "to transform the world in which they lived" – that was what would make them true revolutionaries.[109]

The neosocialists were not the only ones in France who seized on *planisme* as the solution to the country's, and socialism's, problems. By 1934, interest had grown to the point that one observer wrote of "planomania."[110] The main French union federation put forward a plan that closely followed de Man's.[111] "The group *Révolution Constructive* and the *Centre Conféderal d'Études Ouvrières de la C.G.T.* were the principle strongholds" of *planisme*.

---

[102] Ibid., 182.
[103] Zeev Sternhell, *Neither Right nor Left* (Princeton, NJ: Princeton University Press, 1986), 179.
[104] Déat, quoted in ibid., 181–2.
[105] Emily Hartshorne Goodman, "The Socialism of Marcel Deat" (Ph.D. Dissertation, Stanford University, 1973), 127–8.
[106] Joel Colton, "Léon Blum and the French Socialists as a Government Party," *Journal of Politics*, 15, 4, November 1953, 86, and Jackson, *The Politics of Depression*, 142.
[107] Colton, "Léon Blum and the French Socialists as a Government Party," 86.
[108] Ibid., 87, and Goodman, "The Socialism of Marcel Déat," 125.
[109] Ibid., 110, 199.
[110] Jackson, *The Politics of Depression*, 150.
[111] Henry Ehrmann, *French Labor: From Popular Front to Liberation* (New York: Oxford University Press, 1947), 62ff, and Richard Kuisel, *Capitalism and the State in Modern France* (New York: Cambridge University Press, 1981), 109.

In 1934, they adopted their own version of the Plan, which called for increased state control over certain parts of the economy and planning.[112] Union leaders attached to the PSF joined with other dissident socialist groups in an attempt to force *planisme* to the top of the left's agenda, and many also particpated in a "European movement designed to popularize the approach."[113] Despite growing pressure, however, the SFIO leadership remained suspicious,[114] with Blum in particular wary of planning. Not only was he concerned about *planisme*'s overlaps with fascism, he, like so many other socialists, was concerned about its implications for doctrinal purity. Blum noted, for example, that under the Plan, "a substantial private sector [would survive] not as a passage or a transition [phase] but as a relatively stable and durable condition."[115] The party, he felt, had to be wary of becoming associated with "intermediary regimes," and had to take care, during such difficult and confusing times, to "'maintain socialist doctrine in its integrity, its purity'"[116] – even at the price of temporary unpopularity. Similarly, a report presented to the Socialist congress in 1934 stated that *planisme*'s advocates "will not induce the Party to pursue that insane chimera of realizing socialism in a partial and progressive manner by whittling away at the heart of a continuing capitalism."[117]

But as France's domestic and international situation worsened during the mid-1930s, even the SFIO was forced to recognize that a catastrophe loomed.[118] This realization also hit the Soviets at around the same time. Joseph Stalin, who had previously referred to the non-Communist socialists as "social fascists," began to recognize that without left-wing alliances, the right was more likely to triumph. This course shift enabled France's Communists to consider new tactics; as a result, Socialists and Communists put aside their long-standing divisions and joined together in "antifascist" demonstrations. Eventually they even united in the Popular Front, which won a remarkable triumph at the 1936 elections – capturing a majority of seats in parliament, making the Socialists the Chamber's largest party for the first time, and catapulting Blum into the prime ministership. Once in office, the new government – confronted by a country on the verge of chaos and beset by strikes, factory occupations, and fleeing investors – found power to be something of a mixed blessing. Having given relatively little thought to how power might be used to transform the existing

[112] Pierre Rosanvallon, "The Development of Keynesianism in France," in Peter Hall, ed., *The Political Power of Economic Ideas* (Princeton, NJ: Princeton University Press, 1989), 180–1.

[113] Goodman, "The Socialism of Marcel Déat," 243, 245, and Rosanvallon, "The Development of Keynesianism in France."

[114] Jackson, *The Politics of Depression*, 147ff.

[115] Kuisel, *Capitalism and the State in Modern France*, 114.

[116] Ibid., 150.

[117] Rosanvallon, "The Development of Keynesianism in France," 182.

[118] George Codding, Jr., and William Safran, *Ideology and Politics: The Socialist Party of France* (Boulder, CO: Westview Press, 1979), 20; Jackson, *The Politics of Depression*, 115ff; John Marcus, *French Socialism in the Crisis Years: 1933–1936* (New York: Praeger, 1958).

society and economy, Blum lacked either theoretical or practical guidelines for what to do. So he fell back on terms and frameworks he had devised years earlier, announcing that his "government did not represent a Socialist 'conquest' of power which could put through a Socialist program, but merely the 'exercise' of power by an interparty team on a limited program."[119] His task, he insisted, was to "administer the bourgeois state" and "to put into effect the Popular Front program, not to transform the social system."[120] Blum's government did push through a number of innovative reforms, including a forty-hour workweek, paid holidays, collective bargaining, the extension of compulsory schooling, and revision of the statutes of the Bank of France. But he did not attempt to present these as part of a strategy for reshaping the French economy or to stake out a distinctively socialist vision of France's future.

Blum hoped that by acting as the "loyal manager" of capitalism he could gain the support of the bulk of the capitalist class,[121] enabling him to maneuver France through the storm. In practice, however, his attempts at compromise ended up satisfying few and alienating many. The right and much of the business community resented his reforms (and many his Jewishness), while the left was upset by his timidity and conciliation. Most importantly, the government's policies did little to address France's underlying problems, so after an initial wave of reformist euphoria, the country's economy continued to deteriorate and labor unrest revived. When new international challenges in the form of the Spanish civil war and an increasingly aggressive Nazi regime were added to the mix, the government was finally overwhelmed. Blum requested special powers to deal with the country's deteriorating financial situation, but he was turned down, and in response he decided to resign. In June 1937, after just over a year in office, the Popular Front government came to an end.

The turmoil of the French left during the 1930s was a microcosm of the struggle being fought out within European socialism more generally once the Communist left had broken away. Intelligent and well-meaning but politically paralyzed by his traditional doctrines, Blum grabbed the brass ring but could not wear it. His premiership represented the final gasp of the old socialist establishment, which throughout the interwar period had been more adept at outmaneuvering socialist dissidents than at hitting on a successful formula for modern democratic governance. Socialist dissidents, meanwhile, building on the principles laid out by Bernstein and other revisionists a generation earlier, had constructed an entirely new program for the left, one focused on using the state to control capitalism and on a "people's party" strategy and communitarian, even nationalist, appeals. De Man was the most important and influential of these, but such dissidents appeared in all European socialist parties during the interwar years. It was only on the continent's periphery, however, that they

---

[119] Ibid., 176.
[120] B. D. Graham, *The French Socialists and Tripartisme 1944–1947* (Toronto: University of Toronto Press, 1965), 14.
[121] Jackson, *The Popular Front*, 169.

were able to take full control of a party. This left the rest of the continent's dissidents with two choices: They could both submit to the leadership's strictures and remain within parties with which they no longer agreed, or they could break away and find a new political home. More than a few did just that. Their story begins a new historical chapter.

6

The Rise of Fascism and National Socialism

In the early 1930s, Hendrik de Man and Marcel Déat had helped blaze a trail for a new kind of post-Marxist left that would eventually become known as social democracy. But by the end of the decade, they had become known for something much different. Having lost faith in the SFIO in particular and the mainstream socialist movement more generally and becoming convinced that liberal democracy was on the verge of collapse, Déat and many other neosocialists started to look more closely at the communitarianism and anticapitalist critiques of Nazis and Fascists – and liked what they saw. Over time, they decided that these movements were the only ones willing and able to fix capitalism's problems and provide the collective purpose and identity they felt France and Europe desperately needed. In this shift, they were hardly alone. Frustrated by the socialist movement's traditionalism and passivity, disillusioned with the liberal, democratic, capitalist order, and impressed by the vitality of the radical right – particularly its ability to merge communitarian appeals and strategies for controlling capitalism – a surprising number of socialists during these years made the journey from (revisionist) left to (fascist or national socialist) right. By the late 1930s, even de Man had become convinced that neither the mainstream socialist movement nor liberal democracy had a future, and so began advocating authoritarian revisions to the reigning political order in the service of something he called *socialisme national*. And when the Nazis rolled over Europe and German hegemony seemed there to stay, he made his peace with the devil and become a collaborator.[1]

---

[1] On de Man's relationship with Nazism, see James T. Burnett. "The Development of the Political Theory of 'Neo-Socialism.'" (Master's Thesis, New York University, 1963); Erik Hansen, "Hendrik de Man and the Theoretical Foundations of Economic Planning: The Belgian Experience, 1933–40," *European Studies Review*, 8, 1978; Dick Pels, *The Intellectual as Stranger* (London: Routledge, 2000).

The political journey of figures such as Déat and de Man is not as counterintuitive as it has seemed to many,[2] once one understands the striking similarities between the revisionist left and the national, socialist right. As we have seen, both were broadly committed to the primacy of politics and some sort of communitarianism, and both agreed that the time had come for a non-Marxist socialism. And both blossomed into truly independent and distinctive movements with the turmoil unleashed by the Great War. They were able to do so, moreover, because they put forward programs and appeals that were strikingly similar. During the interwar period, social democrats, fascists, and national socialists championed a "third way" in economics that avoided the extremes of free-market liberalism and communism, insisting that the state could and should control capitalism without destroying it. All also appealed to the "people," the nation, and the "common good"; worked to assemble cross-class coalitions; and sought the status of true "people's parties." The main difference was that under Fascists and Nazis, the price to pay for this program was the destruction of democracy and the jettisoning of civil liberties and human rights that accompanied it.

Fascism in Italy

Perhaps the most well-known and consequential exemplar of the shift from revisionist left to fascist right was Benito Mussolini, and so it makes sense to begin our story with him. As noted in Chapter 3, already before the war Mussolini had taken critical steps away from the mainstream socialist movement; the First World War only accelerated this trend and radicalized Mussolini further. The inability of the Socialist International to prevent the outbreak of hostilities – and the decision by almost all of its constituent parties to support the war effort – confirmed for Mussolini the strength of nationalism and the bankruptcy of internationalism. He was soon speaking of the "necessity of shaking oneself free of 'dogma,' 'eternal laws,' and 'iron necessity,' in order to reassess the issue of national problems.... We Socialists," he declared, "have never examined the problems of nations. The International never occupied itself with them," and as a result was overtaken by events. "We must find ... a conciliation between the nation, which is a historic reality, and class, which is a living reality."[3] At the end of 1914, he openly called for a reconsideration of socialist support for neutrality and was finally expelled from the PSI.

As the war progressed, Mussolini drifted further and further away from the mainstream socialist movement, and by the war's end, he had openly abandoned the notion of class struggle (which he now referred to as "a vain formula,

---

[2] Donald Sasson, *One Hundred Years of Socialism* (New York: New Press, 1996), chapter 3, and Dan S. White, *Lost Comrades: Socialists of the Front Generation, 1918–1945* (Cambridge, MA: Harvard University Press, 1992).

[3] A. James Gregor, *Contemporary Radical Ideologies* (Berkeley, CA: University of California Press, 1968), 131.

without effect and consequence"[4]) and replaced it with nationalist rhetoric and an emphasis on social solidarity. Drawing on the idea of Italy as a "proletarian nation" (see Chapter 4), he began to argue that all Italians were united by the need to raise the country's position in the world. This would require expanding the nation's productive capacity while defending it against enemies and competitors – endeavors that would, in turn, create a national solidarity that transcended petty class conflicts.[5] Accordingly, Mussolini also abandoned an exclusive emphasis on the proletariat and began to speak instead of "productive classes" rather than "oppressed" and "oppressors."[6]

In March 1919, Mussolini joined with several like-minded colleagues to form a new political movement, the Fasci di Combattimento, which brought together nationalist and socialist themes. Its first program was strongly anticapitalist, anticlerical, and antimonarchical, calling for an eight-hour day, minimum wages, the participation of workers' representatives in industrial management, "a large progressive tax on capital," "the seizure of all goods belonging to religious congregations," and the confiscation and redistribution of all uncultivated land.[7]

Initially, the Fasci met with little success. On the left, the movement faced a socialist movement still at the height of its popularity and power despite internal divisions (see Chapter 5), while on the right Gabriele D'Annunzio and his Fiume expedition had captured the imaginations of veterans and Italian nationalists.[8] In their first two years, the Fasci remained marginal, with their support essentially limited to northern urban industrial areas, dissatisfied ex-servicemen, and a ragtag bunch of former revolutionary syndicalists and revisionists.[9]

The growing chaos that began to consume Italy during 1920, however, handed the new movement a golden opportunity. As noted in the previous chapter, the acceleration of the country's postwar problems, culminating in the factory occupations of September, further divided the PSI and alienated many workers from the cause while leaving much of the business community and middle classes fearful of the socialists' revolutionary intentions. The liberal regime's seeming unwillingness to take a forceful stand against the occupations and the

[4] Idem, *Young Mussolini and the Intellectual Origins of Fascism* (Berkeley, CA: University of California Press, 1979), 191–2.

[5] Idem, *The Fascist Persuasion in Radical Politics* (Princeton, NJ: Princeton University Press, 1974), 176–8.

[6] Clarence Yarrow, "The Forging of Fascist Doctrine," *Journal of the History of Ideas*, 3, 2, April 1942, 170.

[7] "Platform of the Fasci di Combattimento," in Jeffrey Schnapp, ed., *Italian Fascism* (Lincoln, NE: University of Nebraska Press), 3–5. Also Ivanoe Bonomi, *From Socialism to Fascism* (London: Martin Hopkinson, 1924), 102; F. L. Carsten, *The Rise of Fascism* (Berkeley: University of California Press, 1982), 50; Edward Tannenbaum, "The Goals of Italian Fascism," *American Historical Review*, 74, 4, April 1969, 1185.

[8] Michael A. Leeden, *The First Duce: D'Annunzio at Fiume* (Baltimore, MD: Johns Hopkins University Press, 1977).

[9] Frank Snowden, "On the Social Origins of Agrarian Fascism in Italy," *European Journal of Sociology*, 13, 1972, 270.

socialists, meanwhile, convinced many Italians that the government could not or would not defend their interests. As one observer notes:

> . . . it seems fair to say in the early 1920s the majority of Italians of all classes lost confidence in the liberal regime. The masses of urban and rural workers were hostile to it, and their militant leaders had been openly defying it on numerous occasions. The Nittian and especially Giolittian formulae of neutrality followed by compromise . . . failed to win over the workers while alienating the employers. . . . [T]he landowners, much of big business, and lower middle class people were . . . envious of the workers whose economic status had risen in comparison with theirs, and who feared that any new "concessions" would further threaten their already precarious position in Italian society. Part of [the problem stemmed from these groups'] feeling of bewilderment and helplessness in the face of rapid changes that they did not understand and that seemed to be passing them by.[10]

It was into this breach that Mussolini and the Fasci stepped, seizing the moment to assert themselves as the forces that could restore the order and stability threatened by the actions of the socialists and the inaction of the liberals. Focusing on particular agricultural and rural areas, which felt especially ignored by the government and threatened by the socialists, and under the banner of a "war against Bolshevism," Fascists often took control of entire towns as part of their campaign to restore calm to the countryside and offered jobs and other resources to gain supporters. The strategy proved remarkably successful. While over 1 million strikers stalked the Italian countryside in 1920, the number had dropped to eighty thousand a year later. This triumph, combined with the movement's general vigor – which stood in stark contrast to the government's passivity – brought it support from both landowners and nervous agricultural workers resentful of the socialist labor leagues' monopoly over employment.[11]

The Fascists moved quickly to lock in their newly found support. In June 1921, they published an agrarian program aimed at peasant proprietors that played on the deep unpopularity of the PSI's calls for nationalization of the land and began to chart a new course – one that exploited widespread fears of capitalism, while promising to protect private property. Mussolini declared:

> . . . in opposition to the social-communists we want the land to belong not to the state but to the cultivator. Whereas social-communism tends to disinherit all, and to transform every cultivator into an employee of the State, we wish to give the ownership of the land and economic freedom to the greatest number of peasants. In place of the sovereignty of a central political caste, we support the sovereignty of the peasant.[12]

---

[10] Edward Tannenbaum, *The Fascist Experience: Italian Society and Culture, 1922–45* (New York: Basic Books, 1972), 35. Also, Anthony L. Cardoza, *Agrarian Elites and Italian Fascism: The Province of Bologna, 1901–1926* (Princeton, NJ: Princeton University Press, 1982); Frank Snowden, *The Fascist Revolution in Tuscany 1919–1922* (New York: Cambridge University Press, 1989).

[11] Cardoza, *Agrarian Elites and Italian Fascism*, and Paul Corner, *Fascism in Ferrara* (New York: Oxford University Press, 1975).

[12] Snowden, "On the Social Origins of Agrarian Fascism in Italy," 279. Also, Corner, *Fascism in Ferrara*, 146ff; Adrian Lyttelton, *The Seizure of Power: Fascism in Italy 1919–1929* (London: Weidenfeld and Nicolson, 1973); Snowden, *The Fascist Revolution*, 81ff.

The program also promised the "creation of a new 'rural democracy' based on peasant landownership," and made clear its distaste for absentee or "parasitic" landlords.[13] Alongside the boost that the Fascists got from such refashioned appeals, the party was also bolstered by Giolitti's decision to include them in his 1921 electoral coalition – a fateful choice that gave the movement an added degree of legitimacy and helped it achieve its first electoral break-through.[14]

By the time that the Fascists held their next congress in Rome in November 1921, the movement had been transformed. Two years earlier, it had been a small urban group with 870 members; now it was a mass movement with over 300,000 members widely distributed across the country. Fascism's shifting pro-file was reflected in the new program adopted by the congress, which aimed to appeal to a wide range of voters. In particular, it toned down some of the radicalism of the 1919 program while still appealing to widespread fears of the market and capitalism; it also forcefully emphasized communitarian and nationalist themes. It declared that "disorderly clashes between divergent class and socioeconomic interests [had to] be disciplined," and recognized "national society" as the most fundamental "form of social organization." It offered var-ious ways of reducing class conflict, emphasizing in particular corporatist solu-tions such as the granting of legal recognition to organizations "representing workers and employers so that they may, in turn, be made legally responsible," and thereby help to promote "national solidarity and...the development of production." The program also called for a wide range of social welfare mea-sures and promised that the movement would act for the good of the nation as a whole rather than in the interests of any particular class.[15]

With regard to capitalism and private property, the program presented a mixed message. On the one hand, it declared that "The National Fascist party advocates a regime that would strive to increase our national wealth by unleash-ing individual enterprises and energies – the most powerful and industrious factor in economic production – and by abolishing, once and for all, the rusty, costly, and unproductive machinery of state, society, and muncipality-based control." It thus promised to return a range of state-owned or -controlled enterprises to the private sector and made clear the movement's support for small landowning in the countryside. On the other hand, it signaled Fascism's intent to "restore the ethical principle that governments ought to administer the commonwealth as a function of the nation's supreme interest," and stressed that private property carried responsibilities as well as privileges. "At once a

[13] Ibid., 82.
[14] Paolo Farneti, "Social Conflict, Parliamentary Fragmentation, Institutional Shift, and the Rise of Fascism: Italy," in Juan Linz and Alfred Stepan, eds., *The Breakdown of Democratic Regimes: Europe* (Baltimore, MD: Johns Hopkins University Press, 1978), 23, and Denis Mack Smith, *Italy: A Modern History* (Ann Arbor, MI: University of Michigan Press, 1959), 342, 345.
[15] "Program of the National Fascist Party, 1921," in Schnapp, *A Primer of Italian Fascism*, 10–18.

right and a duty, private property is the form of management that society has
traditionally granted individuals so that they may increase the overall patri-
mony."[16]

Fascism had, in short, morphed into a modern mass party with an appeal,
program, and support base that differentiated it from its competitors. Not easily
placed on either the left or the right, its rhetoric and policy offered something
to practically all groups suffering from or dissatisfied with the existing liberal
order. The Fascists presented themselves as the country's foremost opponents
of "Bolshevism" and the best guardians of private property,[17] while stressing
the "social duties" of property, emphasizing the collective good, and criticizing
absentee landlords and "exploitative" capitalists. The ability to link a fundamental critique of the reigning liberal order and of capitalism's "excesses"
with a commitment to private property and a claim to represent all of Italy's
people enabled Fascism to become the country's first truly mass "people's
party" – one that "came close to representing the overall social structure of
Italy."[18]

While the Fascists were growing in strength, Italy's other parties were in
disarray. As one analyst put it, "[b]y the summer of 1922 the liberals were
disoriented, the *populari* disintegrating, the socialists wrecked."[19] The existing regime had long been losing the "hearts and minds" of Italians, and the
liberal parties most closely associated with the government had been suffering
accordingly. And we have already seen (in Chapter 5) that the socialists had
neither the will nor the ability to mount a strong defense of the system. The
other main force in Italian political life, the Catholic Popular Party, was also
plagued by divisions and disagreements. The result was a growing acceptance
by many governmental and socioeconomic elites that an understanding with
Mussolini and his movement was both desirable and necessary.

The final stage in the drama began in October 1922, when the sitting government fell into crisis and Rome buzzed with talk that the fascists were mobilizing
for a seizure of power. Prime Minister Luigi Facta resigned after the King refused
his request for a declaration of a state of siege (so that the government could
move forcefully against the Fascists). Then the Conservatives, who had hoped to
"tame" Mussolini and the Fascists in a government of their own, stepped aside
when it became clear that Mussolini would not join any government he did not
head. On October 29, with thousands of Fascist cadres waiting for the order

---

[16] Ibid., 15.
[17] Carl T. Schmidt, *The Corporate State in Action* (New York: Oxford University Press, 1939), 40.
[18] Stanley Payne, *A History of Fascism, 1914–1945* (Madison, WI: University of Wisconsin Press,
     1995), 104. A recent analysis is provided by E. Spencer Wellhofer, "Democracy and Fascism:
     Class, Civil Society and Rational Choice in Italy," *American Political Science Review*, 97, 1,
     2003.
[19] Anthony James Joes, *Fascism in the Contemporary World* (Boulder, CO: Westview Press, 1978),
     40. See also Margot Hentze, *Pre-Fascist Italy* (New York: W. W. Norton, 1939), and A. Rossi,
     The Rise of Italian Fascism (London: Metheun, 1938).

to mobilize, the King at last asked Mussolini to form a government. Fascism came to power without firing a shot.[20]

During the next few years, Mussolini concentrated on dismantling the remnants of the liberal regime. He gradually purged non-Fascist ministers from his government, passed an electoral law that all but guaranteed Fascists control of parliament, merged his movement with the Nationalist Association, and chipped away at the power of all parties and organizations not already under Fascist control.[21] Even as he was neutralizing his political enemies, however, discontent and conflict were brewing within his own party between conservative nationalists and revolutionary syndicalists and revisionists. Just as the movement's internal conflicts were growing, however, a crisis intervened to reverse the tide. On May 30, 1924, a Socialist deputy named Giacomo Matteotti gave a speech bitterly denouncing the recently held 1924 elections, claiming (correctly) that the Fascists had engaged in widespread fraud and violence to secure their hold on power. Some days afterward, Matteotti disappeared, and he was later found with a knife stuck in his chest. Five Fascists were eventually arrested for the attack. The murder elicited a storm of protest; the main opposition parties walked out of parliament and the press accused the Fascists of barbarism. The affair also prompted Fascist extremists to threaten a new wave of violence unless Mussolini took forceful action against the opposition. But rather than folding in the face of internal and external pressures, Mussolini went on the offensive against critics both within the party and without. In January 1925, he proclaimed that he alone "assume[d] the political, moral, and historical responsibility for all that has happened.... If fascism has been a criminal association, if all the acts of violence have been the result of a certain historical, political, and moral climate, the responsibility for this is mine."[22] He eliminated the remnants of a free press and suppressed all remaining anti-Fascist activities and parties. (As he would later write, it was at this time that the "foundations of the totalitarian state were laid."[23]) He also tightened his hold over the Fascist movement itself, appointing a new party secretary, purging some old intransigents, abandoning elections for key party posts, and eliminating many local and provincial-level organizations that had previously served as staging grounds for attacks against the central leadership. The result of such moves, as one observer notes, was that "the PNF was not just tamed, it was emasculated."[24]

---

[20] Contrary to popular belief (and Fascist legend), the March on Rome thus happened after all the important political decisions had been made. It was more of a victory parade than a seizure of power.

[21] Carsten, *The Rise of Fascism*; F. Allen Cassells, *Fascist Italy* (London: Routledge and Kegan Paul, 1986); Federico Chabod, *A History of Italian Fascism* (London: Weidenfield and Nicolson, 1963); Lyttleton, *The Seizure of Power.*

[22] Adrian Lyttelton, "Fascism in Italy: The Second Wave," *Journal of Contemporary History*, 1, 1, May 1966, 76.

[23] Carsten, *The Rise of Fascism*, 73.

[24] Martin Clark, *Modern Italy* (New York: Longman, 1984), 238.

By the end of the Matteotti crisis, Mussolini found himself in much firmer control of both the state and his own party than he had been before. Thus began what some scholars have referred to as Fascism's "second wave,"[25] one aspect of which was Mussolini's greater freedom to begin constructing the "New Italy"[26] that Fascism had promised. Scholars have long debated how revolutionary Mussolini and his regime actually were, but there is no doubt that Fascism presented itself as committed to the destruction of the existing order and the creation of a new one. Mussolini himself described the mid- to late 1920s as a time when "Italy's energies [were] totally absorbed in the effort to create... a new type of civilization."[27]

A key component of this effort was a reshaping of socioeconomic relations. In the "New Italy," the state rather than individual interests or economic imperatives would reign supreme. Indeed, while both liberals and orthodox Marxists denigrated it – the former because they wanted to maximize individual freedom and liberty, the latter because they saw the state as a tool of the elite – Fascism placed the state at the center of its transformative vision, portraying it as a powerful entity that stood above the interests of particular individuals or groups. This view they shared with their social democratic counterparts, but they went beyond them by imbuing the state with nearly mystical qualities. As Mussolini put it, for Fascists, "The State... is a spiritual and moral entity because it is the concrete political, juridical, and economic organization of the nation.... Therefore for the Fascist, everything is in the State, and nothing human or spiritual exists, much less has value, outside the State. In this sense Fascism is totalitarian, and the Fascist State, the synthesis and unity of all values, interprets, develops and gives strength to the whole life of the people."[28]

Fascists thought that the state not only enjoyed a certain independence from the governed (as did social democrats), but also that it was free of any direct responsibility to them (something that social democrats denied). As one observer put it, in the Fascist state, "there are no citizens... there are only subjects.... The government [in this view] is not responsive to the will of the people but only to its own conscience."[29] Fascism also rejected one of the key tenets of liberalism (and social democracy): an insistence on the fundamental equality of man, the core argument for democratic rule. "Fascism," according to Mussolini, "denies that the majority can direct human society... and it affirms the immutable, beneficial and fruitful inequality of mankind, which

[25] Alberto Aquarone, "The Rise of the Fascist State," and Renzo de Felice, "From the Liberal Regime to the Fascist Regime," in Roland Sarti, ed., *The Ax Within* (New York: New Viewpoints, 1974); Lyttelton, "Fascism in Italy."
[26] This was a term constantly invoked by Fascist theoreticians and activists. See, for example, Roger Griffin, ed., *Fascism* (New York: Oxford University Press, 1995).
[27] Mussolini, "The Achievements of the Fascist Revolution," in Griffin, ed., *Fascism*, 64.
[28] Ibid, 65, and idem, "The Doctrine of Fascism," in Carl Cohen, ed., *Communism, Fascism and Democracy* (New York: Random House, 1968), 352.
[29] Herman Finer, *Mussolini's Italy* (New York: Grosset and Dunlap, 1965), 204.

can never be permanently leveled through the mere operation of a mechanical process such as universal suffrage."[30]

This view implied that the state had the right – indeed, perhaps the duty – to intervene in almost any aspect of socioeconomic life. As one Fascist put it: "there cannot be any single economic interests which are above the general economic interests of the State, no individual, economic initiatives which do not fall under the supervision and regulation of the State, no relationships of the various classes of the nation which are not the concern of the state."[31] None of this meant that Fascists rejected capitalism or private property. Rather, it meant that Fascists aimed to create a system that could ensure economic growth at the same time that the state made sure that the nation's "needs" and "goals" were not threatened by unregulated markets and "selfish" capitalists.

During Fascism's early years in power, the regime refrained from making any major breaks with economic orthodoxy. But with Mussolini's consolidation of control in the mid-1920s, the outlines of a new type of social and economic organization based on corporatist thinking and institutions began to emerge.[32] The first step toward this new system was taken with the Palazzo Vidoni pact signed by the Confindustria (or CGII, the Italian business association) and the Confederation of Fascist Unions in October 1925. The CGII and the Fascist Unions agreed that all labor negotiations would occur between them, with all non-Fascist labor unions excluded from the process. This new system banned strikes and lockouts since, "as expressions of class interests, they failed to take into account national needs."[33] If for some reason the labor market partners were not able to reach an agreement on their own, the matter was to be referred to labor courts for compulsory arbitration. If business was initially hesitant about the pact, fearing it would lead to further state encroachment on its prerogatives, employers soon realized that a loss of autonomy was balanced by other advantages. Under the new system, any vestiges of power enjoyed by independent labor organizations were eliminated and the CGII was able to extend its control over business groups that had hitherto remained outside its fold.

Another piece of the corporatist edifice was laid the following year with the passage of the Rocco Law, which divided the country's economy into seven branches of economic activity (industry, agriculture, banking, commerce, internal transport, merchant marine, and intellectual community) and set up "syndical confederations" for employees and employers in all but the last. And in 1927, the government put forward the Charter of Labor, which laid out

[30] Ibid., 207, 209.
[31] E.g. Mario Palmieri, *The Philosophy of Fascism*, excerpts reprinted in Cohen, ed., *Communism, Fascism, Democracy*, 381. Also Dick Pels, "Facism and the Primacy of the Political," *Telos*, 10, Winter 1998, and Zeev Sternhell, *The Birth of Fascist Ideology* (Princeton, NJ: Princeton University Press, 1994).
[32] Lyttelton, "Fascism in Italy: The Second Wave"; Payne, *A History of Fascism*, 121; Roland Sarti, *Fascism and the Industrial Leadership in Italy, 1919–1940* (Berkeley, CA: University of California Press, 1971), 58.
[33] Sarti, *Fascism and the Industrial Leadership in Italy*, 72.

the rationale for the corporatist system and the principles governing relations between capital and labor. It proclaimed the right of the corporations ("as representatives of the unified interests of production") to oversee the establishment of production rules, the adjudication of labor disputes, the control of labor exchanges, and the regulation of occupational safety standards. The Charter described the corporatist system as one that promoted capitalism and private initiative while at the same time establishing the state's primary role in ensuring that the economy worked for society as a whole.[34] Corporatism, the Charter proclaimed, considers that private enterprise in the sphere of production is the most effective and useful instrument in the interests of the nation:

In view of the fact that private organization of production is a function of national concern, the organizer of the enterprise is responsible to the State for the direction given to production. Collaboration between the forces of production gives rise to reciprocal rights and duties. The worker . . . is an active collaborator in the economic enterprise, the management of which rests with the employer who is responsible for it. . . .

In the [corporate system] individual initiative is always the fundamental impulse. [E]conomic activity, however . . . had important social reactions [and therefore] must be developed within given juridical limits. . . . [I]t is obvious that the individual must be considered responsible to Society and therefore to the State. . . . [W]hen private initiative is lacking or . . . the interests of the State are involved . . . intervention . . . which may take the form of control, assistance or direct management . . . will [therefore] be necessary.[35]

Fascism's forays into corporatism were accompanied by other initiatives increasing the state's role in the economy. Beginning in the late 1920s, the government established a number of parastatal institutions, such as the Italian Credit Institute (*Instituto Mobiliare Italiano*) and the Italian Financial Society (*Societa Finanziaria Italiana*), that funneled funds to businesses and banks suffering from the economic downturn. In 1933, in response to the Great Depression, the government created the Institute for Industrial Reconstruction (*Instituto per la Riconstruzione Industriale*, IRI) and tasked it with saving Italy's banking system from disaster. To this end, the IRI took over the stockholdings of banks and relieved them of their debts to the Bank of Italy, thereby saving much of the private sector from collapse but making it dependent on the state for capital. By 1939, the IRI "controlled 77 percent of pig iron production, 45 percent of steel, 80 percent of naval construction, and 90 percent of shipping."[36] And banking reform laws passed in the mid-1930s – which among other things nationalized the Bank of Italy – furthered state control over credit allocation.

In the agricultural sphere, meanwhile, the government protected the property of landowners but also extended its control over them by setting production targets and stockpiling important commodities. The result "was the elimination

---

[34] Gaetano Salvemini, *Under the Axe of Fascism* (New York: Viking Press, 1936), 90.
[35] "The Labour Charter," in Benito Mussolini, *The Corporate State* (Florence: Vallecchi, 1938), 122–6.
[36] Alexander De Grand, *Italian Fascism* (Lincoln, NE: University of Nebraska Press, 1982), 107.

of market forces because major producers were allowed to operate in a system of state established prices and quotas."[37] The Fascists also supported social service programs designed to tie labor to the state and compensate it for the loss of autonomy and stagnating wages it was enduring.[38] These programs ranged from traditional welfare measures, such as health insurance, old-age and disability pensions, paid national holidays, the forty-hour work week, and family/maternity benefits, to new services such as the hugely popular *Dopolavoro*, or Leisure-Time Institute, which provided large numbers of Italians with opportunities for education, sport, and recreation.[39] The state also sponsored wide-ranging public works programs, from highway construction to the draining of the Pontine marshes. These programs led to an immense increase in the number of public employees and a doubling of state expenditures between 1922 and 1930-3.[40]

In short, while talk of revolution may be overblown, there is no doubt that Fascism reshaped the relationship among state, society, and the economy in Italy in fundamental and long-lasting ways. The cumulative result of the Fascist regime's efforts was such that by the outbreak of the Second World War, the state had "a control over the economy that was unequalled outside the Soviet Union."[41] Fascism's insistence on the necessity and the desirability of state intervention and even control over the economy was also remarkably popular on both left and right. In particular, many came to believe that Fascism had made real strides toward developing the "third way" between laissez-faire liberalism and Soviet communism that so many Italians (and Europeans) longed for. Fascists recognized this and actively promoted such views. Mussolini, for example, claimed that the regime's corporatist system provided a solution to "the social question of the twentieth century"[42]; Minister of Corporations Giuseppe Bottai argued that corporatism combined "the best aspects of capitalism and socialism"[43]; and former syndicalist and Fascist labor union head Edmondo Rossoni claimed that corporatism embodied the "political principle governing economics.... [Under corporatism] the economy can no longer evade or ignore the higher claims of politics and morals."[44] Some ex-syndicalists and revolutionary revisionists went even further, situating corporatism in socialism's long struggle to find some way to reconcile its revolutionary aspirations with the

---

[37] Ibid., 105.
[38] Cesare Vannutelli, "The Living Standard of Italian Workers 1929–1939," in Sarti, ed., *The Axe Within*.
[39] Schmidt, *The Corporate State in Action*, 86.
[40] Roger Eatwell, *Fascism* (New York: Penguin, 1995), 79, and Schmidt, *The Corporate State in Action*, 128.
[41] Martin Clark, *Modern Italy* (New York: Longman, 1984), 271; Sarti, *Fascism and the Industrial Leadership in Italy*, 124; John Whittan, *Fascist Italy* (Manchester, UK: Manchester University Press, 1995), 65.
[42] Elizabeth Wiskemann, *Fascism in Italy* (London: St. Martin's Press, 1969), 24.
[43] Eatwell, *Fascism*, 79.
[44] Rossoni, "Political and Moral Aspects of the New Economy" (lecture held in Berlin on April 29, 1936, reprinted by Societa Editrice Di Novissima, Rome), 3–5.

reality of capitalism. Sergio Panunzio, for example, claimed that the corpo-ratist system "finally brought to a close the long crisis in the socialist tradition that began in the late 1890s."[45]

In short, Fascism's insistence on the primacy of politics – its willingness to assert the power of the state vis-à-vis the market – strengthened the regime's position both at home and abroad. When Mussolini proclaimed that "the malaise of the past is no more," and that the regime was well on its way to cre-ating a new civilization "which reconciles traditions with modernity, progress with faith, the machine with the spirit, and which synthesizes the thought and advances of two centuries,"[46] a surprisingly large number of Italians were inclined to agree. And the attention that Fascism was generating abroad had by the 1930s made Italy – as the leading contemporary critic of Fascism, Gaetano Salvemini, noted – a "Mecca for political scientists, economists, and sociolo-gists looking for the basis of a new order in a world trapped between capitalist depression and communist autocracy."[47] The buzz had reached a point where Cole Porter could enshrine it in cultural amber. Compiling a list of superlatives for a song in his new musical *Anything Goes*, he registered just how far Italian Fascism had come in a decade and a half: "You're the top, you're Mussolini!"

National Socialism in Germany

The story of Hitler's rise to power has been told so often that the milestones along the way are practically common knowledge. What is less accepted is that national socialism in Germany can be fully understood only if it is viewed as part of the broader political and ideological trends that were sweeping the continent.[48] As was the case in Italy, the new right in interwar Germany drew on intellectual and political currents that predated the war but blossomed only with the political, social, and economic chaos of the postwar years. Unlike Italy, which had emerged from the war exhausted but at least victorious, Germany in 1918 had to deal with the psychological trauma of a shattering defeat. Unable to accept Imperial Germany's collapse and blaming leftists and democrats for the country's humiliation, a wide range of right-wing thinkers and activists

---

[45] David Roberts, *The Syndicalist Tradition and Italian Fascism* (Chapel Hill, NC: University of North Carolina Press, 1979), 316.

[46] Mussolini, "The Achievements of the Fascist Revolution," in Griffin, ed., *Fascism*, 63–5.

[47] Eatwell, *Fascism*, 79.

[48] This analysis is in contrast to the view that the rise of National Socialism was merely a conse-quence of peculiarly German trends or problems. The most well-known examples of this type of analysis are associated with the *Sonderweg* school, good discussions of which include Geoff Eley, *From Unification to Nazism* (Boston: George Allen and Unwin, 1986); Geoff Eley and David Blackbourn, *The Peculiarities of German History* (New York: Oxford University Press, 1984); Richard J. Evans, *Rethinking German History* (London: Unwin Hyman, 1987); Roger Fletcher, "Recent Developments in German Historiography," *German Studies Review*, 7 (1984); Gordon Martel, ed., *Modern Germany Reconsidered* (New York: Routledge, 1992); Robert G. Moeller, "The Kaiserreich Recast?" *Journal of Social History*, 17 (1984); Thomas Nipperdey, "1933 und die Kontinuität der Deutschen Geschichte," in Nipperdey, *Nachdenken über die Deutsche Geschichte* (Munich: C. H. Beck, 1986).

(as well as the far-left Communist Party, or KPD)[49] began a vociferous and often violent campaign against the Weimar Republic as soon as it was born.

The most important intellectual attacks came from a group of right-wing academics, journalists, and scribblers known collectively as the "conservative revolution."[50] Continuing along the trail blazed by prewar figures such as Paul de Lagarde and Julius Langbehn, they were defined by a contempt for liberalism and democracy and a desire for a new order based on a unified *Volk*. Among the most important figures in this movement were Arthur Moeller van den Bruck, Oswald Spengler, and Werner Sombart.

Identified by more than one scholar as the "single most important figure of the conservative revolution,"[51] the cultural critic and historian Moeller devoted his most influential work, *Das Dritte Reich* (*The Third Reich*), to developing a truly "German" alternative to the liberal order he despised. This alternative, he argued, would have to combine elements of the nationalist and socialist traditions in order to create the national unity that Germany so desperately needed.[52] Moeller's so-called socialism, however, had little to do with Marxism. As he put it, "German socialism began where Marxism ended," and the "task of German socialism... was to dissolve all traces of liberalism [remaining in the movement]."[53] Achieving this objective required purging socialism of materialism and class conflict, transforming it "from a class socialism to a people's socialism." Only with such a transformation would it be possible to wean workers from the "false doctrines of Marxism"[54] and create the social cohesion that the *Volk* would need. The precise outlines of this "German" socialism were somewhat vague. On the economic front, Moeller envisioned some type of "third way" between communism and unfettered capitalism – one in which the needs of the *Volk* would take precedence over those of the market, but private property and free enterprise would remain more or less intact.[55]

---

[49] In fact, like the Nazis, the KPD developed its own "paramilitary" units that it eagerly employed, particularly toward the end of the Republic. See Ben Fowkes, *Communism in Germany* (London: Palgrave Macmillan, 1984), and Eric Weitz, *Creating German Communism* (Princeton, NJ: Princeton University Press, 1996).

[50] The literature on this group has by now become immense. To begin, see Stefan Breuer, *Anatomie der Konservativen Revolution* (Darmstadt: Wissenschaftliche Buchgesellschaft, 1993); Jeffrey Herf, *Reactionary Modernism* (New York: Cambridge University Press, 1984); Armin Mohler, *Die Konservative Revolution in Deutschland* (Darmstadt: Wissenschaftlich Buchgesellschaft, 1972); Herbert Rauschning, *The Conservative Revolution* (New York: G. P. Putnam's Sons, 1941); Otto-Ernst Schuddekopf, *Linke Leute von Rechts* (Stuttgart: W. Kohlhammer, 1960); Christoph Werth, *Sozialismus und Nation* (Opladen: Westdeutscher Verlag, 1996); Roger Woods, *The Conservative Revolution in the Weimar Republic* (London: Macmillan, 1996).

[51] E.g., Herf, *Reactionary Modernism*, 37.

[52] Schueddekopf, *Linke Leute von Rechts*, 103ff.

[53] Herf, *Reactionary Modernism*, 37.

[54] Fritz Stern, *The Politics of Cultural Despair* (Berkeley, CA: University of California Press, 1961), 243. Also Woods, *The Conservative Revolution in the Weimar Republic*, 64.

[55] Reflecting this desire, Moeller had originally thought to title his book *The Third Force* (*Die Dritte Kraft*) rather than the *The Third Reich*. George Mosse, *Germans and Jews* (New York: Howard Fertig, 1970), 119.

The writer Oswald Spengler took up many of the same themes, seeking in particular to bring an updated nationalism together with a reconfigured socialism. Spengler believed that for this to happen, the former would have to be "cleansed of all feudal-agrarian narrowness," and the latter would have to be liberated from Marx.[56] Indeed, as far as Spengler was concerned, Marxism was a "false" socialism, "a variation of Manchesterism, [a] capitalism of the lower classes, anti-statist and English-materialistic through and through,"[57] and he saw it as his duty to come up with a "German" or "Prussian" alternative. He was, however, equally critical of capitalism, especially its disruptive effects on national unity, its promotion of unfettered materialism, and its insistence on the primacy of economics. While he did not believe that correcting these problems would require destroying the system entirely,[58] he favored a new type of order where "productive" rather than "parasitic" economic activity would be encouraged and where "politics, not economics, [would be] the decisive force" – where a strong state and leader would ensure continued economic and technological progress while protecting against materialism, social disruption, and spiritual malaise.[59] In his *Preussentum und Sozialismus (Prussianism and Socialism,)*[60] and elsewhere, accordingly, he traced the outlines of a national political community that transcended all class conflicts and an economic order in which "the economy is disciplined by political authority" and property is viewed as in the "service of the general public."[61]

The social scientist Werner Sombart went beyond many of his colleagues in interwar discussions of national socialism by explicitly linking his evaluation of different systems to racial categories. For Sombart, the driving force behind liberalism and capitalism was the Jews, and any truly "German" or national alternative to it would therefore have to rid itself of them. Like Moeller and Spengler, he sought to correct the failings of not only liberalism and capitalism but also of Marxism, which he too saw as fatally flawed by virtue of its insistence on the primacy of economics.[62] Sombart's proposed alternative, which he too called "German socialism," was characterized by a belief that "the economy [was not]...destiny," but rather something that the state could and should control in the service of the *Volk*.[63]

These conservative revolutionaries both reflected and furthered the wide-spread discontent of interwar German society. By providing an intellectual justification for antidemocratic and anticapitalist sentiment and the longing for an alternative, they contributed to the Republic's ultimate demise. And although few of them actually played important roles in the Nazi regime, they

[56] Herf, *Reactionary Modernism*, 49–50.
[57] Quoted in Werth, *Sozialismus und Nation*, 43.
[58] Herf, *Reactionary Modernism*, 52, 59.
[59] Ibid., 57.
[60] Oswald Spengler, *Prussianism und Sozialismus* (Munich: Beck, 1920).
[61] Werth, *Sozialismus und Nation*, 49.
[62] Ibid., 199–200.
[63] Ibid., 217ff.

helped lay the intellectual groundwork for it and would see many of their arguments taken up by important Nazis and incorporated into the movement's program.

Among the welter of *völkisch* and nationalist groups that sprung up on the heels of the German defeat, the German Workers' Party was noteworthy because in 1919 a young Austrian named Adolf Hitler attended one of its meetings. He was soon persuaded to join and by the end of the year had become its propaganda chief. In early 1920, the party changed its name to the National Socialist German Workers' Party (NSDAP) and published a program that mixed nationalist, socialist, and anti-Semitic themes. In addition to calling for "the union of all Germans in a greater Germany" and promising to combat "the Jewish-materialist spirit," the program included many planks designed to help the party fight Marxism (and the SPD), in part by appropriating some of its main themes, particularly its critique of capitalism. It argued "that the state be obligated first of all to ensure the gainful employment and the livelihood of the citizens," and demanded the confiscation of war profits, the nationalization of trusts, profit sharing, and land reform. It pledged that if the National Socialists came to power, they would replace the "ruthless competition" and egoism of capitalism with a new system whose basic principle was that "public interest comes before self-interest."[64]

The party's first attempt to come to power, the Beer Hall Putsch of 1923, was a flop that ended with Hitler in jail and the party banned. The episode made Hitler recognize the dangers of an insurrectionary route to power, and so after his release and the party's refounding (in 1924 and 1925, respectively), it adopted a legal, parliamentary strategy instead.

At first the party retained a heavy "socialist" tinge, concentrating its attention on urban areas and blue-collar workers – a strategy associated with Gregor Strasser, the key figure in the party's more "radical" northern wing and its most outspoken advocate of a "German" socialism. Strasser's "German" socialism differed greatly from that of "Jewish-led Marxism," he insisted, "not only [in] its fervent national outlook, but [also because of] something deeper: the rejection of the materialistic world view.... We hate from the bottom of our souls the leveling, comprehensively idiotic Marxist ideology! Socialism does not mean the domination of the masses, the leveling of achievement and reward, but rather socialism is the deeply felt Prussian German idea of 'service to all.'"[65]

Strasser's strategy, however, met with little success, and most of the working class remained committed to the SPD and KPD, leaving little political space for another party aimed at this constituency. As a result, during the mid- to late 1920s the NSDAP gained few votes, saw its membership stagnate, and

---

[64] Program reprinted in J. Noakes and G. Pridham, eds., *Nazism 1919–1945*. Vol 1: *The Rise to Power* (Exeter, UK: University of Exeter Press, 1994), 14–16.

[65] Quoted in Peter Stachura, *Gregor Strasser and the Rise of Nazism* (London: George Allen and Unwin, 1983), 42–3. See also Max Kele, *Nazis and Workers: National Socialist Appeals to German Labor* (Chapel Hill, NC: University of North Carolina Press, 1972).

experienced financial difficulties.[66] But rather than fading into obscurity as they seemed destined to do, the Nazis, like their Italian counterparts, were handed a golden opportunity by democracy's continuing difficulties and the mainstream parties' inability to attract increasingly alienated and disillusioned middle-class and rural groups. Although the Weimar Republic had managed to stabilize itself somewhat during the mid-1920s, its foundations remained weak and its support relatively shallow among broad swathes of German society. The Great Inflation was followed by a crushing stabilization, which hit white-collar workers and the middle classes particularly hard.[67] During the second half of the decade, tension continued to grow as economic dislocations made all groups more jealous of their socioeconomic interests and more strident in their political demands, and middle-class and rural groups became particularly resentful of both workers and big business, who were seen as having a disproportionate influence over the national government and political parties. SPD support for measures such as the eight-hour workday and better wages was seen as serving workers' interests above all else, and its limited but real success only highlighted middle-class impotence, generating paroxysms of antisocialist fervor. At the same time, middle-class and rural groups were becoming increasingly frustrated with the inability of liberal and conservative parties such as the DDP (the left liberal party), DVP (the National Liberals), and DNVP (the main conservative party) to fight for their needs on the national political stage. These parties came to be seen as the tools of big capitalists and financial interests, run by and for an unrepresentative elite. And so their share of the vote dropped precipitously, especially during the latter part of the 1920s.

Recognizing the political opening that this dissatisfaction created, the NSDAP abandoned the failed Strasserite strategy of targeting urban workers and began to shift its focus to middle-class and rural groups fed up with the Republic and traditional parties. During the late 1920s, the party's rhetoric changed accordingly: Radical themes were toned down and national ones with greater cross-class appeal were emphasized instead. The party stressed its commitment to serving the entire German *Volk*, its strong law-and-order stance, its pledge to seek a revision of the Versailles Treaty, and its anti-Marxism, while at the same time downplaying the expropriation plank in its official program (which was now interpreted as applying only to Jews) and declaring its firm support for private property.[68] Also helping to facilitate the NSDAP's

---

[66] Dietrich Orlow, *The History of the Nazi Party* (Pittsburgh, PA: University of Pittsburgh Press, 1969), 88ff.

[67] Gerald Feldman, *The Great Disorder: Politics, Economics and Society in the German Inflation, 1919–1924* (New York: Oxford University Press, 1993), and Jürgen von Krüdener, "Die Entstehung des Inflationstraumas: Zur Sozialpsychologie der Deutschen Hyperinflation, 1922–23," in Feldman et al., eds., *Consequences of Inflation* (Berlin: Colloquium Verlag 1989).

[68] Werner Angress, "The Political Role of the Peasantry," *Review of Politics*, 21, July 1959; J. E. Farquharson, *The Plough and the Swastika* (London: Sage, 1976); Horst Gies, "The NSDAP

"rebirth" were a series of organizational changes that centralized power within the party and gave Hitler firm control over all major political decisions, while its grassroots organization and ties to a wide range of civil society groups were expanded.[69] As a result, by the early 1930s, the NSDAP had "perhaps the most efficient and best equipped organizational structure in German politics."[70] These ideological and organizational changes left the NSDAP well positioned to take advantage of the chaos that began to consume the country in the 1930s.

The Great Depression hit Germany particularly hard. From 1929 to 1932, industrial production dropped by almost half, national income decreased by about a third, stock prices collapsed, savings evaporated, investment disappeared, and during the winters of both 1931–2 and 1932–3 unemployment shot above 6 million. This led to a rise in support for the KPD and emboldened its attacks on the Republic and capitalism, trends that served only to frighten business, middle-class, and rural groups further. Meanwhile, as noted in the previous chapter, the SPD – the Republic's largest and most important party – essentially sat on its hands. Having rejected a cross-class approach, the party could not take advantage of the growing desperation of Germany's farmers and middle classes, and having failed to come up with a viable "socialist" approach to economic policy during the interwar years – and having rejected the unorthodox solutions to the Depression presented to it, such as the WTB plan – the SPD had little to offer an electorate desperate for some alternative to what was increasingly seen as capitalism's failure. Into this void stepped the NSDAP.

During the early 1930s, the Nazis continued their efforts to reach out to almost all strata of German society, especially rural and middle-class groups. They had already begun to tone down their attacks on the existing economic order, though this did not entail eliminating criticism of free-market capitalism or calls for dramatic socioeconomic change. The Nazis attempted to square this circle by invoking the difference between "rapacious" (*raffendes*) and "creative" (*schaffendes*) capital that national socialists had developed generations before (see Chapter 4). The former was associated with finance, commerce, and Jews and was seen as serving no good purpose; the latter was linked to industry and production, reflected "German" values and virtues, and was necessary for the health of society and the economy. This distinction between *raffendes* and *schaffendes* capital was, as one observer notes, "indeed almost a

---

and Agrarian Organization in the Final Phase of the Weimar Republic," in Henry Turner, ed., *Nazism and the Third Reich* (New York: New Viewpoints, 1972); Charles Loomis and J. Allan Beegle, "The Spread of Nazism in Rural Areas," *American Sociological Review*, 11, December 1946.

[69] Sheri Berman, "Civil Society and the Collapse of the Weimar Republic," *World Politics*, 49, 3, 1997.

[70] Stachura, *Gregor Strasser and the Rise of Nazism*, 71. See also Orlow, *The History of the Nazi Party*.

stroke of genius; it permitted the Nazi party to assume an anticapitalist stance
without frightening off the business world whose financial and political support
it sought."[71]

As the Depression persisted and Germany's situation deteriorated, the political situation became ever more volatile and frustration grew while the government and the traditional parties dithered. The Nazis once again responded
vigorously, attacking both Heinrich Brüning and the SPD for their passivity and
promising that if given power they would make jump-starting the economy and
alleviating the suffering of *all* Germans their primary goal. Strasser emerged as
a key figure in the Nazis' efforts, and in May 1932 he gave a speech criticizing
the government's economic policies and helping to set the agenda for the Nazi
alternative:

> This great anti-capitalist longing... which is going through our nation and which has
> gripped perhaps as many as 95 percent of our people is interesting and valuable. It
> by no means represents a rejection of property which is morally justified because it
> has been produced through work and saving. Above all, it has nothing to do with the
> senseless, unsuccessful, and destructive tendencies of the International. It is rather the
> protest of the productive sections of the nation against a degenerate theory of eco-
> nomics and it demands... the state... break with the demons of gold, the world econ-
> omy, materialism... and reestablish a situation in which honest labor receives an honest
> reward. This great anti-capitalist longing is proof... that we are on the threshold of a
> great, a tremendous new epoch: the overcoming of Liberalism and the emergence of a
> new kind of economic thinking and a new attitude towards the state.... [With regard to
> current crisis of unemployment and the question of work creation,] the state must never
> ask: Have I got the money for it? But rather, there is only one question: What should
> I use the money for? There is always money for work creation and in the last resort
> one should use productive credit creation (i.e. deficit spending), which is economically
> entirely justified.... In the case of work creation, therefore, the only question can be:
> where should one begin?[72]

(After hearing Strasser's speech, Fritz Tarnow, one of the authors of the WTB
plan, remarked, "This speech should have been given by one of us."[73])

In the election campaign leading up to the July 1932 elections, the NSDAP
promised to fight the Depression and solve the problem of unemployment,
contrasting these promises with the meekness of the government and the SPD.
It distributed six hundred thousand copies of its economic program, which was
organized around the basic principle that, "Our economy is not sick because
there is a lack of production opportunities, but rather because the available

---

[71] Avraham Barkai, *Nazi Economics* (New Haven, CT: Yale University Press, 1990), 23.
[72] Speech reprinted in E. J. Noakes and G. Pridham, *Nazism 1919–1945*, Vol. 2: *State, Economy,
and Society* (Exeter, UK: Exeter University Press, 1983), 347–58.
[73] G. Bombach, H. J. Ramser, M. Timmermann, and W. Wittmann, eds., *Der Keynesianismus:
Die Beschäftigungspolitische Diskussion vor Keynes in Deutschland* (Berlin: Springer, 1976),
Vol. 3, 382–3. Apparently, some within the Nazi movement returned Tarnow's "compliment,"
expressing sympathy for the WTB plan. Barkai, *Nazi Economics*, 53.

production opportunities are not being put to use."[74] The election results were nothing less than remarkable: For the first time since 1912, the SPD lost its status as the country's largest party (capturing only 21.6 percent of the vote) and was replaced by the NSDAP (with 37.3 percent of the vote; the KPD, meanwhile, was able to capture 14.5 percent of the vote). As important as the size of the NSDAP's victory was its nature. The 1932 elections revealed that the reorientation that the party had undergone over the past years had helped it achieve something that no other Weimar party had: It had become a true "people's party," with a support base that was "more equally distributed among the different social and demographic categories than any other major party of the Weimar Republic."[75]

In the months that followed, the situation remained fluid. The conservative Catholic Fritz von Papen continued to eviscerate what remained of Weimar democracy. Lacking a strong base of support, however, von Papen lasted only a few months in power. His government suffered a vote of no confidence in September and new elections were called for November. Ironically, at just that moment, for the first time in many years the NSDAP appeared to be suffering. Financial troubles and political differences caused internal tensions, while the end of reparations payments in the summer of 1932 robbed the Nazi appeal of some of its force. As a result, for the first time in four years, the Nazi vote declined: In the November 1932 elections, the NSDAP lost 2 million votes and thirty-four Reichstag seats. Yet despite this setback, the fact that no other party was able to mount a convincing challenge to the Nazis or offer any real possibility of forming a working coalition in the Reichstag (combined with the behind-the-scenes machinations of von Papen, Oksar von Hindenburg, Alfred Hugenberg, and others) led President Paul von Hindenburg finally to name Hitler chancellor of Germany on January 30, 1933.

The Nazis consolidated power much faster than their Italian counterparts had. Within a month, civil liberties had been suspended and freedom of the press abolished; within two months, an enabling law had given Hitler dictatorial powers; and within six months all other parties had been banned. Hitler also rapidly consolidated his internal position, eliminating Strasser and other rivals in the "Night of the Long Knives" in June 1934. Despite the Nazis' rapid evisceration of democracy, however, the regime was committed to cultivating and retaining the support of the German public – and to do this it had to find some way of living up to its promises and doing something about the Depression

---

[74] Ibid., 40, and Heinrich August Winkler, *Der Weg in die Katastrophe: Arbeiter und Arbeiterbewegung in der Weimarer Republik, 1930–1933* (Berlin: J. H. W. Dietz, 1987), 638.

[75] Jürgen Falter, "The First German Volkspartei," in Karl Rohe, ed., *Elections, Parties and Political Traditions: Social Foundations of German Parties and Party Systems* (Providence, RI: Berg, 1990), 79, 81.

and unemployment.[76] The Nazis, accordingly, proclaimed full employment a central goal. Trumpeting slogans such as "the right to work," the Nazis began a number of highly publicized work-creation programs, stepping up highway, canal, house, railway, and other types of construction projects (financed essentially by central bank credits)[77] and took every opportunity to exhort "business to take on extra workers and restrict hours of work and overtime."[78]

The regime also undertook a variety of other measures to jump-start the economy. It restarted the flow of credit, which had essentially dried up during the Depression; lowered interest rates; consolidated and secured government debts; and exercised greater control over the banking system. It gave industry and businesses subsidies and tax relief to encourage hiring and spending. Hitler, unwilling to alienate important business constituencies, had taken a relatively cautious approach to government expenditures in his first years in power, but by 1935 he was ready to accept more aggressive and "creative" measures. During the second half of the decade, accordingly, government spending increased dramatically.[79] Although Hitler and especially Hjalmar Schacht (Reichsbank president from 1933 to 1939 and minister of economics from 1934 to 1937) were often loath to admit it, what they were engaged in was "fiscal adventurism; they conducted a policy of deficit spending that was unprecedented in peacetime economies."[80] In 1933, Germany's national debt was 1.6 billion RM; by 1938, the last fiscal year before the war, it had ballooned to at least 30 billion RM.[81]

Germany's economy rebounded and unemployment figures improved almost miraculously. When Hitler came to power in 1933, almost 6 million Germans

---

[76] Timothy Mason, "The Primacy of Politics," in S. J. Woolf, ed., *The Nature of Fascism* (New York: Random House, 1958), and idem, *Social Policy in the Third Reich* (Oxford, UK: Berg, 1993). See also Barkai, *Nazi Economics*, 168–9, and R. J. Overy, *War and Economy in the Third Reich* (Oxford, UK: Clarendon Press, 1994), 38.

[77] C. W. Guillebaud, *The Social Policy of Nazi Germany* (New York: Howard Fertig, 1971), 15–16 and chapter 3; Overy, *War and Economy in the Third Reich*; Dan Silverman, *Hitler's Economy: Nazi Work Creation Programs, 1933–1936* (Cambridge, MA: Harvard University Press, 1998).

[78] Overy, *War and Economy in the Third Reich*, 55. When work-creation programs were originally proposed during the end phase of the Weimar Republic, many businesses objected, viewing the government spending and intervention in the market that they implied as dangerous. However, once the Nazis came to power, such criticism essentially stopped. As one observer notes:

> ... by August 1933 businessmen who had resisted work creation two years earlier were now doing their part to support the Hitler government's battle for jobs. The new attitude reflected not only an improved economic outlook, but also the fact that under the developing Nazi dictatorship 'the price of insurance against unpleasant forms of government intervention had risen considerably.' By destroying the German trade unions, Hitler had finished the job begun by Brüning. In return, the government expected industry to cooperate in providing jobs for the unemployed. If that cooperation had not been forthcoming ... German industrialists might have faced unpleasant consequences" (Silverman, *Hitler's Economy*, 8).

[79] Ibid., chapter 2.

[80] Barkai, *Nazi Economics*, 166. For a more circumspect judgment, see Overy, *War and Economy in the Third Reich*, e.g., 56.

[81] Gustav Stolper, *The German Economy* (London: Weidenfeld and Nicolson, 1967), 143.

had been unemployed; by the end of 1934, this number had dropped to 2.4 million, and by 1938 the country enjoyed essentially full employment. Scholars have long debated the role that Nazi programs played in the recovery. What now seems clear is that while these programs probably did contribute something, most of the upswing was attributable to a simultaneous upturn in the international economy.[82] But even if they were relatively unimportant economically, *psychologically* the Nazi programs were critical. By showing that the government was committed to winning the "Battle for Work" and getting the economy moving again, the programs gave large numbers of Germans renewed confidence in the future, making the recovery something of a self-fulfilling prophecy.[83] And even more important were the political consequences of the regime's Depression-fighting policies. Most Germans gave the regime credit for the economic turnaround that occurred on its watch and this boosted its popularity and legitimacy.

In addition to the specific measures undertaken to fight the Depression and unemployment, the Nazi regime expanded its control over the economy in other ways, always with an eye to the primacy of politics. Although Hitler never took the radical anticapitalist stances of a Strasser, he was fully committed to the old national socialist formula *Gemeinnutz geht vor Eigennutz* – national interest above private interest. The Nazi movement, according to Hitler, considered the economy "merely a necessary servant in the life of our people and nationhood. [The movement] feels an independent national economy to be necessary, but it does not consider it a primary factor that creates a strong state; on the contrary, only the strong nationalist state can protect such an economy and grant it freedom of existence and development." He once remarked that "the fundamental idea in [the Nazi] party's economic program [is quite clear] – the idea of authority.... I want everyone to keep the property that he has acquired for himself ... [but] the Third Reich will always retain its right to control the owners of property."[84]

Like the budding social democrats, Hitler and the Nazis operated on the belief that to achieve their goals, "the essential thing was not the taking over ownership, but that of control."[85] Destruction of the capitalist system and the elimination of private property would not only hinder production and create a political backlash, but were also unnecessary, since control could be exerted in a number of other ways. Businesspeople (with the obvious exception of Jews and other "undesirables") were thus allowed to retain their enterprises and much of their profits, but almost all their other activities "were fettered

[82] R. J. Overy, *The Nazi Economic Recovery* (London: Macmillan, 1982); idem, *War and Economy in the Third Reich*, 38; Silverman, *Hitler's Economy*, 245.
[83] Overy, *War and Economy in the Third Reich*, 80.
[84] Barkai, *Nazi Economics*, 26–7.
[85] Hendrik De Man, *Gegen den Strom* (Stuttgart: Deutsche Verlagsanstalt, 1953), 211, and Peter Dodge, *Beyond Marxism: The Faith and Works of Hendrik de Man* (The Hague: Martinus Nijhoff, 1966), 139.

(*gebunden*) or at least directed (*gelenkt*) by state agencies"[86] – through extensive
regulation, wage and price controls, the preferential awarding of contracts, and
the management of credit and investment funds. The result was that although
business, and especially big business, probably benefited materially more than
any other group from the Nazi regime, these benefits were accompanied by a
dramatic loss of autonomy.[87]

Agriculture suffered a similar fate, but received less in exchange for sub-
mitting to the state. Soon after the Nazis came to power, the entire agricultural
sector was organized into cartels known as *Reichsnährstand*. Marketing boards
(*Marktverbände*) were set up to fix prices, regulate supplies, and basically oversee all aspects of agricultural production. As time passed, regulation grew to
the point where talking of a market in agriculture became something of a misnomer, since the state determined everything from what seeds and fertilizers
were used to how land was inherited.[88] And even though farmers were granted
a moratorium on debt payments and protection from food imports, the cumulative result of Nazi policies was predictable: Agricultural production and the
rural standard of living declined and farms were sold off in record numbers.
Despite the Nazi romanticization of peasants and talk of the importance of
"Blod and Boden," the Third Reich witnessed "a mass migration [from the
land] comparable only to that of the late nineteenth century."[89]

Thus, by the end of the 1930s, the state's role in the economy had expanded
dramatically: Controls and regulations touched every sphere of economic life,
public spending as a share of the gross national product (GNP) had grown
spectacularly (from 17 percent of GNP in 1932 to 33 percent in 1938),[90] and
the government essentially controlled the provision of credit.[91] Indeed, as many
observers have noted, although the German economy remained at least nomi-
nally capitalist and private property was never fundamentally threatened, "The
scope and depth of state intervention in Nazi Germany had no peacetime prece-
dent or parallel in any capitalist economy, Fascist Italy included."[92]

The Nazis justified state control of the economy and the accompanying
loss of autonomy as the price that had to be paid for the creation of a true

---

[86] Barkai, *Nazi Economics*, 3.
[87] As several observers have noted:

> ...there is no question that, compared to other strata, the industrial community enjoyed a
> preeminent and protected position under Nazi rule and was less exposed to...terror. It is also
> true that the Nazis allowed that community a considerable measure of self-management as
> long as it kept to the straight and narrow and painstakingly strove to achieve the prescribed
> objectives. However, to describe this state of affairs as a "coalition of equal partners" is a gross
> exaggeration (Barkai, *Nazi Economics*, 16–17).

[88] Stolper, *The German Economy*, 137.
[89] David Schoenbaum, *Hitler's Social Revolution* (New York: W. W. Norton, 1966), 174.
[90] For comparison, the comparable figures for Great Britain and the United States were 23 percent
and 10 percent respectively. See Walter Laqueur, *Fascism: Past, Present, Future* (New York:
Oxford University Press, 1996), 67, and Overy, *The Nazi Economic Recovery*, 35.
[91] Ibid., 42.
[92] Barkai, *Nazi Economics*, 3.

Volksgemeinschaft – a system in which the good of the national community took precedence over all else. In addition to the previously discussed measures that were designed to temper or control markets, the regime also initiated a wide variety of policies that aimed not only to ensure the security and relative prosperity of ordinary Germans but also to bring a level of equality to what had long been a deeply divided and hierarchical society. As one recent scholar has put it, Hitler's policies

... benefited around 95% of all Germans. They did not experience National Socialism as a system of tyranny and terror but rather as a regime of social warmth, a sort of "warm and fuzzy" dictatorship (*wohlfühl-Diktatur*). Social reforms ... and real possibilities for social advancement, explain the regime's rising or at least stable [levels of popular support].[93]

Hitler took particular pride in the fact that "in this Reich we have opened the way for every qualified individual – whatever his origins – to reach the top if he is qualified, dynamic, industrious and resolute."[94] Although the rhetoric undoubtedly got ahead of the reality, the Nazis did offer, in a perverse kind of way, "real social opportunity for those who enjoyed it, opportunities that neither the Weimar Republic nor the Empire had offered them."[95]

Hitler also provided ordinary Germans with an expanded welfare state that included free access to higher education, help for families and child support, high pensions, and health insurance. Also extremely popular were the wide range of publically supported entertainment and vacation options provided by the regime:

Seats in theater and concert halls were made available for a nominal entrance fee of 50 pfenning and for 7 marks one could take an eight-hour excursion on the Mosel River. In total, 9 million Germans availed themselves of the opportunity to join these cheap excursions and more people traveled abroad than ever before. This was an age of festivals. The Olympic games of 1936 and the annual party conventions in Nuremberg were the most widely publicized, but there were also harvest festivals and various parades celebrating some historical or current political event.[96]

Tax policies were also designed to favor ordinary Germans: To pay for the war, it wasn't workers, peasants, and the lower middle classes who had to sacrifice, but rather the wealthy and corporations. For example, between 1936 and the beginning of the war, the corporate tax rate was raised from 20 percent to 40 percent – a policy that was explicitly designed to show that the cost of German power was to be divided "fairly and equitably." Similarly, in 1935 Hitler stated that in case of war "higher incomes would be squeezed" while German workers, farmers, white-collar workers, and civil servants would be protected.[97] These policies were designed to make clear that the regime was

[93] Götz Aly, "Die Wohlfühl-Diktator," *Der Spiegel*, October 2005, 56.
[94] Schoenbaum, *Hitler's Social Revolution*, 238.
[95] Ibid., 273.
[96] Laqueur, *Fascism*, 68–9. Also Mason, *Social Policy in the Third Reich*.
[97] Aly, "Die Wohlfühl-Diktator," 57.

committed to egalitarianism and social justice – and to a surprising degree, Germans responded as desired.[98] Of course, all these goodies had to be paid for some way, and in addition to some squeezing of the wealthy and corporations, the real brunt of this burden was borne by Jews, other minority groups, and the societies conquered by the Nazi war machine.

In the final analysis, there is little doubt that the Nazi boast that the year "1933 was revolutionary and opened a new epoch in German history" was accurate.[99] In addition to instituting a regime of unprecedented violence and barbarism, the Nazis managed to reshape the relationship among the state, society, and the economy in Germany in fundamental ways. Most obviously, they instituted a "genuine revolution"[100] in economic affairs, rejecting both laissez-faire liberalism and Soviet communism. Instead, the Nazi system was predicated on a belief in the primacy of politics, the insistence that the state and its leader had the right – indeed, the duty – to intervene in all spheres of life, including the economy. And intervene the Nazis did, exerting their dominance over socio-economic actors and the direction and nature of economic development through myriad indirect measures (and the constant, if often implicit, threat of force).

The consequences of these changes were profound. The Nazis' seeming success in overcoming the Depression, their insistence that capitalism and capitalists had to serve the "national interest," and their constant assertion that class cleavages, conflicts, and hierarchies had no role to play in a true *Volksgemeinschaft* played a critical role in stabilizing and legitimizing the regime during the 1930s. Hitler enjoyed genuine popular support in Germany because most Germans associated National Socialism first and foremost not with racism, violence, and tyranny, but with an improved life, national pride, and a sense of community: "...economic leveling and social mobility domestically, collective and palpable prosperity for the *Herrenfolk* at the cost of the so-called *Minderwertiger*, this was the simple and popular magic formula of the National Socialist state."[101] De Man and Déat were not alone, in other words, in concluding that the Third Reich might actually have found solutions to many of modernity's contemporary problems – a claim that by the 1930s the mainstream left could no longer make.

Epilogue

Despite important differences, fascism and national socialism shared many critical similarities, perhaps the most important of which were a commitment to the

---

[98] Eg. Alf Lüdtke, "What Happened to the 'Fiery Red Glow'? Workers' Experiences and German Fascism," in idem, ed., *The History of Everyday Life* (Princeton, NJ: Princeton University Press, 1995), and Detlef Muehlberger, "Conclusion to Hitler's Followers," in Christian Leitz, ed., *The Third Reich* (Boston: Blackwell, 1999).

[99] Peter Stachura, "Introduction," in idem, ed., *The Nazi Machtergreifung* (London: George Allen and Unwin, 1983), 6.

[100] E.g. Barkai, *The Nazi Economy*, 10, 18, and Stolper, *The German Economy*, 129.

[101] Aly, "Die Wohlfühl-Diktator," 62

primacy of politics and nationalism. During the interwar years, these principles were translated into a program that paralleled in many ways the one developed by budding social democrats – all advocated a "third way" between laissez-faire liberalism and Soviet communism and advocated people's party strategies and communitarian appeals. Such programs help explain why, despite their violence and barbarism, the Italian Fascist and German National Socialist regimes enjoyed a surprising degree of support. This political and economic mix proved popular not just in Italy and Germany but in many other parts of the continent as well.

In France, for example, scholars have long debated whether any of the right-wing movements that sprung up during the interwar years deserves to be called fascist or national socialist. The fact is, however, that when examined from a comparative perspective, it is very clear that many if not most of these groups shared several critical characteristics with each other and with fascist and national socialist movements in other countries, characteristics that differentiated them from traditional conservative parties. These characteristics are by now familiar: Many made real efforts to attract a mass base and a cross-class constituency, employed communitarian and nationalist appeals, and groped toward a "third way" in economics. During the early 1920s, the most important of the radical right-wing groups were the Légion (led by Antoine Rédier), the Jeunesses Patriotes (JP, led by Pierre Taittinger, into which the Légion merged in 1925), and the Faisceau (led by George Valois). All vociferously attacked the left and democracy more generally and favored replacing the Republic with a corporatist system that would foster national cohesion.[102] These movements claimed not to represent any particular class, but "all France." The Légion, for example, purported to stand "above the interests of a single group," and sought "to gather all those ... who put the salvation of France above all else."[103] The JP's 1926 program, meanwhile, declared that the movement wanted not "class struggle but class collaboration."[104]

The late 1920s and the early 1930s saw the rise of a second wave of right-wing groups like Solidarité Française (SF), the Parti Populaire Français (PPF), and the Croix de Feu (CF, which later morphed into the Parti Social Français, or PSF). As with their earlier counterparts, all of these were fervent opponents of both the traditional left and the Republic and declared their advocacy of some sort of fascist or national socialist alternative to the reigning order. In addition, all claimed to be working in the interests of the nation as a whole rather than any particular group or class and tried to attract a broad constituency. The SF, for example, claimed to be a "defender of the people, even of the proletariat,"[105] while the PPF, at least during the earlier stages of its development, attracted a

---

[102] E.g., Robert Soucy, *French Fascism: The First Wave, 1924–1933* (New Haven, CT: Yale University Press, 1986), 28, 161ff.
[103] Ibid., 30.
[104] Ibid., 69.
[105] Ibid., 89.

relatively large number of workers as well as other defectors from the left.[106] The CF, finally, along with its successor the PSF, which grew to be the largest of the interwar new right movements,[107] also attracted a surprisingly broad constituency. As one observer notes, the CF/PSF was the "first modern, cross-class, mass-mobilized French rightist party.... Its initial membership was strongly middle class, but as the movement grew, farmers made up 25 percent of the total, and an increasing number of workers were mobilized."[108] Reflecting this, one of its leaders, Colonel François de La Rocque, proudly proclaimed that it was the only movement that could not "be classed a priori, a posteriori right or left.... Instead it had achieved a fusion of all classes in which individual wealth had no bearing on the choice of its leaders.... One sees generals, great artists, great scholars, [and] high dignitaries of the Legion of Honor proud to obey workers and clerks who wear the Military Medal or the Croix de Guerre."[109]

All of these movements showed a fondness for state intervention in the economy while at the same time proclaiming their intention of protecting bourgeois and peasant interests. The JP criticized the "egoism of the rich" and supported a wide range of social reforms, including health and unemployment insurance, retirement plans, and improved housing programs. Its leader, Taittinger, declared that the JP differed from the traditional left in that it was "inspired by...[a] social nationalism...which recognized a solidarity uniting the interests of all Frenchmen, not by a Marxist internationalism which pitted one class against another."[110] Similarly, the Faisceau and Valois took great pains to convince the French that they were "no lack[eys] of capitalism, but [rather]...friend[s] of the worker." Reflecting this, the group's paper denounced the "'yoke of money' that 'plutocracy' had imposed on the nation and [to] proclaim its own devotion to social justice." Valois was even known to imply that "big business was as decadent as parliamentary democracy."[111]

None of these parties, however, called for the complete destruction of capitalism, markets, or private property, and they had no problem with a bourgeoisie that would "amass wealth" and work "for the good of the people and the grandeur of the country."[112] As Valois once remarked, such stances indicated

---

[106] Its leader, Jacques Doriot, was a former Communist. Ibid., 236, 247.

[107] There is real debate in the literature about whether the CF and PSF should be considered fascist. Clearly, this book takes the position that they should. On this issue, see William Irvine, "Fascism in France and the Strange Case of the Croix de Feu," *Journal of Modern History*, 63, June 1991, and Robert Soucy, *French Fascism: The Second Wave, 1933–1939* (New Haven, CT: Yale University Press, 1995).

[108] Payne, *A History of Fascism*, 295. Also Irvine, "Fascism in France."

[109] Soucy, *French Fascism: The Second Wave*, 178.

[110] Idem, *French Fascism: The First Wave*, 69.

[111] Ibid., 92.

[112] Ibid., 166–7. Also Kalus-Juergen Mueller, "French Fascism and Modernization," *Journal of Contemporary History*, 11, 1976.

that fascism properly understood "was 'neither of the right nor of the left,'" as Mussolini put it, but was instead simply "a friend of the people."[113]

Although their economic plans were often vague, what all these parties shared was a pledge to "temper" capitalism and create an economy that took societal needs into account.[114] However fuzzy and unrealistic such promises may have been, they proved quite attractive in France as elsewhere. While no party was able to achieve its stated goal of toppling the Republic, this does not mean that some parties did not enjoy a high degree of support. As Robert Soucy notes, "when Hitler came to power in Germany in 1933, the total membership of the NSDAP was about 850,000...that is, about 1.5 percent of a national population of about sixty million. In 1937 the CF alone had nearly a million members in a population of forty million. France was not as allergic to fascism as some scholars have claimed."[115]

In short, in France as in Italy and Germany (and many other parts of Europe), the political and economic policies and appeals offered by fascists and national socialists proved to be widely popular. Tapping into widespread longing for some alternative to the reigning capitalist system and for an end to class conflict and social divisions, fascists and national socialists managed to achieve a surprising degree of support, despite the violence and barbarism so clearly associated with them.

But an appreciaton of the nature and significance of fascism's and national socialism's program is necessary not only for understanding their success during the interwar years: These programs also helped shape the trajectory of their nations in later decades. Several critical "innovations" championed by fascists and national socialists – such as the notion of a "people's party" and an economic order that aimed to control but not destroy capitalism – became central features of Europe's postwar order. Before moving on to examine that order, however, it is worth turning to another regime that managed to achieve a "national socialist" revolution during the interwar era, but in this case without sacrificing democracy and human rights: Swedish social democracy.

---

[113] Ibid., 167.

[114] Soucy, *French Fascism: The Second Wave*, 184. Also Kevin Passmore, *From Liberalism to Fascism* (New York: Cambridge University Press, 1997), chapter 8.

[115] Soucy, *French Fascism: The Second Wave*, 36. See also idem, *French Fascism: The First Wave*, xii.

7

The Swedish Exception

In the years after the First World War, democratic revisionists waged a war for the soul and the future of the international socialist movement. Confronted with an exhausted orthodox Marxism and a rising radical right, the sharpest revisionists developed a new strategy for the left based on state control of the market and communitarian appeals. Although these insurgents gained followers in countries across Europe, they were unable to capture control of any major socialist party on the continent. Only in Scandinavia – and particularly in Sweden – did socialists embrace the new course wholeheartedly. And it was thus only in Sweden that socialists were able to outmaneuver the radical right and cement a stable majority coalition, escaping the collapse of the left and democracy that occurred elsewhere in Europe. The key to understanding the Swedish SAP's remarkable success in the interwar years lies in the triumph of democratic revisionism several decades earlier.

Democratic Revisionism in Sweden

From its inception, the SAP's view of Marxism was flexible and undogmatic, a stance facilitated by the party's peripheral position in the international socialist movement and by the long-term leadership of Hjalmar Branting (the SAP's leader from its founding in 1889 to his death in 1925).[1] Branting was a democratic revisionist through and through, and, having started his career in liberal circles, his views were shaped by his continuing relationship with them; this not only allowed for extensive cooperation between socialists and liberals, but also

---

[1] On the early development of the SAP, see Seppo Hentilä, *Den Svenska Arbetarklassen och Reformismens Genombrott Inom SAP före 1914* (Helsingfors: Suomen Historiallinen Seura, 1979); John Lindgren, *Det Socialdemokratiska Arbetarpartiets Uppkomst i Sverige, 1881–1889* (Stockholm: Tiden, 1927); G. Hilding Nordström, *Sveriges socialdemokratiska arbetarparti under genombrottsåren, 1889–1894* (Stockholm: KF, 1938); Birger Simonson, *Socialdemokratiet och Maktövertagandet* (Göteborg: Bokskogen, 1985).

manifested itself in Branting's conviction that socialism was the next logical step toward liberalism's completion. His longevity and extraordinary talents enabled him to exert an unparalleled influence over his party's development. As one of his colleagues noted in 1920, "faith in Branting has become so universal in our country that no counterpart to it ... is likely to be found ... in this or any other country during the last quarter of a century."[2]

Even though the SAP considered itself a Marxist party, it never asserted that Marxism was a complete guide for action across time and space.[3] Indeed, the revisionist position that Marx and Engels needed updating had become widespread within the party by the end of the nineteenth century. In his 1902 introduction to Engels' *Socialism's Development from Utopia to Science*, Branting noted that Marx and his colleagues, writing a generation earlier, could not have foreseen the developments of the last years "any more than the utopians of a half a century ago could have understood the socialism of Marx and Engels." Modifications to socialism were therefore necessary, even if the core of the socialist world view remained the same: "Just as capitalism was at one time a bitter historical necessity, so will it move aside for socialism. But the possibility to fight and bridle capitalism [is] much better than it was at the time when Marx and Engels began. Class society ... is beginning to change ... [and the] reasons for this are to be found in [socialist] political activity."[4] And in 1906, Branting argued that

... contemporary [socialism's] fundamental idea ... preserves the essentials of Marxism, but does not swear by the master's words as infallible, least of all those passages dated by changing historical circumstances. Moreover, these modifications [of theory] according to new developments ... are in a deeper sense in complete harmony with Marxism's own spirit. Only a Marxism that failed to conceive of itself properly as a doctrine of development could wish to proclaim the validity of Marxist propositions referring to social conditions that since his time have changed completely.[5]

Over the years, accordingly, the SAP increasingly presented Marxism as valuable not primarily for its "scientific" pretensions or insistence on historical or economic necessities, but for its emphasis on changing the world and its promise of a better, more just future.

This early and relatively widespread acceptance of an undogmatic Marxism helped liberate the SAP from the ideological and political struggles that paralyzed many of its sister parties in the Second International. Not only was

[2] Gustav Möller, "Hjalmar Branting," in *Hjalmar Branting: Festschrift* (Stockholm: Tiden, 1920), 9.
[3] Mats Dahlkvists, *Staten, Socialdemokratien och Socialism* (Stockholm: Prisma, 1975); Gunnar Gunnarsson, *Socialdemokratisk Idearv* (Stockholm: Tiden, 1979); Simonson, *Socialdemokratin och Maktövertagendet*.
[4] Hjalmar Branting, "Förord och Noter till 'Socialisms Utveckling' av Engels," in idem, *Tal och Skrifter I: Socialistisk Samhällssyn* (Stockholm: Tiden, 1926), 271ff.
[5] Idem, "Partinamn och Partigränser," reprinted in idem, *Tal och Skrifter: Stridsfrågor inom Arbetarrörelsen,* (Stockholm: Tiden, 1929), 114.

questioning Marxism itself considered acceptable, but shifts in strategy were
never subjected to ideological litmus tests. As early as 1886, Branting urged
his followers to remember that even when "we have a clear goal it remains for
us to investigate the means and ways the workers movement can use to bring
itself closer to its future ideals."[6] Similarly, Axel Danielsson, another early SAP
leader, argued in 1890 that, "We are skeptics, opportunists, where tactics are
concerned. To dogmatically maintain that a certain tactic is relevant for all
parties, under all conditions is insanity."[7] Decades later, Per Albin Hansson,
Branting's successor as party leader, noted that "we have never demanded that
all party members should swear on each point in our program. Within the
framework of a common [socialist] world view we leave the freedom to . . . think
differently."[8] This willingness to let a hundred flowers bloom helped generate
a high level of research and debate within the party on contemporary problems
facing socialism – and was central to the SAP's ability to adapt to changes in
its environment.[9]

When it came to facing the thorny question of how to handle the quest for
political reform, Sweden's political backwardness (during the late nineteenth
century, it was one of the least democratic countries in Europe[10]) may actually have furthered the party's revisionist tendencies. Unlike the situation in
France or Germany in the late nineteenth century, the young SAP was essentially shut out from any political influence or representation, making it natural
for the party to give political reform a high priority. Thus as early as 1887
the Swedish labor movement passed a resolution declaring: "Because universal
suffrage can end the injustice that the largest part of society's citizens should
have heavy obligations but no rights, because universal suffrage is a necessary
prerequisite for people becoming masters in their own house, . . . and because
universal suffrage is the only way to solve the social question peacefully . . . this
meeting demands universal, equal, and direct suffrage."[11] Over time, the

[6] Idem, "Vaför Arbetarrörelsen Måste bli Socialistisk," in idem, *Tal och Skrifter I*, 107.
[7] Axel Danielsson in *Arbetet*, July 4, 1890. Also, Herbert Tingsten, *Den Svenska Socialdemokratiens Ideutveckling*, Vol. 2 (Stockholm: Tiden, 1941), 29.
[8] Per Albin Hansson, "De Kristna och Partiet," reprinted in Anna Lisa Berkling, ed., *Från Fram
till Folkhemmet: Per Albin Hansson som Tidningsman och Talare* (Stockholm: Metodica, 1982),
223.
[9] Tolerance, however, was not unlimited. In 1908, for example, the party expelled obstreperous
anarchist leaders.
[10] On the struggle for democracy in Sweden, see Nils Andren, *Från Kungavälde till Folkstyre*
(Stockholm: Ehlins Folkbildningsförlaget, 1955); Sheri Berman, *The Social Democratic Moment:
Ideas and Politics in the Making of Interwar Europe* (Cambridge, MA: Harvard University
Press, 1998), chapters 3 and 5; Rudolf Kjellen, *Rösträttsfrågan, 1869–1909* (Stockholm: Hugo
Gebers, 1915); Leif Lewin, Bo Jansson, and Dag Sörblom, *The Swedish Electorate, 1887–1968*
(Stockholm: Almqvist and Wicksell, 1972); Dankwart Rustow, *The Politics of Compromise*
(Princeton, NJ: Princeton University Press, 1985); Torbjörn Vallinder, *I Kamp för Demokratin:
Rösträttsrörelsen i Sverige, 1886–1900* (Stockholm: Natur och Kultur, 1962); Douglas Verny,
Parliamentary Reform in Sweden, 1866–1921 (Oxford, UK: Clarendon Press, 1957).
[11] Quoted in Vallinder, *I kamp för demokratin*, 16.

SAP's leadership remained united behind the goal of political reform, with both Branting and Danielsson presenting democracy as the prerequisite for achieving other socialist goals as well as a central component of the socialist vision.[12]

Since the limited franchise excluded most workers, moreover, the SAP faced a stark tactical choice: It could pursue alliances with non-socialist parties or remain impotent. It chose the former, reaching out in particular to left-Liberals, the other main group in Swedish society favoring political liberalization. Branting worked hard to make his fellow socialists recognize that cross-class collaboration was in their long-term interest, arguing that, "As long as a victory for the Liberals over [the reactionaries] is more likely than a victory for [socialists]... we friends of freedom in Sweden [would do well] to [support this group's] fight."[13] As a result, during the 1890s the SAP invited left-Liberals to help organize and participate in "people's parliaments" *(folksriksdagen)* – popularly elected bodies that would confront the government with a demand for democratization – and engaged them in electoral alliances and other forms of political cooperation. Indeed, it was thanks to left-Liberal support that Branting, in 1896, became the first Socialist elected to Sweden's lower house of parliament.

By the turn of the century, under the banner "Democracy is our goal!" SAP election manifestos were already proclaiming that

[I]n a majority of [electoral districts] the situation is such that a purely labor candidate has little chance of winning in the contemporary situation. The task [for those workers who are eligible to vote is therefore] ... to support those candidates ... favoring universal suffrage.... Universal, equal, and direct suffrage, without any restrictions and reservations, through which a class of ... citizens would [no longer] remain without the vote – our old demand – is the firm point to which Sweden's workers should unshakably hold themselves and test those who desire their votes.[14]

At first, these priorities were defended with the argument that political liberalization would ultimately improve the position and power of the labor movement and that increasing the number of workers who could vote would naturally increase the SAP's representation in parliament and hence its ability to pressure the old regime. Over time, however, democratizing Sweden's political system came to be seen not only as a means but also as an end. Unlike many of its continental counterparts, therefore, the SAP early on freed itself from the tendency to dismiss democracy as a "bourgeois" system. Instead, democracy came to be

[12] E.g., Hjalmar Branting, "Rösträtt och Arbetarrörelse" (1896), reprinted in idem, *Tal och Skrifter: Kampen för Demokratin I* (Stockholm: Tiden, 1927), 145–56, and Matts Danielsson, "Anarki eller Socialism," *Arbetet*, May 27, 1891.

[13] Hjalmar Branting in *Folkviljan*, November 11, 1884, quoted in Nils-Olof Franzen, *Hjalmar Branting och Hans Tid* (Stockholm: Bonniers, 1985), 103.

[14] Election manifesto from 1902 reprinted in Sven-Olof Håkansson, ed., *Svenska Valprogram: 1902–1952*, Vol. 1 (Göteborg: Göteborgs Universitet, Statsvetenskapliga Institution, 1959).

seen as an integral component of the identity and goals of a socialist party –
indeed, the form that socialism would take once it arrived.

The SAP was also early on firmly dedicated to reform work. Already in 1889,
Branting asserted, "I believe ... that one benefits the workers ... so much more
by forcing through reforms which alleviate and strengthen their position, than
by saying that only a revolution can help them."[15] Socialism "would not be
created by brutalized ... slaves," he noted, but rather by "the best positioned
workers, those who have gradually obtained a normal workday, protective
legislation, minimum wages."[16] Since reforms helped provide workers with
"the will, the insight, and ability to create ... a thoroughgoing transformation,"
it was the task of social democracy to obtain "all the reforms ... that [could be]
forced from bourgeois society."[17]

And as time passed, many Swedish socialists began to argue that incremental reforms were more than just a way to remedy contemporary injustices or
improve the material resources of the working class; they were steps on the way
to socialism. Frederick Ström's influential 1907 essay "The Working Woman
and Socialism," for example, argued that socialists "must try to [win] from
contemporary society ... all that which can ensure the working class a materially and spiritually acceptable existence and raise the working class to a higher
culture, while at the same time step by step driving the social order over to
socialism and thereby approaching its final goal. Both of these tasks are in
their fundamentals, one and the same."[18] What is crucial here is not merely
the emphasis on reforms – since all socialist parties eventually came to embrace
some reform work – but rather a growing acceptance within the SAP of the revisionist view that reform work could contribute directly to the achievement of
socialism itself. Thus by the early twentieth century, reform work had become
absolutely central to the SAP's understanding of its nature and tasks, clearly differentiating it from most of its European counterparts. As Branting once noted:

> ... a dividing line runs between reformist and negative socialism. ... I have met a narrow-
> mindedness that says: vote against this [proposal], it will pass in any case. Then later the
> decision can be attacked, one can beat one's breast, pointing to the fact that one voted
> against it in order to create better conditions for the working classes. For my own part I
> believe that such tactics are completely valueless for a large party. ... Above all it should
> be observed, that in debates about social reforms one should never ... present [them] as
> relatively unimportant or [act] indifferently [toward them].[19]

---

[15] In a letter to Axel Danielsson in jail (1889), reprinted in *Från Palm to Palme: Den Svenska
Socialdemokratins Program* (Stockholm: Rabén and Sjögren), 189–90, quote on 189.

[16] Quoted in Zeth Höglund, *Hjalmar Branting och Hans Livsgärning*, Part I (Stockholm: Tiden,
1928), 194.

[17] Hjalmar Branting, "Den Revolutionära Generalstrejken" (1906), reprinted in idem, *Tal och
Skrifter: Stridsfrågor inom Arbetarrörelsen*, 125.

[18] Quoted in Simonson, *Socialdemokratin och Makövertagendet*, 54.

[19] Branting in a speech to the Riksdag, May 21, 1913, in idem, *Tal och Skrifter: Ekonomisk och
Social Arbetarepolitik* (Stockholm: Tiden, 1928), 280.

In typical democratic revisionist fashion, that is, the SAP had exchanged orthodoxy's insistence that socialism would emerge from economic developments with a conviction that socialists could and should use political power to reshape the world around them.

The SAP's departures from orthodoxy did not stop with its disavowal of historical materialism. The party gradually abandoned orthodoxy's second pillar, class struggle, as well. From early in its history, it advocated a relatively mild view of class conflict. This was manifested not only in the acceptance of alliances with non-socialist parties, but also in the SAP's refusal to cultivate for itself an image as exclusively a worker's party. Indeed, some have even argued that the SAP conceived of itself as a "people's party" from its birth. Hansson noted, for example, that the first social democratic newspaper in Sweden was entitled the *People's Will (Folkviljan)*, the SAP's original paper was entitled the *People's Paper (Folkbladet)*, and public places built by the party were called things such as the People's House (*Folkets hus*) and the People's Park (*Folkets park*).[20] This may oversimplify matters, but there is no doubt that the SAP began to reach out to groups outside the industrial proletariat much earlier than did most of its European counterparts.

By 1890, for example, Danielsson was already arguing that the SAP must "come in closer contact with the people, in particular the people who do not yet feel themselves revolutionary, but who want to improve their political situation.... We must become a people's party." Reflecting this, when the first issue of his newspaper *Arbetet* came out in 1887, it was designed to appeal not only to the workers of his city, Malmö, but also to the "economically dependent" middle class.[21] Branting was another early advocate of a "big tent" view of the class struggle, declaring that it "should... be carried out in such a way that it does not close the door to an expansive solidarity among more than just [manual workers]. The goal... is through struggle to come to a solidarity that... stretches across the entire nation and through this... includes all human beings."[22] In 1886, he wrote:

In a backward land like Sweden we cannot close our eyes to the fact that the middle class increasingly plays a very important role. The working class needs the help it can get from this direction, just like the middle class for its part needs the workers behind it, in order to be able to hold out against [our] common enemies. And... we would only be doing the task of the reactionaries if under contemporary conditions we were to fully isolate ourselves and... be equally hostile to *all* old parties.[23]

---

[20] Per Albin Hansson, "Folk och Klass," *Tiden*, 1929, 330. Also Lars Christian Trägårdh, "The Concept of the People and the Construction of Popular Culture in Germany and Sweden, 1848–1933" (Ph.D. Dissertation, University of California, Berkeley, 1993), esp. 123–4.

[21] Quote in *Från Palm till Palme*, 38–9. Also, Axel Danielsson, *Om Revolution i Sverige* (Stockholm: Arbetarkultur, 1972), esp. 28–9.

[22] Hjalmar Branting, "Socialism i Arbetarrörelsen," reprinted in Alvar Alsterdal and Ove Sandel, eds., *Hjalmar Branting: Socialism och Demokrati* (Stockholm: Prisma, 1970), 72.

[23] Branting, "De Närmaste Framtidsutsikterna," (1886), reprinted in idem, *Tal och Skrifter: Kampen för Demokratin I*, 33.

As a result of such views, by the turn of the century the SAP's electoral manifestos were addressed not merely to the proletariat but to "Sweden's working
people" (*Sveriges arbetande folk*) or to "all progressive citizens in the city and
country" (*all frisinnade medborgare i stad och på land*).[24]

By the turn of the century, several key figures within the party also began to
debate the SAP's relationship with, and policies toward, other sectors of Swedish
society, especially the peasantry. The relationship between farmers and workers
was as strained in Sweden as it was in many other parts of Europe, but many key
figures within the SAP began to argue that even if small farming was destined
to fade away over the long run, it was politically unwise (as well as morally
unjustified) to hope or work for this sector's collapse. In 1894, Danielsson
reasoned that "whether or not small farming is doomed to die it is not the
task of [socialists] to hasten the impoverishment of agriculture.... [We] don't
expect, as do the anarchists, that intensive poverty will bring forth socialist
change.... Let [us try to reach a] compromise with farmers...through this [we
will] solve some of our most urgent tasks...and move from being a sect, as
Bebel wants, to becoming a people's party."[25] Similarly, Branting, who was
quite skeptical about the future of small farming, was nevertheless critical of
the inflexible orthodoxy exhibited by many of his German counterparts, who
insisted "that one should not hold out to the farmers the prospect of their
situation being improved."[26]

The publication of Eduard David's *Sozialismus und Landwirtschaft* in
1903[27] reignited the debate over agricultural policy in Sweden (as it had in
Germany). Advocates of agricultural reform within the SAP were heavily influenced by David's rejection of large-scale agriculture and celebration of the
virtues of small farming, and they succeeded in persuading increasing numbers of Swedish socialists that, given time and effort, small farmers could be
made to see some community of interest with workers. The 1908 SAP party
congress, accordingly, decided to devote more resources to agitation in rural
areas. It even published a brochure proclaiming: "concerning agriculture, we
[socialists] have no desire other than...to bring about relationships as favor-
able as possible in the countryside.... On the other side it should be near to
the hearts of those [working in the agricultural sector to see] the wages and
working conditions of industrial workers improve [so that] their purchasing
power and need for foodstuffs will grow."[28]

Three years later, a committee appointed by the party executive to come up
with a new agricultural program sought to increase the party's appeal to small
farmers and agricultural workers through a variety of social, financial, and

[24] Håkansson, *Svenska Valprogram*, and Hansson, "Folk och Klass," 330.
[25] Danielsson, *Arbetet*, November 27, 1894.
[26] Hjalmar Branting, "Industriarbetarparti eller Folkparti?" (1895), reprinted in idem, *Tal och
Skrifter: Stridsfrågar inom Arbetarrörelsen* (Stockholm: Tiden, 1929), 50–1.
[27] See footnote 77 of Chapter 2 in this book.
[28] Quoted in Simonson, *Socialdemokratien och Maktövertagendet*, 192–3.

educational policies. The committee stressed the insecurity that both workers and farmers faced, and stated that small farmers, peasants, and agricultural workers belonged, along with industrial workers, to the exploited classes.[29] And it argued that since within capitalism there could be areas where workers owned the means of production, in such areas, "it was only right that the fruits of labor fell to [the owner]."[30] This twist allowed the party to exclude farms from the category of private property that would be eliminated under socialism, thus making its platform less threatening to rural voters.

On the eve of the First World War, therefore, the Swedish SAP was in a very different position from most of its counterparts in the Second International. The party had already placed democracy and reform work at the center of both its political strategy and its understanding of socialism, had developed alliances with non-socialist parties, and had reached out to other groups in Swedish society. It had essentially abandoned an economistic and deterministic orthodox Marxism and accepted all the key tenets of democratic revisionism – leaving it much better positioned than other European socialist parties to deal with the challenges it would face in the tumultuous years ahead.

The Challenges of the Interwar Era

The period leading up to the First World War was particularly tense in Sweden, with society bitterly divided over democratization. The outbreak of the war temporarily postponed the conflict, as both Liberals and socialists pledged to support the government's neutrality policy during the crisis. But by 1916, the domestic truce had ended.[31] Both the Liberals and the SAP increased their attacks on the government, with the latter in particular intensifying its demands for full democratization.

All parties recognized that the 1917 elections would be crucial, and the labor movement set for itself an ambitious goal: an SAP victory great enough to force change. The SAP's election manifesto asked: "Shall Sweden be the last refuge of reaction? ... Isn't it an infamy for our country that when all of Europe stands like never before in the shadow of democracy and freedom, our Swedish people ... should remain under the authority of industrialists and large landowners, of big capitalism and bureaucracy. ... Sweden's people must ... [vote] for the party that above all carries forward the demand for a

---

[29] Lars Björlin, "Jordfrågan i Svensk Arbetarrörelse, 1890–1920," *Arbetarrörelsens Årsbok*, 1974, 105–9.

[30] Per Thullberg, "SAP och Jordbruksnäringen 1920–1940: Från Klasskamp till Folkhem," *Arbetarrörelsens Årsbok*, 1974, 129.

[31] The best summary in English of this period is Carl-Göran Andrae, "The Swedish Labor Movement and the 1917–1919 Revolution," in Steven Koblik, ed., *Sweden's Development from Poverty to Affluence, 1750–1970* (Minneapolis, MN: University of Minnesota Press, 1975).

democratization of our constitution . . . [the SAP]."[32] The response to the SAP's call was impressive: the Liberals claimed 27.6 percent and the SAP 31.1 percent of the vote.

As discussed in earlier chapters, the question of whether socialists should settle for shared power when it became possible had troubled almost all parties in the Second International. For fear of tarnishing their ideological purity, many of them could not bring themselves to take the plunge into governance during the interwar years – even when the fate of democracy hung in the balance. The SAP, however, approached the transition from opposition to government party with much less trepidation thanks to its long grappling with the issue of cross-class cooperation and the high priority it had always placed on democratization. In 1904, for example, the Swedes had clearly placed themselves on the revisionist side of the issue by voting against the condemnation of *ministerso-cialism* presented at the International's Amersterdam congress (see Chapter 3). When the SAP became the largest party in the Swedish parliament a decade later, it started to consider just what responsibilities such a position carried. Many argued that if the SAP were asked to help govern and refused, the result would be continued right-wing rule. As Branting noted, "If such a situation were to occur our voters would get the impression that voting [socialist] did not bring any practical result."[33] In addition, such a refusal would also conflict with the party's long-term commitment to using its political power to achieve incremental progress and political reform.

Nevertheless, a small radical minority in the party adamantly opposed cross-class cooperation in general and the idea of joining a non-socialist government in particular. Branting had tried to assure the party's 1914 congress that it was a win-win situation, since they would agree to join a coalition only if it was devoted to a clearly delineated democratic program. Should the Liberals accept this condition, the SAP would get what it wanted, while if the Liberals rejected it, they and not the socialists would be the ones stuck with the blame for continued right-wing rule. But Zeth Höglund, the main speaker for the opposition, argued that the Liberals could not be trusted and urged the delegates to recognize that "our party is faced with a decision whether it will be a bourgeois reform party or the [socialist] party which up until now has been so . . . victorious."[34]

The issue came to a head at the party's 1917 congress, which ultimately passed a resolution overwhelmingly condemning the radicals, who promptly broke off to form the Swedish Social Democratic Left Party (*Sveriges Socialdemokratiska Vänsterparti*),[35] freeing Branting and his supporters to do

[32] Manifesto reprinted in Håkansson, *Svenska Valprogram*, Vol. 1.
[33] Branting, *Tal och Skrifter: Kampen för Demokratin*, Vol. 2, 181–4. Also, Agne Gustafsson, "Branting och Partivänstern," *Tiden*, 9, 1960, 581.
[34] Branting, *Tal och Skrifter: Kampen för Demokratin*, Vol. 2, 200.
[35] Its main basis was the former Social Democratic Youth League headed by Höglund. However, the party's opposition to the mainstream social democrats hid important internal splits: Within the left socialists there were Bolshevik sympathizers as well as a group committed to the achievement

what they wanted. When the elections later that year returned a left majority, therefore, the SAP was ready to cooperate, and on October 17, 1917, it joined a national government for the first time in Swedish history.[36] A year later, after fighting off last-ditch challenges by conservatives and the King, that government presided over Sweden's transition to full parliamentary democracy.

With full democratization accomplished, however, the SAP's relationship with its left-Liberal partners became more problematic. The two parties had cooperated on fighting conservatives and promoting political reform, but their success dissolved the glue that held their alliance together. When the SAP tried to turn the government's attention from political to economic reform, the left-Liberals balked and the coalition broke apart, throwing Sweden's political system into turmoil.[37] In subsequent years, the SAP remained the largest party in parliament but was unable to gain a majority on its own.[38] The non-socialist part of the Swedish political spectrum, meanwhile, remained split among liberal, farmer, and conservative groups, and the liberal movement in particular declined, making it difficult to form stable center or center-right governments. The result was a revolving door, with Sweden suffering through ten different governments between 1919 and 1932.

On the economic front, things did not look much better. Although Sweden had remained neutral, World War I and its aftermath hurt the country nonetheless. Wages, prices, and the cost of living tripled during the war,[39] and the depression that swept across the continent in its wake hit Sweden hard. Interest rate policy during the early 1920s accentuated the downswing and had especially devastating effects on unemployment and industrial

of democracy. On the background and makeup of this new party, see Leif Bureborgh, "Sverige och WWI," in *Från Palm till Palme*, 85–6; Sigurd Klockare, *Svenska Revolutionen, 1917–18* (Luleå: Föreningen Seskaröspelen, 1967), 22–35; Jan Lindhagen, *Socialdemokratiens Program: I Rörelsens Tid, 1890–1930* (Stockholm: Tiden, 1972), 51–66; idem, *Socialdemokratins Program: Bolsjevikstriden* (Stockholm: Tiden 1974); Tingsten, *Den Svenska Socialdemokratiens Ideutveckling*, Vol. 1, 229–41.

[36] One important sticking point was Branting's position in the new government. Branting had been ill and was not eager to take over any particular ministry, preferring instead to be a sort of overall advisor. Nils Eden (the Liberal leader) was adamant on having him in the government, however, and it was finally agreed that Branting should take over the finance ministry. This was a particularly inauspicious choice, and Branting resigned from this post before the government's term of office was due to expire.

[37] Sten Carlsson, "Borgare och Arbetare," in Sten Carlsson and Jerker Rosen, eds., *Den Svenska Historien: Vår Egen tid från 1920 till 1960-Talet* (Stockholm: Bonniers, 1968), 16–20; Gunnar Gerdner, *Det Svenska Regerinsproblemet, 1917–1920* (Stockholm: Almqvist and Wicksell, 1946), 34, 86, 122–39; Olle Nyman, *Parlamentarism i Sverige* (Stockholm: Bokförlaget Medborgarskolan, 1963), 24, 37.

[38] During the 1920s, the SAP did form minority governments, but these were short-lived and the party remained out of power during the later part of the decade.

[39] Svante Beckman with Hans Chr. Johansen, Francis Sejersted, and Henri Vartiainen, "Ekonomisk Politik och Teori i Norden under Mellankrigstiden," in Sven Nilsson, Karl-Gustag Hildebrand, and Bo Öhngren, eds., *Kriser och Krispolitik i Norden under Mellankrigstiden* (Uppsala: Almqvist and Wiksell, 1974), 28.

production.[40] By the mid-1920s, things were looking up, but unemployment levels remained high[41] and labor-market conflict was fierce.[42] As a government minister remarked during this time, "one lamentable fact is that during the last years our country has become the land of strikes, boycotts and lockouts. In this respect we have broken all world records."[43]

The 1920s, in short, were a difficult time for Sweden. As the decade wore on, growing numbers of Swedes felt betrayed by capitalism and disillusioned by the new democratic political system that seemed unable to produce either stable governments or forceful policy initiatives. The result was growing societal tensions, frustration, and alienation. In other parts of Europe, such conditions fed the rise of radical right-wing movements, as fascists and national socialists offered a vision of a harmonious national community and the promise of a government able and willing to deal creatively and forcefully with society's and the economy's problems. In Sweden, however, something very different occurred. Rather than the radical right, it was the social democratic left that emerged triumphant from the chaos of the 1920s and 1930s, although for similar reasons: The SAP offered the most creative response to the problems generated by capitalism and democracy and was therefore rewarded with the opportunity to reshape the political and economic environment in the years ahead.

The Transition to Social Democracy in Sweden

After the collapse of the SAP-Liberal government in 1920, the SAP, as a plurality rather than a majority party in a democratic system (the situation facing most of its counterparts in Western Europe), had two real options if it wanted to avoid impotence: It could abandon its commitment to democracy and take the insurrectionary route to power (the communist approach), or it could find some way to assemble a majority in favor of its program so it could win power through elections (the revisionist approach). As we saw in Chapter 5, many socialist parties proved unable to commit fully to either approach; the Swedes, on the other hand, forcefully chose the latter. During the 1920s, the party reached out to groups beyond the industrial proletariat. Embracing concepts such as "people" and "nation" that the radical right was exploiting successfully elsewhere, the SAP was able to claim the mantle of national unity and social solidarity during the chaos of the early 1930s.

[40] Svante Beckman et al., "Ekonomisk Politik och Teori i Norden under Mellankrigstiden," 31–2, and Erik Lundberg, *Ekonomiska Kriser för och nu* (Stockholm: Studieförbundet Näringsliv och Samhälle, 1983), 42.

[41] Beckman et al., "Ekonomisk Politik," 32; E. H. Phelps Brown with Margaret Browne, *A Century of Pay* (New York: St. Martin's Press, 1968), 209–19; Erik Lindahl et al., *National Income of Sweden* (Stockholm: P. A. Norstedt och Söner, 1937), 232–52.

[42] Per Holmberg, *Arbete och Löner i Sverige* (Stockholm: Raben och Sjögren, 1963), 62, 223.

[43] Quoted in Knut Bäckström, *Arbetarrörelsen i Sverige*, Vol. 2 (Stockholm: Arbetarkultur, 1963), 126.

The key figure in the party during this period was Per Albin Hansson, who became party chair in 1928.[44] His key contribution was to cast the SAP vision's of the socialist future as the *folkhemmet,* or "people's home." His most well-known explanation of the concept came in a speech he made in 1928, and it is worth quoting at length:

The basis of the home is community and togetherness. The good home does not recognize any privileged or neglected members, nor any favorite or stepchildren. In the good home there is equality, consideration, co-operation, and helpfulness. Applied to the great people's and citizens' home this would mean the breaking down of all the social and economic barriers that now separate citizens into the privileged and the neglected, into the rulers and the dependents, into the rich and the poor, the propertied and the impoverished, the plunderers and the plundered. Swedish society is not yet the people's home. There is a formal equality, equality of political rights, but from a social perspective, the class society remains and from an economic perspective the dictatorship of the few prevails.[45]

Interestingly, although the idea of Sweden as the "people's home" would become indelibly linked to Hansson and the SAP, it originated on the right. In fact, it was central to the critique of modern, capitalist, liberal society that in other parts of Europe formed part of the foundation upon which fascist and national socialist movements were built.

The first known political use of the term came in a 1909 talk by Alfred Petersson i Påboda, a leading figure in Sweden's farmers' movement. "Our society," Petersson asked, "what is it other than a *människohem* [home for mankind], a *folkhem* [great people's home]? It should provide work ... and sustenance for farmers as well as workers. ... [and provide] hope for the future. To strive to achieve this goal ... is not to build 'castles in the sky' but to satisfy the most basic human needs."[46] The idea was then taken up by the most influential Swedish nationalist of the day, Rudolf Kjellén. Like his counterparts elsewhere in Europe, Kjellén sought to re-create the national solidarity and sense of community lost in modern society. He was a particularly harsh critic of liberalism, seeing it as the root of almost all contemporary problems. For Kjellén, the main problem with liberalism was its focus on private and individual interests rather than those of the nation or state. No mere reactionary, he was also critical of old-fashioned conservatives, favoring instead the creation of a new movement

---

[44] On Hansson's background, see Anna Lisa Berkling, ed., *Från Fram till Folkhemmet: Per Albin Hansson som Tidningsman och Talare* (Stockholm: Metodica, 1982), and Timothy Tilton, *The Political Theory of Swedish Social Democracy* (Oxford, UK: Oxford University Press, 1990), 125–6.

[45] Berkling, *Från Fram till Folkhemmet*, 227–30, and Tilton, *The Political Theory of Swedish Social Democracy*, 126–7.

[46] Fredrika Lagergren, *På Andra Sidan Välfärdsstaten* (Stockholm: Stehag, 1999), 55–6. On the background of the use of the term *Folk,* see idem and Lars Trägårdh, "Varieties of Volkish Ideologies. Sweden and Germany, 1848–1933," in Bo Stråth, ed., *Language and the Construction of Class Identities* (Göteborg: Göteborg University Press, 1990), and Trägårdh, "The Concept of the People."

that could stimulate the national "rallying" or cooperation (*nationell samling*) that he believed was the prerequisite for the achievement of national greatness and expansion.[47] As he once put it, "In our country, key groups experience the social gulf between themselves and the powerful more than they do the gulf between [Swedes] and others. Correcting this abnormality is now the task of us all."[48] In order to achieve this goal, Kjellén advocated a wide range of social and political reforms that could help bring Sweden's workers and other alienated groups back into the national fold. He also favored joining nationalism with a new type of socialism, one that promoted "state power instead of individual rights; solidarity that was not limited to particular individuals or classes but encompassed an entire people (*folk*); the [primacy] of kinship (*samhörighet*) rather than freedom. [Current socialists] limit these ideas to the working class.... [Let's] extend these ideas to the entire people – imagine a national socialism rather than a class socialism!"[49]

Not surprisingly, Kjellén viewed the SAP as a critical stumbling block to the achievement of his goals, since it represented a powerful alternative to the liberalism and old-fashioned conservatism that he hoped to supplant. Indeed, it was precisely in a debate with Branting in 1912 (ostensibly over the changing international situation but really aiming at questioning the SAP's loyalty to the nation) that Kjellén offered up his vision of Swedish society as *folkhemmet*.[50] He used the term to conjure the image of a strong, solidaristic nation in contrast to the divided society that he believed was the logical corollary of mainstream socialism:

The Sweden we long for and work for – a Sweden made great by ... the subordination of classes to the ... whole, happy in the common loyalty to the land that fostered us ... this Sweden has not yet arrived. And it will not come before the false prophets have been revealed and vanquished. One thing is clear: only upon its own foundation can Sweden be turned into the fortunate people's home (*folkhemmet*) that it is meant to be. Only in nationalism is there salvation from the contemporary voices, which in the name of misguided internationalism try to attract broad groups of [our] people to disloyalty to [the nation and their most basic needs].[51]

During the interwar years, Sweden's nationalist movement took up Kjellén's attacks on mainstream socialism for fostering societal divisions and working against the national interest. Recognizing the resonance of such attacks – and pragmatic enough to appropriate a good idea when they heard it – SAP leaders decided to steal the nationalists' thunder. Hansson was determined to fight the

---

47 Lagergren, *På Andra Sidan Välfärdsstaten*, and Eric Wärenstam, *Fascism och Nazismen i Sverige* (Stockholm: Almqvist and Wicksell, 1970), 14–15.
48 Erik Åsard, *Makten, Medierna, och Myterna* (Stockholm: Carlssons, 1996), 156.
49 Ibid., 157. Also Mikkael Hallberg and Tomas Jonsson, *"Allmänanda och Självtukt": Per Albin Hanssons Ideologiska Förändring och Folkhemretorikens Framväxt* (Uppsala: Avdelningen för Retorik, 1993).
50 Ibid.
51 Åsard, *Makten, Medierna, och Myterna*, 162, and Lagergren, *På Andra Sidan*, 56.

charge that the SAP was antinational or disloyal to the nation in any way and by the early 1920s was groping toward the *folkhemmet* idea as the perfect way to recast the party's image and appeal. In 1921, he remarked: "We have often been called unpatriotic. But I say: there is no more patriotic party than [the SAP since] the most patriotic act is to create a land in which all feel at home."[52] Hansson argued that outflanking the right and creating a majority coalition required nothing more than continuing along the path the party had set out upon long ago. From its founding, he maintained, "the party had refused to isolate itself, declaring that it was prepared to cooperate with those groups 'which were seriously [committed] to protecting and expanding the people's rights.'"[53]

Hansson's concerns about the SAP's minority position, the threat from the right, and the general health of Swedish democracy only grew as the decade progressed. This was especially true after 1928, when the bourgeois parties banded together in electoral alliances and tried to portray the SAP as a stalking horse for communism. The election results that year revealed the potency of this strategy, as the SAP's share of the vote dropped somewhat and it lost fifteen seats in parliament.[54] The outcome helped convince Hansson that for the SAP to succeed, it needed to convince the broad masses that it represented neither a threat to their interests nor those of the nation more generally. At the party's 1928 congress, accordingly, Hansson urged his colleagues to recognize

...that the SAP currently faced a critical juncture, one whose mastery would require wisdom and unity. The progressive democratization policy, which began so promisingly ten years ago with the revision of the constitution and the institutionalization of the eight-hour day, has come to a dead end. Social reform work has stagnated and the bourgeois parties have mobilized a campaign of fear and hostility against [our policies]. The old left cooperation [between the SAP and left-Liberals] has...come apart and behind [recent] bourgeois electoral cooperation one senses a...politics that aims at conserving existing conditions and thwarting the continuation and completion of the democratization [of society]. Our country is currently suffering from a governance crisis [*regeringslösheten*] that is subverting faith in the parliamentary system and generating widespread political dissatisfaction.

The prerequisite for dealing with these problems, he argued, was for the SAP to commit itself to ending its minority status:

As the country's largest political party, it is our responsibility to try to bring about a better situation, to restore respect for parliamentary principles...and secure democracy...while at the same time mobilizing [greater support for our policies]. We

[52] Mikkael Hallberg and Tomas Jonsson, "Vägen till Folkhemmet," *Göteborgs Posten*, May 5, 1994.
[53] Alf W. Johansson, *Per Albin och Kriget* (Stockholm: Tiden, 1988), 27.
[54] Leif Lewin, *Planhushållningsdebatten* (Stockholm: Almqvist and Wicksell, 1967), 16–17; John Lindgren, *Från Per Götrek till Per Albin: Några Drag ur den Svenska Socialdemokratiens Historia* (Stockholm: Bonniers, 1936), 248–50; Åke Thulstrup, *Reformer och Försvar:konturerna av Sveriges historia, 1920–1938* (Stockholm: Bonniers, 1938), 101–2.

are already firmly rooted in different groups of working people in both city and country. We are now striving to expand the party further, to make it into a true, great people's party, that with the support of a majority of the people can realize the dream of the... *folkhemmet*. The precondition for such a gathering is a politics that takes into consideration the needs of different groups and without prejudice experiments with different ways of satisfying legitimate demands from wherever such demands may come.[55]

Hansson took pains to reassure his colleagues that the *folkhemmet* strategy was not only consistent with the party's history, but in fact the logical culmination of the SAP's long-standing emphasis on reform-based societal transformation and cross-class alliances. Furthermore, he saw no necessary trade-off between appealing to workers and appealing to other social groups, arguing that "[t]he expansion of the party to a people's party does not mean and must not mean a watering down of socialist demands."[56]

It was largely under Hansson's leadership, therefore, that in Sweden communitarian and even nationalist appeals became associated with the left. But he was hardly working alone. Throughout the 1920s, others within the SAP also began to consider new ways for the party to reach out to larger swaths of Swedish society and thus undercut the right's nationalist appeals. One such advocate, Rickard Lindström, even referred to what the SAP was striving to create as "national socialism."[57] The most important consequence of these efforts was the continuation of the SAP's outreach to farmers. A new agricultural program adopted in 1920 reiterated that workers and small farmers should stand together since both were exploited by the capitalist system. And while the SAP favored societal ownership of large landholdings and natural resources, it reaffirmed that it would otherwise leave private land ownership untouched.[58]

Later in the decade, under pressure from deteriorating conditions in the countryside, key figures in the party pushed for further outreach to farmers. At a meeting of the party executive in 1928, for example, leading activist Gustav Möller argued that "we must find ways to bring our party closer to a real people's party. We should carefully accumulate experience concerning the relationships and mentality of farmers. We should direct ourselves towards breaking down the distrust which rises up against us from many directions." The executive decided to arrange a conference to help rethink these issues,[59] and in the coming period a growing number of Swedish socialists began to argue that things like cash support payments to farmers might be a reasonable price

---

[55] *Protokoll från Sverges Socialdemokratiska Arbetarpartis Trettonde Kongress i Stockholm*, June 3–9, 1928, 7–8.

[56] Hansson, "Folk och Klass," 80.

[57] Lars Trägård, "Crisis and the Politics of National Community," in Nina Witoszek and Lars Trägård, eds., *Culture and Crisis: The Case of Germany and Sweden* (New York: Berghahn, 2003).

[58] Ibid., 129–30.

[59] "SAP Partistyrelsens Möte," September 25 (?), 1928, Arbetarrörelsens arkiv och bibliotek (AAB). See also Torsten Svensson, *Socialdemokratins Domins* (Uppsala: Skrifter Utgivna av Statsvetenskapliga Föreningen, 1994), 81ff.

to pay not only to avoid a catastrophe on the land, but also to buy the support of key rural groups for other SAP policies.[60]

When the Great Depression hit Sweden, the SAP was thus already armed with the *folkhemmet* idea and committed to a strategy that emphasized the party's desire to help not merely workers, but the "weak," the "oppressed," and "people" more generally – and had worked at least to neutralize the fears of some farmers and peasants, groups that provided critical support for fascist and national socialist movements in other parts of Europe. Alongside this, the party increasingly organized its appeals around the concept of *folk* rather than *klass* and proclaimed its desire to become a true "people's party."[61] This further helped undercut the right's monopoly on communitarian and nationalist appeals.

Alongside this political reorientation, an economic one had been brewing as well. As revisionist pleas to abandon the passivity of orthodox Marxism failed across Western Europe – leaving the right to pick up the mantle of economic activism and benefit from the widespread anticapitalist sentiment that accompanied the Depression – the SAP once again bucked the trend, and reaped great rewards from doing so.

The "Third Way"

As Branting put it at the party's 1920 congress, with the achievement of the SAP's central political demand (that is, full democratization), it was "only natural that economic questions should come to the fore."[62] Thus began a vigorous debate about the future of the SAP's economic agenda. A key figure in it was Gustav Möller, who argued that the basic problem with capitalist economies was their inability to provide for the needs of all citizens. Möller felt that the party had to figure out some way of enlarging the economic pie so that all could get larger slices of it.[63] "The point," he noted, "is not to present a specific socialization program, but . . . investigate what measures are needed to increase production. That is the only way genuinely to improve the social position of the great mass of people. Just as constitutional questions previously were the natural focus of our electoral platform, so now socialization questions must become fundamental."[64] Others agreed, and the notion that economic reforms had to be judged at least partly on their ability to contribute to growth became an increasingly important theme of SAP debates.

---

[60] An example of such rural groups is agricultural workers. See Gustav Möller, *Landsbygdens Fattiga Folk och Den Svenska Arbetarrörelsen* (Stockholm: Tiden, 1930), and idem, *Lantarbetare Vart Går Du?* (Stockholm: Tiden, 1932).

[61] Trägård, "Crisis and the Politics of National Community."

[62] *Protokoll från Sverges Socialdemokratiska Arbetarpartis Elfte Kongress i Stockholm*, February 8–20, 1920 (Stockholm: A-B Arbetarnas Tryckeri, 1920), 3.

[63] Gustav Möller, "Den Sociala Revolution," *Tiden*, 1918, 243. Also idem, *Revolution och Socialism* (Stockholm: Tiden, 1975).

[64] Möller, *Partistyrelsens Möte*, May 16, 1919, AAB.

In 1926, Nils Karleby, another key player, published *Socialism in the Face of Reality.*[65] It argued that a mix of idealism and pragmatism was the defining characteristic of the SAP, differentiating it, for example, from its more influential German counterpart:

[The SPD presents itself] as the true administrator of [Marx's] heritage. Not on a single point has this party been able to create something independent, not on a single point has this party been able to more than uncritically take up (and as a rule, in the process coarsen the content of) the Master's word. Those who have had to confront practical tasks and have tried to find guidelines for action within [the SPD] have been terribly disappointed.... [If, on the other hand, one studied the SAP's] practical work and intellectual life, one would come to the conclusion that this party ... was fundamentally superior to the German both in questions of theoretical clarity and independence and in questions of practical capabilities.[66]

Karleby urged socialists to view bourgeois property relations as involving not simple all-or-nothing possession, but a bundle of rights. If ownership were only the conglomeration of a number of individual rights, then these rights could be separated from one another and gradually made subject to societal influence. "This conception," he noted, "gives [socialists] a rationale for gradually stripping away the prerogatives of capitalists, like layers of an onion, until nothing remains."[67]

Karleby argued, on this basis, that any reforms that limited capitalists' control over societal and economic resources would be a step in the direction of a socialist society. The fact that any particular reform left some capitalist structures in place did not mean that society was not fundamentally changing: "All social reforms ... resulting in an increase in societal and a decrease in private control over property [represent a stage in] social transformation.... [Furthermore], social policies are, in fact, an overstepping of the boundaries of capitalism ... an actual shift in the position of workers in society and the production process. *This is the original [and uniquely] Social Democratic view.*"[68] He suggested, in short, that "[r]eforms do not merely prepare the transformation of society, they are the transformation itself."[69]

Karleby's book had an immense impact on the Swedish labor movement, providing for a generation of SAP leaders an intellectual foundation that reinforced the party's traditional emphasis on attaining incremental reform and working within existing structures to achieve long-term goals. Future

---

[65] Nils Karleby, *Socialism Inför Verkligheten* (Stockholm: Tiden 1976 [1926]). For an English summary of Karleby's work and influence, see Chapter 4 in Tilton, *The Political Theory of Swedish Social Democracy.*

[66] Karleby, *Socialism Inför Verkligheten*, VII.

[67] Tilton, *The Political Theory of Swedish Socialism*, 81. Also Rickard Lindström, "Bor Socialdemokratiska Partietsprogramm Revideras," *Tiden*, 1928, 154–5.

[68] Karleby, *Socialism Inför Verkligheten*, 83, 85. Emphasis in the original.

[69] Tilton, *The Political Theory of Swedish Socialism*, 82.

prime minister Tage Erlander recalled how the book was "read with a feeling of...emancipation.... [Karleby] taught us that socialization was [only] one instrument for socialist transformation among many others and by no means the most important."[70]

Alongside Karleby, others within the SAP were coming to accept that the best way of transforming society was not by the state taking over economic functions, but rather through partial state control or economic planning.[71] They argued that exerting influence, even indirect, over the production and distribution of resources could allow socialists to reach many of their goals without the potential inefficiency and loss of freedom that accompanied traditional nationalization strategies. The party thus placed increasing emphasis on developing reform strategies capable of giving workers greater control over their jobs and lives and figuring out how to use the power of the state to control the capitalist system.[72]

During the Depression, the SAP championed a number of innovative economic policies, including a form of "Keynesianism before Keynes." This success had many fathers,[73] but the most important of them was Ernst Wigforss, who served as an SAP parliamentarian from 1919 to 1953 and as finance minister from 1932 to 1949. Although not trained as an economist, Wigforss began studying the subject after the war in order to help the party devise new means for achieving traditional ends. He recognized that, "What is missing in our Swedish [socialist party], as well as in the large part of the international socialist movement is...clarity regarding the ways [to achieve our goals. If we could create this,] then we could also create the self-confidence that is necessary in order to succeed."[74]

Looking around for ways to liven up the SAP's economic policy agenda, Wigforss was drawn to some of the new economic ideas coming out of England. By studying the English radical Liberals, Wigforss became convinced that the way to conquer the economic crisis was through stimulating aggregate demand. In his 1928 article "Savings, Wastefulness and the Unemployed," he argued: "...if I want work for 100 people I do not need to put all 100 to

[70] Erlander in his introduction to Karleby, *Socialism Inför Verkligheten*, 21.

[71] On this point, see Lewin, *Planhushållningsdebatten*.

[72] Tage Erlander, "Introduction," in idem, *Ide och Handling: Till Ernst Wigforss på 80-års Dagen* (Stockholm: Tiden, 1960); Winton Higgins, "Ernst Wigforss: The Renewal of Social Democratic Theory and Practice," *Political Power and Social Theory*, 5, 1985; Ernst Jungen, "Socialpolitik och Socialism," *Tiden*, 1931; Paul Lindblom, *Ernst Wigforss: Socialistisk Idepolitiker* (Stockholm: Tiden, 1977); Timothy Tilton, "A Swedish Road to Socialism: Ernst Wigforss and the Ideological Foundations of Swedish Social Democracy," *American Political Science Review*, 73, 1979; Ernst Wigforss, "Personlig Frihet och Ekonomisk Organisation," in idem, *Vision och Verklighet* (Stockholm: Prisma, 1967); idem, "Socialism in Social-demokrati," *Tiden*, 4, 1949.

[73] Rickard Lindström and Gustav Möller have already been mentioned, and Gunnar Myrdal was another devotee of note.

[74] Ernst Wigforss, *Minnen II 1914–1932* (Stockholm: Tiden, 1951), 350 (the statement was made originally at the 1932 party congress). See also "Partistyrelsens Möte," May 12, 1929, AAB.

work.... [I]f I can get an unemployed tailor work, he will get the opportunity to buy himself new shoes and in this way an unemployed shoemaker will get work.... This crisis is characterized above all by a relationship which is called a vicious circle.... One can say the crisis drives itself once it begins, and it [will] be the same once recovery begins."[75]

Wigforss outlined his new approach to economic policy in a pamphlet called *The Economic Crisis.* He argued that the main problem with capitalism was that it allowed productive resources to go to waste, thereby artificially lowering demand and most people's standard of living. His solution was to put these resources back into use through state-sponsored work programs. He thus insisted that government-initiated work creation, and the rise in purchasing power it would encourage, was the only way to get the economy back on its feet. Such policies, he asserted, would free the economy and the great masses of Swedish society from the chains placed on them by capitalists. During the early 1930s, debates over economic policy grew heated since, as elsewhere in Europe, the increasing impact of the Depression made economic issues and unemployment in particular the focus of election campaigns. But whereas in Germany it was the Nazis who championed work creation and an active, state-led attack on the crisis (see Chapter 6), in Sweden it was the socialists who pushed that agenda.

During the 1930s, Wigforss and his fellow advocates of a "Keynesian" course shift undertook an intensive campaign to convince their party and then the electorate of the viability of these new economic ideas. For example, in 1930 Wigforss argued that

It cannot be logical that a society should say: "here we have unemployed workers, here we have access to capital, here we have raw materials – all that we need, but there is no way to put people to work to use the raw material, to put the capital to use in producing useful products." We socialists [cannot accept a system]... where during all times, even the best, up to 10% of the workers must be unemployed, and during worse times, even more. We refuse to admit that this is necessary and natural despite how much people come armed with theories stating that this must be so.[76]

The bourgeois parties, of course, rejected Wigforss's arguments and the SAP motion; but Wigforss's ideas also faced resistance within the SAP as well.

Wigforss continued his crusade for an economic course shift at the SAP's critical 1932 party congress. Here he was particularly eager to win over the minority of delegates who favored a renewed emphasis on more traditional "socialization" or nationalization measures. Hansson opened the meeting by urging the assembled delegates to recognize the significance of the party's

[75] Ernst Wigforss, "Sparen, Slösaren och den Arbetslöse," *Tiden,* 1928, 501, 504.

[76] Idem, quoted in *Andra Kammars Protokoll,* 47, 1930, 24. See also Karl-Gustav Landgren, *Den "Nya" Ekonomien I Sverige* (Stockholm: Almqvist and Wicksell, 1960), 66. For a fascinating parallel, compare this with Gregor Strasser's speech in the Reichstag, discussed in the previous chapter.

work-creation program and the need for positive action during such a dangerous time:

From its beginning... our party has fought the struggle for democracy..... and [has never given in to the] tendency... to denigrate democracy as only a "form" that when the time comes can be exchanged for something better.... [Furthermore], the best way to strengthen and protect the democratic order is to make sure that all citizens feel secure and comfortable under it.... The policy expressed in our 1930 program is designed to assist those hurt most by the current crisis and is nothing more than a continuation of our party's traditional line.... The number who have lost faith in the capitalist system and bourgeois politics is continually growing. Not just workers are suffering... but also farmers see their security threatened, and deep in the middle class a feeling of insecurity is growing, as well as the desire for a radical change. People are looking for leadership and it is our task to give it to them![77]

After this, many members of the leadership came forth to explain the rationale behind the crisis program. Rickard Sandler urged his colleagues to recognize that the SAP could not sit by and wait for the economic cycle to run its course: "We must abandon the view that we or our children will enjoy some kind of 'freebie' socialism, which ...'developments' will place in our hands."[78] The only way society would move in a socialist direction, Sandler argued, was if the party actively pushed it along this path. In response to Sandler's comments, many others spoke up to agree. Fredrick Ström, for example, argued that if the party did not offer an aggressive approach to the crisis soon, there was a danger that "the masses [would] travel the same path that they have done in many other countries – for example in Germany, where they are in the process of being divided up into Communists and Nazis."[79] And Möller argued that since the work-creation program would increase society's control over economic development, it was perfectly consistent with the goal of socialization, even if it might not appear so at first.[80]

Not surprisingly, Wigforss was the program's most pointed and skillful advocate. Like Möller, he stressed that it would enable the SAP to use the power of the state to organize and control the market and that it should be seen as part of an overall strategy of "economic planning." Such a strategy, he argued, would help the party reshape traditional political and economic patterns:

Against the... harmful line pursued by the bourgeois [parties]... I do not think it will suffice to put forth negative [arguments].... Instead we must put forth a positive socialist politics, which can convince people that we can create order just as well as the bourgeois [parties], while at the same time bringing about for the people an easing of their burdens.... If we at this congress can unite around a declaration which shows that we will bring these socialist ideas to [fruition], if we can unite around not just pushing them

[77] *Protokoll Från Sveriges Socialdemokratiska Arbetarpartis Fjortonde Kongress i Stockholm,* March 18–23, 1932 (Stockholm: Tiden 1932), 6–9.
[78] Ibid., 452.
[79] Ibid.
[80] Ibid., 448ff.

here at the congress but also out in our districts in an entirely new way than previously, take them up in discussions, convince all our fellow [citizens] that this is timely politics, then the congress... will have made a real contribution.[81]

After some further debate, the congress united behind the new program and joined it to a clear people's party approach, concluding with the following statement:

In the contemporary situation [the SAP sees] as [its] most important task working with all [its] energy to help all groups suffering from the unprovoked effects of the economic crisis.... The party does not aim to support and help [one] working class at the expense of the others. It does not differentiate in its work for the future between the industrial working class and the agricultural class or between workers of the hand and workers of the brain. The party begins from the premise that society... has the responsibility... to ensure care for those who are suffering, regardless of what group they belong to. Only such a policy, which aims at securing the best for all working people, is a 'people's policy' in the true meaning of the phrase.... Against the bourgeois majority's opposition to this democratic policy we appeal to Sweden's people.... We appeal for support around a policy that without consideration to group or class interest will strengthen and expand democracy to ensure the security of the common good.[82]

Still smarting from its 1928 electoral defeat,[83] the party paid close attention to the popular desperation that the crisis was creating and marshaled all its resources and its most popular figures in an all-out offensive stressing its own activism in contrast to others' passivity.[84] Commenting on the campaign afterward, Wigforss declared:

Again and again we were struck by the recognition that we... could link our explanations of the party's economic policy to the clear interest of the majority of the population and express viewpoints on the economy that, without theoretical detours, addressed themselves to everyday common sense.... Against this simple common sense, it was now our opponents who had to appeal to often incomprehensible theories about the economic context.[85]

Hansson's electoral brochure, meanwhile, declared that the SAP's "view of transformative work does not follow a fatalistic belief that everything will arrange itself.... On the contrary, our view... emphasizes daily politics – at every situation trying to do the most and best possible for the people. In the

[81] Ibid., 475.
[82] Ibid., 515–16. Also Per Albin Hansson, "Socialdemokraten Inför Valet" (SAP electoral brochure, 1932).
[83] Sven-Anders Söderpalm, "The Crisis Agreement and the Social Democratic Road to Power," in Koblik, ed., *Sweden's Development from Poverty to Affluence*.
[84] For information on the campaign and the party's propaganda efforts, see *Socialdemokratiska Partistyrelsens Berättelse för år 1932* (Stockholm: Arbetarnas Tryckeri 1932).
[85] Ernst Wigforss, *Skrifter i Urval, VIII: Minnen, 1914–1932* (Stockholm: Tiden, 1980), 54. Also Higgins, "Ernst Wigforss," 223. Steiger also notes how concerned Wigforss was with the political as well as the economic side of his program. *Studien zur Entstehung der neuen Wirtschaftslehre in Schweden* (Berlin: Duncker und Humboldt, 1971), 84.

current crisis [the SAP] interprets its... next task as working with all its energy for speedy and effective help for those... citizens who have had to suffer... as a result of the crisis."[86] The party's 1932 election manifesto combined Wigforss's economic strategy and Hansson's political strategy into a seamless whole:

We [see] a crisis developing which claims victims in all sectors of society.... In the middle of abundance... misery and unemployment prevails.... At the same time that [the SAP] strives for measures for lasting improvement of the situation [it also] devotes its efforts towards inducing the state to bring effective help to the innocent victims of the crisis. [The SAP] does not question... whether those who have become capitalism's victims... are industrial workers, farmers, agricultural laborers, forestry workers, store clerks, civil servants or intellectuals.[87]

And in the end, all the strategizing paid off: the SAP received its hitherto largest share of the vote, 41.7 percent.

Since it did not quite manage to get a majority, however, the SAP still needed at least one ally to form a government and put its program into effect. The party turned first to the Liberals, hoping to base a marriage on shared free-trade sentiment. But the Liberals balked at some provisions of the SAP's program.[88] So the party then turned its attention to the farmers, who like their counterparts elsewhere in Europe had been suffering through an agricultural crisis since the late 1920s. During the run-up to the election, the party had issued brochures and sent speakers to rural areas to explain the SAP's new thinking. And the SAP signaled its pro-farmer intentions by putting forward soon after the election a budget bill that included restrictions on foreign imports of milk and dairy products, as well as other regulations benefiting domestic farmers.[89]

Still, the farmers were uneasy about the idea of a socialist-agrarian alliance. So Hansson took it upon himself to intervene, trying to convince the farmers that the SAP could offer them more than the other bourgeois parties (who were themselves working fervently to cobble together a majority coalition of their own). In May 1934, these efforts paid off and the two groups agreed to their famous "cow-trade," with the SAP accepting protectionist measures for certain agricultural products and the farmers helping the party to true governing power.[90]

[86] Hansson, "Socialdemokraten Inför Valet."
[87] Reprinted in Håkansson, ed., *Svenska Valprogram*, Vol. 2.
[88] "Partistyrelsens Möte," September 21–3, 1932 (AAB). See also Gustav Möller, *Kampen Mot Arbetslösheten: Hur den Förts och Hur den Lyckats* (Stockholm: Tiden, 1936), 5; Clas-Erik Odhner, "Arbetare och Bönder Formar den Svenska Modellen," in Klaus Misgeld et al., *Socialdemokratins Samhälle*, 97–8; Göran Therborn, "Den Svenska Socialdemokratin Träder Fram," *Arkiv für Studier I Arbetarrörelsens Historia*, 27–8, 1984 8; Thulstrup, *Reformer och Försvar*, 137–8.
[89] Thullberg, "SAP och Jordbruksnäringen," 164.
[90] The party executive's vote on the agreement occurred at a leadership meeting (*Partistyrelsens möte*) on May 27, 1933. In addition, while the agrarians conceded the principle that state work programs should not be a form of poor relief but instead a form of productive unemployment compensation, the two parties had difficulty coming to an agreement on the exact level of wages

The formation of the SAP-led government and the subsequent passage of the SAP's crisis package ushered in a new era in Swedish politics. As with the similar policies instituted by the Nazis around the same time, it is probably true that the SAP's economic stimulus program really only accelerated an economic upswing caused by international trends beyond the government's control.[91] Still, the fact that the recovery coincided with the accession and activism of a new regime was political gold, and the SAP, like the NSDAP, mined it for all it was worth. As Gunnar Myrdal later mused, "if it can possibly be said that we had [at] this time unbelievably good luck, we can however be allowed to attribute to [ourselves] a certain skillfulness in exploiting our good fortune."[92]

Again like the NSDAP, the SAP stressed not only the success of its economic policies, but also its willingness to work for the good of the people as a whole. Hansson kept repeating that the SAP's crisis program was

...committed not to helping one working class at the cost of the others. The party and its policies don't differentiate between progress for the industrial proletariat and the agricultural classes or workers of the hand and brain. [Instead] the party's efforts are based on the conviction that society...has a special responsibility to ensure care for those most in need, regardless of who they are. This is 'people's politics' (*folkpolitik*) in the word's truest meaning.[93]

As the decade progressed, the SAP used the success of its crisis program to lock in its gains and push new ones. Politically, it worked to solidify its standing as a "people's party."[94] It also used the improvement in conditions to help stabilize Swedish democracy more generally. Party leaders recognized that in order to compete with the dictatorships in Italy, Germany, and elsewhere, democracies needed to show their citizens that they were capable of forceful and direct action. The party's 1934 May First Manifesto declared that "in the long term the most effective measure against the anti-democratic contagion is to conquer its foundation and that will happen through effective welfare policies that conquer the economic crisis, help those suffering from it and provide hope and confidence to the people."[95]

---

to be paid. The compromise that was reached set the "market" wages at the level of an unskilled worker. In addition, the SAP had to settle for somewhat less funding for its programs than it had hoped. The other negative aspect of the compromise for the SAP was that it did not contain a fixed agreement on unemployment insurance.

[91] Edgar H. Clark, "Swedish Unemployment Policy," (Ph.D. Dissertation, Harvard University, 1939), 222–3; Lars Jonung, "The Depression in Sweden and the United States," in Karl Brunner, ed., *The Great Depression Revisited* (Boston: Martins Nijhoff, 1981); Richard Lester, *Monetary Experiments* (Princeton, NJ: Princeton University Press, 1936), 225–82; Arthur Montgomery, *How Sweden Overcame the Depression* (Stockholm: Bonniers, 1938).

[92] Gunnar Myrdal, "Tiden och Partiet," *Tiden*, 1, 1945.

[93] Per Albin Hansson, "Den Stora Krisuppgörelsen," *Tiden*, 1934, 11–12.

[94] Idem, "Democratisk Samverkan Eller Nationell Splittring?" (Stockholm: Tiden, 1934), 3.

[95] "1934 Förstamajmanifest," reprinted in *Socialdemokratiska Partistyrelsens Berättelse för år 1934* (Stockholm: Tiden, 1935), 7.

On the economic front, meanwhile, the SAP used the success of its crisis program to argue for a new tranche of economic and social reforms. The party maintained that Sweden's experience during the Depression proved that the state could be a positive force in the economy, and that its powers should be expanded in order to help prevent future crises and protect the welfare of all citizens.[96] The party's 1936 election manifesto, for example, declared that "the experience of the last years has shown that state power can and must assist in ensuring the... security of the people. The terrible crisis has once again revealed private enterprise's inability to alone care for the livelihood of the people.... The only way to ensure that there is not a repeat of the crisis is for private enterprise and the state's representatives to join together and through general oversight and management, achieve a better control over economic life."[97]

The SAP fought the 1936 elections under the slogan "We Conquered the Crisis," trumpeting its previous successes and promising that it would continue to use its political power to tame and direct the capitalist system. As one observer put it, "At no earlier point in [Swedish history] had a party so systematically grounded its electoral propaganda... on what had already been accomplished and on [an argument] that the politics of the future should go further on [the same] path."[98] The strategy paid off handsomely, with the party winning a full 46 percent of the vote and easily forming a second SAP-led government. Social democratic hegemony in Sweden had begun.

Epilogue

In the subsequent years, the SAP left orthodox Marxism even further behind, implementing a bold political and economic program that broke new ground. In the political realm, the SAP appealed to "the people," communal solidarity, and the collective good, identifying itself as the protector of the Swedish nation – an approach that, in an era of dislocation and disorientation, proved more attractive than the divisive class struggle perspective of orthodox Marxists or the individualism of classical liberals. As Wigforss put it in 1940:

One hears so much talk of the unity that now characterizes the Swedish people.... One should not neglect to note that this is connected with the fact that the economic situation for the broad masses of our citizens has improved. It is also connected with the overall political program that [we have] driven over the past years that has aimed at creating work, improving housing and lightening the burdens of the society's worst-off. It is not

---

[96] See the 1936 election manifesto in Håkansson, ed., *Svenska Valprogram*, Vol. 2, and also Valter Åmen, "Vad lär oss Tyskland," *Tiden*, 25, 1933.

[97] "Partistyrelsens Manifest to 1936 Andrakammarvalen," in *Socialdemokratiska Partistyrelsens Berättelse för år 1936*, 11.

[98] Tingsten, *Den Svenska Socialdemokratiens Ideutveckling*, Vol. 1, 377.

least these measures which have created the foundations of the national solidarity that we are currently so pleased about.[99]

Economically, the party sought out a "third way" based on state intervention – a course which tapped the material wealth and technological advances generated by capitalism but checked the market's "degenerative" and anarchic effects. Hansson declared the SAP's ideal to be

...a society of free and equal individuals in democratic cooperation, where common resources are used to ensure security and well being for all. We Social Democrats do not accept a social order with political, cultural and economic privileges or one where the privately-owned means of production are a way for the few to keep the masses of people in dependence.... [Yet] we have no desire to interfere [economically] in such a way that will hold back or injure production. Our main interest is in getting the most out of our nation's productive capacity...so that we can [ensure] a better distribution of welfare.... Sweden belongs to us all, it has resources for all and everything should be done for the good [of the whole]. That has always been the starting point of our work. We have only to continue along the same path.[100]

In short, although by the early 1930s revisionists across Europe had succeeded in fully exchanging the remnants of orthodox Marxism for a new, truly social democratic ideology and strategy, it was only in Scandinavia, and particularly in Sweden, that a unified party embraced the new approach wholeheartedly. This is why one must turn to Sweden to observe the full dimensions, and potential, of the new and truly social democratic alternative. Not only did the transition to social democracy help the SAP outflank the right and place Swedish democracy on a firmer footing during the interwar years, it also laid the foundation for the distinctive political and economic order for which the country would become famous during the postwar years.

---

[99] Quoted in Karl Molin, *Försvaret, Folkhemmet och Demokratin: Socialdemocratisk Riks-dagspolitik, 1939–1945* (Stockholm: Allmänna Förlaget, 1974), 32.

[100] Per Albin Hansson, *Socialdemokratiska Idéer och Framtidsutsikter* (Frihets, 1944?), 10, 12, 23.

8

The Postwar Era

World War II was the culmination of the most violent and destructive period in modern European history. Over 30 million people died from the fighting and the Nazis' crimes.[1] Motorized armies and strategic bombing flattened the continent's urban and industrial areas, and postwar inflation, migration, and shortages further ravaged already devastated economies. As the 1947 Report of the Committee of European Economic Cooperation declared, "The scale of destruction and disruption of European economic life was far greater than that which Europe had experienced in the First World War. . . . The devastated countries had to start again almost from the beginning."[2]

And indeed 1945 was a new beginning, as Europe struggled to rebuild economically while trying to head off the political and social instability that had led to ruin in the past. There was a widespread conviction that unchecked capitalism could threaten goals in all three spheres. One observer notes that, "If the war had shattered anything, it was the already damaged belief that capitalism, if left to its own devices, would be able to generate the 'good society.'"[3] The political chaos and social dislocation of the 1930s were held to have been caused by the Great Depression, which in turn was held to have been the consequence of unregulated markets – and so actors from across the European political spectrum agreed on the inadvisability of taking that path again.

The war itself, moreover, profoundly changed many people's views of the appropriate roles of states and markets:

All European governments assumed responsibility for managing the economy and controlling society during the war, but after the war they did not withdraw from economic and social life as most attempted to do after the First World War. . . . The experience of

---

[1] In addition, millions more died in Stalin's collectivization of agriculture, mass purges, and "deportations of enemy nations" at around this time.

[2] Reprinted in Shepard B. Clough, Thomas Moodie, and Carol Moodie, eds., *Economic History of Europe: Twentieth Century* (New York: Harper and Row, 1968), 328.

[3] Donald Sassoon, *One Hundred Years of Socialism* (New York: Free Press, 1996), 84.

the war [seemed to] demonstrate conclusively that, contrary to the received wisdom of the 1920s and 1930s, central governments could in fact control economic development effectively.[4]

Such beliefs were by no means limited to the left. The 1947 program of the German Christian Democrats, for example, declared that, "The new structure of the German economy must start from the realization that the period of uncurtailed rule by private capitalism is over." In France, meanwhile, the Catholic Mouvement Republican Populaire declared in its first manifesto in 1944 that it supported a "revolution" to create a state "liberated from the power of those who possess wealth."[5]

After 1945, therefore, Western European nations started to construct a new order, one that could ensure economic growth while at the same time protecting societies from capitalism's destructive consequences.[6] This order decisively broke with the relationship among state, economy, and society that existed before the war. No longer would states be limited to ensuring that markets could grow and flourish; no longer were economic interests to be given the widest possible leeway. Instead, after 1945 the state became generally understood to be the guardian of society rather than the economy, and economic imperatives were often forced to take a back seat to social ones.

This chapter will draw on the story told in the previous chapters to situate the postwar order historically and intellectually. It will not provide another analysis of the genesis and functioning of this order's constituent elements (for example, Keynesianism, the welfare state, and planning); many excellent examples of such analyses exist and this chapter will draw on them.[7] Instead, it will show how the postwar order is best understood against the background of debates and developments that had occurred during the previous decades. It will also argue that its nature and significance have been fundamentally misinterpreted.

Scholars have long recognized that the postwar order represented a clear repudiation of the radical left's hopes for an end to capitalism.[8] What many have failed to appreciate, however, is just how much this order represented a refutation of traditional liberalism as well. Based on a belief that political forces should control economic ones and determined to "re-create through political

[4] Frank Tipton and Robert Aldrich, *An Economic and Social History of Europe from 1939 to the Present* (Baltimore, MD: Johns Hopkins University Press, 1987), 6, 48.
[5] Sassoon, *One Hundred Years of Socialism*, 140.
[6] Philip Armstron, Andrew Glyn, and John Harrison, *Capitalism Since 1945* (New York: Basil Blackwell, 1991); Geoffrey Denton, Murray Forsyth, and Malcom Maclennan, *Economic Planning and Policies in Britain, France and Germany* (London: George Allen and Unwin, 1968); Stephen Marglin and Juliet Schor, eds., *The Golden Age of Capitalism* (New York: Clarendon Press, 1991).
[7] See notes 18–20 in Chapter 1.
[8] Charles Maier, "The Two Postwar Eras," *American Historical Review*, 86, 2, April 1981, and Clas Offe, "Comparative Party Democracy and the Welfare State," *Policy Sciences*, 15, 1983.

means the social unity which modernization has destroyed,"[9] the postwar order fundamentally broke with classical liberalism's theory and long-standing practice. The most common term used to describe the postwar system, John Ruggie's concept of "embedded liberalism,"[10] is thus a misnomer. If liberalism can be stretched to encompass an order that saw unchecked markets as dangerous, that had public interests trump private prerogatives, and that granted states the right to intervene in the economy to protect the common interest and nurture social solidarity, then the term is so elastic as to be nearly useless. In fact, rather than a modified and updated form of liberalism, what spread like wildfire after the war was really something quite different: social democracy.

The Postwar Order

Sixty years on, it is easy to forget how profound a break with the past the postwar order was. Even Americans, least affected by the war and most committed to the restoration of a global liberal free-trade order, recognized that there was no going back to the status quo ante. Reflecting this, in his opening speech to the Bretton Woods conference, U.S. Treasury Secretary Henry Morgenthau noted, "All of us have seen the great economic tragedy of our time. We saw the worldwide depression of the 1930s.... We saw bewilderment and bitterness become the breeders of fascism and finally of war." To prevent a recurrence of this phenomenon, Morgenthau argued, national governments would have to be able to do more to protect people from capitalism's "malign effects."[11] And so instead of a return to the gold standard as after World War I (a system in which the need to maintain the balance of payments severely curtailed state autonomy), after World War II, "no country was expected to suffer severe unemployment or inflation to protect its balance of payments. Henceforth, the balance of payments would become subject to national policy objectives and not dictated by international conditions."[12]

At the domestic level, the shift was even more striking. Throughout Western Europe, states explicitly committed themselves to managing capitalism and protecting society from its most destructive effects. In essence, the liberal understanding of the relationship among state, economy, and society was abandoned. A "large area of economic action [came to] depend on political, not market processes,"[13] and "the 'economic' and the 'social' were no longer [to be] distinct

---

[9] Samuel Huntington, *Political Order in Changing Societies* (New Haven, CT: Yale University Press, 1968), 73.

[10] John Gerard Ruggie, "International Regimes, Transactions, and Change: Embedded Liberalism in the Postwar Economic Order," *International Organization*, 36, 2, Spring 1982, 386.

[11] G. John Ikenberry, "A World Economy Restored," *International Organization*, 46, 1, Winter 1992. Also idem. "Workers and the World Economy," *Foreign Affairs*, May/June 1996.

[12] Massimoi De Angelis, *Keynesianism, Social Conflict and Political Economy* (New York: St. Martin's Press, 2000), 72.

[13] Robert Skidelsky, "Introduction," in idem, ed., *The End of the Keynesian Era* (London: Macmillan, 1977), vii.

but [instead] became totally interwoven."[14] The two most often noted manifestations of these changes were Keynesianism and the welfare state.

Keynesianism's significance lay in its rejection of the view that markets operated best when left to themselves and its call instead for substantial state intervention in economic affairs. As one observer put it:

>...for classical liberal economists of the nineteenth century, the artifical notion of eco-
> nomic policy had to be meaningless since all adjustments were held to be governed
> by "natural" laws of equilibrium. Their only preoccuption was to keep the state from
> abusing its institutional role....In the end, economists of Marxist allegiance essentially
> believed the likewise, crises in capitalism were inevitable, and only a change of regime –
> the progression to socialism – could modify this given.[15]

John Maynard Keynes rejected such views and argued that state action would
often be necessary to help avoid economic crises that could threaten both
democracy and the capitalist system itself. Having experienced the rise of the
Soviet Union and the Great Depression, Keynes understood that markets were
socially and politically dangerous. As his biographer has noted, "Keynes was
quite consciously seeking an alternative to dictatorship...a programme on
which to fight back against fascism and communism."[16] He hoped to undercut the appeal of left-wing calls for capitalism's destruction by showing how it
could be rescued from its flaws, and hoped to undercut the appeal of fascism
by reconciling democracy with increased state management of the economy.

With regard to the former, Keynes provided arguments for those who wanted
to ensure prosperity while avoiding extensive nationalizations and a command
economy. In particular, he showed how the state could use fiscal and monetary
policy to influence demand, thus stabilizing profits and employment without
actually socializing ownership itself.[17]

But Keynes believed that a more active state and a more "managed" capitalist system were necessary for political reasons as well. He was aware of the
appeal of fascism's economic stance and the widespread view that capitalism
and democracy were incompatible. As one analyst of Keynesianism has noted,
fascism "promised an anti-socialist solution to the crisis of capitalism...[and]
offered a political critique of liberalism's ineffectiveness in the face of [that]
crisis."[18] Keynes, by offering a system that "held out the prospect that the
state could reconcile the private ownership of the means of production with
democratic management of the economy,"[19] showed that there was another,
non-totalitarian solution to the problem.

[14] Pierre Rosanvallon, "The Development of Keynesianism in France," in Peter Hall, ed., *The Political Power of Economic Ideas* (Princeton, NJ: Princeton University Press, 1989), 188.
[15] Ibid.
[16] Skidelsky, "The Political Meaning of Keynesianism," in ibid., 35–6.
[17] Stuart Holland, "Keynes and the Socialists," in Skidelsky, ed., *The End of the Keynesian Era*, 68.
[18] Skidelsky, "The Political Meaning of Keynesianism," 35–6.
[19] Adam Przeworski, *Capitalism and Social Democracy* (Cambridge, MA: Cambridge University Press, 1985), 207.

Like Keynesianism, the welfare state helped transform the relationship among states, markets, and societies during the postwar era. It represented a repudiation of the view that a "good" state was one that interfered in the economy and society least, and embodied instead a view of the state as the guardian of society and promotor of social unity. As C. A. R. Crosland noted, after 1945, "it was increasingly regarded as a proper function and indeed obligation of Government to ward off distress and strain not only among the poor but almost all classes of society."[20]

But welfare states were important not only because they altered the relationship among state, market, and society; they also transformed the meaning or nature of society itself. In particular, welfare states gave renewed importance and significance to membership in a national community, since they both required and fostered a sense of kinship and solidarity among citizens: They could be sustained only if individuals believed that ensuring a basic level of well-being for all was a worthy goal. With the development of full-fledged welfare states, governments became committed to doing, on a massive, impersonal scale, what families and local communities had done in pre-capitalist times – namely, take care of people when they couldn't help themselves. Welfare states thus marked a significant break with a liberal *gesellschaft* and a move toward a more communitarian *gemeinschaft*: No longer was one's subsistence dependent on his or her position in the marketplace; instead, it came to be "guaranteed as a moral right of membership in a human community."[21] This "delinking… of social support from market position" also went a long way toward eliminating "the economic whip of hunger," and "made political resources rather than markets the main basis for the distribution of resources."[22] Postwar welfare states worked, in other words, to significantly decommodify labor.[23] Decommodification, in turn, shifted the balance of power in society. Guaranteed a certain level of welfare, workers became less deferential to employers and found it less necessary to hold on to particular jobs.[24]

But the break with liberalism and the move toward social democracy did not end there. Alongside a general acceptance of Keynesianism and an expansion of the welfare state, European nations also developed a variety of other policies that used the power of the state to manage capitalism and protect society from its most destructive effects.

---

[20] C. A. R. Crosland, *The Future of Socialism* (London: Fletcher and Son, 1967), 98.

[21] Karl Polanyi, *The Great Transformation* (Boston: Beacon Press, 1944), and also T. H. Marshall, "Citizenship and Social Class," in idem, *Class, Citizenship and Social Development* (New York: Anchor Books, 1965), 86ff.

[22] Walter Korpi, "Power, Politics, and State Autonomy in the Development of Social Citizenship," *American Sociological Review*, 43, June 1989, 313.

[23] Although the extent of this decommodification varied. Gøsta Esping-Andersen, *Three Worlds of Welfare Capitalism* (Princeton, NJ: Princeton University Press, 1990), and John Huber and Evelyn Stephens, *Development and Crisis of the Welfare State* (Chicago: University of Chicago Press, 2001).

[24] E.g., Michal Kalecki, "Political Aspects of Full Employment," in idem, *The Last Phase in the Development of Capitalism* (New York: Monthly Review, 1972).

In France, for example, during the war, members of the Resistance became convinced that the country had to transcend "liberalism, which had brought egotism, disorder and backwardness under the republic." They envisioned a postwar republic *"pure et dure"* alongside "an organized, yet free, economy dedicated to human dignity, economic equality, growth and the national interest."[25] In practice, this meant a state willing and able to control economic resources and actors. The most straightforward manifestation of this tendency was nationalization. Thus Charles De Gaulle argued that France's postwar health and prosperity depended on ensuring that "the main sources of common wealth are worked and managed not for the profit of a few individuals, but for the benefit of all."[26]

The most substantively important policy undertaken by the French state to help steer economic development, however, was not nationalization but rather planning. Planning in postwar France was associated above all with Jean Monnet (better known for his role in European integration). Like other members of the French elite, Monnet believed that ensuring the country's health and prosperity required greater state influence over the economy. But unlike some of his colleagues, he thought this influence should not be too direct or heavy-handed. He argued instead that the state could and should intervene indirectly, by offering incentives for certain types of behavior and activity rather than by trying to command or force them. The system that he helped design reflected these beliefs and came to be known as "indicative" planning; it involved the state's putting forward broad goals for the economy and then using a variety of tools to induce economic actors to comply with or contribute to them. The state manipulated the credit supply, for example, to get businesses to undertake certain types of investments and projects rather than others.[27]

The distinctive feature of the postwar Italian economy, in contrast, was a large state sector. As one analyst noted, "Italy is the most extreme example ... of public sector enterprise and intervention in the whole of Europe."[28] Indeed, during the 1950s and 1960s, the state controlled approximately 20–30 percent of Italian industry. The largest public sector corporations, ENI and IRI, were responsible for over one-fifth of all capital investment in manufacturing, industry, transport, and communications. The energy giant ENI alone controlled over two hundred concerns in areas ranging from oil to rubber and gas stations to motels, while IRI was Italy's largest commercial

---

[25] Richard Kuisel, *Capitalism and the State in Modern France* (New York: Cambridge University Press, 1981), 188.

[26] Andrew Shennan, *Rethinking France: Plans for Renewal 1940–1946* (Oxford, UK: Clarendon Press, 1989), 251.

[27] Denton et al., *Economic Planning and Policies in Britain, France and Germany*, 164; Andrew Shonfield, *Modern Capitalism* (New York: Oxford University Press, 1969); John Zysman and Stephen Cohen, *Modern Capitalist Planning: The French Model* (Berkeley, CA: University of California Press, 1977).

[28] Shonfield, *Modern Capitalism*, 177.

enterprise.[29] The large Italian state sector was viewed as part of a broader strategy for using the power of the state to ensure economic growth as well as general social health and well-being. This new vision of the correct relationship among economy, society, and the state was enshrined in Italy's postwar constitution, which declared the country a democratic republic "founded on labor," and promised that all "economic and social obstacles" to workers' advancement would be demolished. Recognizing the primacy of certain societal goals and needs, the constitution also refrained from according private property the status of "absolute right...instead emphasiz[ing] its social obligations and limitations." And it promised Italian citizens a whole range of new benefits, including the right to employment, health care, and education.[30]

In Germany, the picture was more complicated. Here a commitment to economic liberalism and a desire to break with the Nazis' extreme statism were central features of the postwar economic order. Indeed, the self-professed "neo" or "ordo" liberals who provided the intellectual foundations and much of the leadership for postwar reconstruction "were firm believers in...market forces."[31] Yet even here the new political reality intruded, forcing the state to intervene in the economy in myriad ways and commit itself to social protection. In particular, the German state practiced what some scholars have referred to as "discriminatory intervention," whereby resources were used to help promote and protect favored "national champions." By the 1950s, for example, the German state was already absorbing about 35 percent of the gross domestic product (GDP) in taxes, which it used to influence aggregate demand as well as to "discriminate actively between one industry, and one purpose, and another."[32] The state also played a large role in steering savings and investment, with perhaps "half the capital formation in the Federal Republic...directly or indirectly financed by public means."[33] And German industry was highly organized, with its *Verbände* (industrial associations) playing an "important public role, as guardians of the long-term interests of the nation's industries."[34]

Although not nearly as extensive as the state sector in Italy, in postwar Germany, "about one-third of the output of iron ore, one-fourth of coal, more than two-thirds of aluminum production, one-fourth of shipbuilding and, until 1960, about half of automobile production,"[35] were under the government's

[29] Walter Laqueur, *Europe Since Hitler* (Baltimore, MD: Penguin, 1973), 223; Sima Lieberman, *The Growth of European Mixed Economies, 1945–70* (New York: John Wiley and Sons, 1977) 262; Shonfield, *Modern Capitalism*, 184.

[30] Spencer M. Di Scala, *Italy: From Revolution to Republic* (Boulder, CO: Westview Press, 1998), 283, and Harold James, *Europe Reborn* (New York: Longman, 2003), 257.

[31] Laqueur, *Europe Since Hitler*, 217.

[32] Shonfield, *Modern Capitalism*, 282.

[33] Denton et al., *Economic Planning and Policies*, 223, and Gustav Stolper, *The German Economy 1870 to the Present* (London: Weidenfeld and Nicolson, 1967), 277.

[34] Shonfield, *Modern Capitalism*, 245.

[35] Stolper, *The German Economy*, 277.

control. And the German state's commitment to protecting society from the kind of economic and social turmoil that had contributed to the rise of Hitler was unmistakable. Alongside traditional remedies like the welfare state, Germany also developed a number of innovative policies, such as codetermination, which gave workers the ability to oversee, and in some cases even help direct, business decisions and activity. This system proved very successful, and for decades helped workers and management view each other as "social partners" rather than adversaries. Even in Germany, in short, the postwar political economy was characterized by a fairly activist and interventionist state, a firm commitment to protecting society from capitalism's most disruptive effects, and a belief in the need to foster social unity.

Not surprisingly, the most dramatic postwar transformation in the relationship among state, market, and society came in Sweden. As one observer noted, in Sweden there was a widespread recognition that

...political power [had become] separated from economic power.... Public power [could therefore now be used]...to encroach upon the power of capital. Through economic policies, the business cycles would be evened out. The level of employment, of crucial importance for the welfare of the working class, would be kept high through political means, and thereby partly withdrawn from the control of capital. State intervention would be used to induce structural changes in the economy in order to increase its efficiency. Public power, above all, would be used to affect the distribution of the results of production. Through fiscal and social policies a more equal distribution of income would be achieved. Political power, founded in control of organizations would be pitched against economic power.[36]

In essence, the postwar Swedish state was charged with two tasks: the promotion of growth and the protection of society.[37] These goals were seen not as contradictory but as complementary. As Gunnar Adler-Karlsson, a well-known theorist of the postwar Swedish order, noted:

All the parties of the economic process have realized that the most important economic task is to make the national cake grow bigger and bigger, because then everyone can satisfy his demanding stomach with a greater piece of that common cake. When instead, there is strong fighting between the classes in that society, we believe that the cake will often crumble or be destroyed in the fight, and because of this everyone loses.[38]

To achieve these goals, the Swedish state employed a wide range of tools including planning, the manipulation of investment funds and fiscal policy, and the encouragement of cooperation between labor market partners. (Interestingly, one tool that the Swedish state did not use much was nationalization, which was viewed as both economically unnecessary and politically unwise.)

---

[36] Walter Korpi, *The Working Class in Welfare Capitalism* (London: Routledge and Kegan Paul, 1978), 82.
[37] Lars Trädgårdh, "Statist Individualism: On the Culturality of the Nordic Welfare State," in Bo Stråth, ed., *The Cultural Construction of Norden* (Gothenburg, Sweden: Gothenburg University, 1990), 261, and also Korpi, *The Working Class in Welfare Capitalism*, esp. 48–9.
[38] Gunnar Adler-Karlsson, *Functional Socialism* (Stockholm: Prisma, 1967), 18.

But perhaps the two most distinctive features of Sweden's postwar political economy were the Rehn-Meidner model and the welfare state, both of which were distinguished by their promotion of decommodification and social solidarity.

The Rehn-Meidner model featured a centralized system of wage bargaining that set wages at what was seen as a "just" level (which in practice seems to have meant ensuring "equal pay for equal work," consistently rising incomes, and improvements for the worse-off to reduce inequality). Wages would be set "too high" for some firms (those that were inefficient or uncompetitive) and "too low" for others (the highly productive and competitive). Firms that fell in the former category faced the choice of either improving or going out of business, while those in the latter would increase their profitability (since the wages they paid would be less than they could otherwise afford). To compensate workers who lost their jobs, the state committed itself to retraining and relocating them for new ones. The system aimed to do a number of seemingly contradictory things at once: promote rising business efficiency and productivity while generating a more equal wage structure and increasing social solidarity. In addition, the Rehn-Meidner model also promoted decommodification, since it attenuated "the relationship between the marginal productivity of individual firms and their wage rates." It also helped eliminate "unemployment ('the reserve army of labour')... as a disciplinary stick" (since the government committed itself to doing whatever was necessary to help the unemployed obtain new jobs). And finally, by encouraging labor market participation, it helped prevent "a fiscal overload on social policy programmes such as unemployment insurance, and thus ensured that social benefits based on the de-commodification principle were rendered compatible with capital accumulation."[39]

In comparison to its European counterparts, the Swedish welfare state was larger and more generous as well as distinguished by its explicit promotion of both decommodification and social solidarity. As one of its most perspicacious observers noted, the Swedish welfare state "both establish[ed] universal solidarity and marginalize[d] the market as the principal agent of distribution and the chief determinant of people's life chances."[40] It did this by providing a range of programs and benefits that dwarfed most other welfare states and by "socializing" (that is, bringing into the public sector) a broad spectrum of services and resources (such as health care, education, and child care) that in many other countries remained at least partially the provenance of the market, families, or civil society organizations.[41] The Swedish welfare state was more universalistic than most others and did a much better job of promoting

[39] Magnus Ryner, *Capital Restructuring, Globalisation and the Third Way* (London: Routledge, 2002), 85.
[40] Gøsta Esping-Andersen, *Politics Against Markets* (Princeton, NJ: Princeton University Press, 1985), 245.
[41] Trädgårdh, "Statist Individualism," 263.

socioeconomic equality.[42] This, along with an explicit attempt to design policies that could appeal to a broad cross-section of the population, helped promote social solidarity and unprecedented cross-class support.[43]

For these and other reasons, Sweden has long been recognized as a social democratic showplace. Yet even if other countries did not go as far along the same path, a close look shows that their postwar orders were far more social democratic than classically liberal. In France, for example, even though many scholars refer to indicative planning as "neoliberal"[44] because it differed greatly from Soviet-style command planning and left capitalism and markets intact, it actually represented a dramatic break with liberalism. Both intellectually and practically, it was a descendant of the 1930s *planisme* (put forward by social democratic revisionists following Hendrik de Man) as well as the Vichy regime's efforts to "steer between the extremes of prewar liberalism and wartime dirigisme."[45] Furthermore, planning was just one part of a larger strategy employed in France during the postwar years that was decidedly unliberal. Its goal was to temper capitalism by "public economic management and heightened self-organization among private interests,"[46] and it was overseen by a state whose role had changed both quantatively and qualitatively from the prewar period. "After 1945 . . . the state provided the principal cement holding together a scattered and spent France. . . . The activism of the state was no longer viewed simply as a temporary and reversible intervention, as it had been after World War I; it became part of a long term perspective."[47] As across much of Europe, in other words, during the postwar period a central role of the French state became guarding and promoting the "collective good" and social unity.[48]

Something similar could be said of Italy, although here the postwar order's intellectual and practical roots in the Fascist period were even clearer. The large Italian state sector discussed previously was essentially the product of Mussolini's nationalizations, and postwar social policy, tax policy, bureaucratic structures, and business relations were all crucially shaped by developments during the Fascist era as well. Most importantly, perhaps, the postwar assumption that markets needed to be controlled and that the state was responsible for protecting society was a mainstay of Fascist propaganda (as well as the work of social democratic revisionists such as Carlo Rosselli).

---

[42] For example, Huber and Stephens find that Sweden has the lowest posttax transfer Gini (the most common measure of inequality) and the highest level of redistribution resulting from taxes and transfers. See *Development and Crisis of the Welfare State*, 103.

[43] Esping-Andersen, *Politics Against Markets*, and idem, *The Three Worlds of Welfare Capitalism*.

[44] E.g., Kuisel, *Capitalism and the State*.

[45] Ibid., 155. As one observer put it, "the architects of postwar innovation could not always avoid building upon Vichy legislation or legislating in parallel directions. For good or evil, the Vichy regime had made indelible marks on French life." Robert O. Paxton, *Vichy France: Old Guard and New Order, 1940–1944* (New York: Columbia Press, 1972), 331.

[46] Ibid., 248–9.

[47] Rosanvallon, "The Development of Keynesianism in France," 186–7.

[48] Shonfield, *Modern Capitalism*, 133ff.

Even in Germany, where the self-professed liberals who guided reconstruction were committed to a firm break with the past and markets, competition, and free enterprise, the postwar political economy drew much more on National Socialist themes and policy "innovations" than many have recognized. The German state's tendency toward "discriminatory intervention," for example, was both a clear violation of liberal teachings and a carryover from the Nazi economy.[49] It was during Hitler's reign that the state began identifying "national priorities" and developed the tools to control private enterprise and direct economic development. And the cultivation of "national champions" such as Volkswagen, the hierarchical and organized nature of German industry, and the special role played by the *Verbände* were all at least partially legacies of the Nazi era.[50]

Beyond policies and institutions, meanwhile, many of the central principles or values undergirding the postwar German political economy also represented a significant break with classical liberalism. The architects of the social market economy were not only committed to social protection, but also argued that "higher values" should guide economic development and that unregulated markets and laissez-faire policies were socially dangerous and politically irresponsible. Even such supposed "neoliberals" as Walter Eucken, for example, argued that the whole "experience of laissez-faire [proved] that the economic system cannot be left to organize itself," while Ludwig Erhard described the Manchester school of liberalism as "virtually outmoded," and thought it wrong to "accept without reservation and in every phase of development the orthodox rules of a market economy." Similarly, Wilhelm Ropke argued that, "like pure democracy, undiluted capitalism is intolerable."[51] It would be grossly unfair to identify such sentiments with national socialism, but there is no doubt that the Nazi state's insistence on "harnessing capitalism to politics" and its "assumption that it is legitimate for state officials ... to intervene pervasively ... at the micro-level in both public and private sector enterprises"[52] continued to influence the German economy long after Hitler's demise.

Across Europe, in short, the postwar order represented something quite unusual. Crosland pointed out that it was "different in kind from classical capitalism ... in almost every respect that one can think of,"[53] while Andrew Shonfield questioned whether "the economic order under which we now live and the social structure that goes with it are so different from what preceded them that it [has become] misleading ... to use the word 'capitalism' to describe them."[54] Capitalism remained, but it was a capitalism of a very different type – one tempered and limited by political power and often made subservient to

[49] Simon Reich, *The Fruits of Fascism* (Ithaca, NY: Cornell University Press, 1990), 62.
[50] Ibid., and Shonfield, *Modern Capitalism*.
[51] Alan Peacock and Hans Willegrodt, eds., *German Neo-Liberals and the Social Market Economy* (London: Macmillan, 1989), 109–10.
[52] Reich, *The Fruits of Fascism*, 44. See also Chapter 6 of this book.
[53] Crosland, *The Future of Socialism*, 34.
[54] Shonfield, *Modern Capitalism*, 3.

the needs of society rather than the other way around. This was a far cry from both what orthodox Marxists and communists had wanted (namely, the elimination of markets and private enterprise) and from what liberals had long advocated (namely, as free a reign for markets as possible). What it most closely corresponded to was the mixture of economic policies championed by social democrats, fascists, and national socialists together with the commitment to democracy that social democrats displayed but that fascists and national social-ists decidedly did not.

Postwar Social Democracy

Ironically, although the postwar order represented a clear triumph for social democratic principles and policies, it was less of a victory for actual social democrats themselves – both because many on the left continued to cling to less promising ideological approaches and because many non-leftists moved quickly to appropriate central planks of the social democratic program.

After the war, all democratic socialist parties turned themselves into cham-pions of policies such as Keynesianism and the welfare state, but this practical reorientation was not always matched by an equivalent ideological one. Main-stream socialists, that is, may have embraced the revisionists' words, but many still didn't hear the music and continued to proclaim their dedication to classic, prewar ideological goals such as transcending capitalism entirely. Over time, all parties of the left recognized this as a disastrous political strategy, and so eventually all did break decisively with the past and with orthodox Marxism in particular. Unfortunately, by the time they did so, other actors had gotten a jump on them politically, and the true lineage of the new arrangements had been forgotten.

The loss of a vibrant, organic connection between democratic revisionism and the postwar order was partially a result of generational change on the left. By the war's end, many of the socialist movement's pioneering activists and intellectuals had either died or emigrated from Europe. As leftist parties reori-ented themselves toward gaining political support and power, meanwhile, they naturally selected as leaders technocrats and managers rather than intellectu-als and activists – people comfortable with, and good at, the ordinary politics of ordinary times. These new leaders often presided over unprecedented power and political success, but they lacked the old-timers' hunger, creative spark, and theoretical sophistication. As a result, by the last decades of the twentieth cen-tury, the democratic left had largely become estranged from social democracy's original rationale and goals, clinging only to the specific policy measures that their predecessors had advocated decades before. Few recognized that these policies, while crucial achievements in their day, had originally been viewed as only a means to larger ends, and fewer still tended enough of the movement's original fires to be able to forge innovative responses to contemporary chal-lenges. This left them vulnerable to other political forces offering seemingly better solutions to pressing problems.

The classic and most consequential unfolding of this drama occurred in Germany. After the collapse of the Third Reich, it was widely assumed both within the SPD and without that the leadership of Germany would naturally fall to the socialists. The SPD expected to benefit from the wave of anticapitalist sentiment that spread across Germany and the continent after the war, as well as its long-standing resistance to National Socialism and the heroic story of its leader, Kurt Schumacher (who had managed to survive over a decade in Nazi concentration camps). Yet despite these advantages, the SPD soon found itself relegated to essentially the same minority status it had enjoyed before the war – and for similar reasons.

In essence, despite the radically changed environment, after the war the SPD offered Germans a rehashed version of its prewar program and appeal.[55] The theoretical and historical sections of the party's program, for example, spoke in traditional Marxist tones not dramatically different from those invoked at Erfurt more than half a century earlier. Schumacher, who dominated the leadership until his death in 1952, proclaimed:

> The crucial point [of the SPD's contemporary agenda] is the abolition of capitalist exploitation and the transfer of the means of production from the control of the big proprietors to social ownership, the management of the economy as a whole in accordance not with the interests of private profit but with the principles of economically necessary planning. The muddle of the capitalist private-economy...cannot be tolerated. Planning and control are not socialism; they are only prerequisites for it. The crucial step is to be seen in drastic socialisation.[56]

In addition to offering a bleak and intransigent view of capitalism's possibilities and calling for widespread nationalization, the SPD also more or less returned to its traditional emphasis on workers and suspicion of other parties. As one observer notes, Schumacher "was so convinced of his party's destiny that he insisted throughout the first postwar election that the SPD could only cooperate with those parties who confirmed the SPD's legitimate right to govern Germany."[57] In addition, Schumacher "could not suppress his hatred of 'capitalist' and 'reactionary' ruling elites, nor could he overcome his deep seated distrust of the Roman Catholic hierarchy." He also never fully put aside his belief that class struggle or at least polarization were the necessary corollaries of capitalism.[58] Such views obviously hindered his ability to reach out to broad sectors of German society.

---

[55] This is perhaps easier to understand if one recognizes that many of the party's initial postwar leaders came from its prewar ranks. William Carr, "German Social Democracy Since 1945," in Roger Fletcher, ed., *From Bernstein to Brandt* (London: Edward Arnold, 1987), and Susan Miller and Heinrich Potthoff, *A History of German Social Democracy* (New York: St. Martin's Press, 1986), esp. 152.

[56] Schumacher, "What Do the Social Democrats Want?" speech delivered in Kiel on October 27, 1945, reprinted in ibid., 274.

[57] Diane Parness, *The SPD and the Challenge of Mass Politics* (Boulder, CO: Westview Press, 1991), 53.

[58] Ibid., 51–2.

Making matters worse were Schumacher's foreign policy positions, which included opposition to the Federal Republic's integration into Western institutions such as the European coal and steel community (on the grounds that they were stalking horses for capitalist expansion and barriers to eventual German reunification). Not surprisingly, these stances proved unattractive to a German public desperate for prosperity, security, and some semblance of normalcy. Under Schumacher, in short, "the party slid all too easily into the oppositional stance of the Weimar days, supremely confident that it could spurn co-operation with bourgeois parties and win power effortlessly through the logic of history."[59]

But if Schumacher and his cronies were comfortable with such a position, others in the party, and especially its younger echelons, were not. As the SPD's membership declined during the 1950s, it became painfully clear that without a change it was heading for permanent minority status. The contrast between the increasingly dictatorial regime in the East and the Federal Republic's prospering economy, meanwhile, helped many to realize that a fully socialized economy was inimical to both democracy and growth.[60] In 1955, therefore, Schumacher's successor Erich Ollenhauer set up a commission to reevaluate the party's direction and appeal.

The ultimate outcome was a full reconsideration of the SPD's course in German politics, the famed Bad Godesberg program. Essentially, it committed the SPD to the two main pillars of a modern social democratic program – a people's party strategy and a commitment to reform capitalism rather than destroy it. In particular, Bad Godesberg proclaimed that the party "no longer considered nationalization the major principle of a socialist economy but only one of several (and then only the last) means of controlling economic concentration and power."[61] In the program's well-known phrase, it committed the SPD to promoting "as much competition as possible, as much planning as necessary."

Bad Godesberg also attempted to reach beyond the working class by making clear the party's desire for better relations with the churches and its commitment to defending the country and supporting its military. It abandoned, as one observer noted, the view that the party needed "to redeem an isolated, alienated and repressed working class [and] formally accepted the position that progress could be made through reform and power attained in parliament."[62]

Finally, the Bad Godesberg program marked the triumph of social democracy through its clear, if implicit, severing of socialism from Marxism. It proclaimed:

Democratic socialism, which in Europe is rooted in Christian ethics, humanism and classical philosophy, does not proclaim ultimate truths – not because of any lack of understanding for or indifference to philosophical or religious truths, but out of respect

---

[59] Carr, "German Social Democracy Since 1945," 194.

[60] Ibid., 196.

[61] Gerard Braunthal, *The German Social Democrats Since 1969* (Boulder, CO: Westview Press, 1994), 18.

[62] Parness, *The SPD and the Challenge of Mass Politics*, 70.

for the individual's choice in these matters of conscience in which neither the state nor any political party should be allowed to interfere.

The Social Democratic party is the party of freedom of thought. It is a community of men holding different beliefs and ideas. Their agreement is based on the moral principles and political aims they have in common. The Social Democratic party strives for a way of life in accordance with these principles. Socialism is a constant task – to fight for freedom and justice, to preserve them and to live up to them.[63]

Bad Godesberg marked a clear shift in the SPD's stated identity and goals. Yet if somewhere Bernstein was smiling about his ultimate triumph over Kautsky, he might also have been a bit troubled, because the shift was at least as much pragmatic as it was principled, motivated by a desire to break out of a political ghetto rather than a decision to chart a bold course for the future. In a country where national socialism was a recent memory and "real, existing" socialism was being built next door, the wish to avoid ideology and grand projects is perhaps easy to understand. And it was made possible by the leadership transition to Ollenhauer, "a solid, loyal party functionary, a man dedicated to oiling the wheels of a smoothly running bureaucratic machine [who] was as far removed from the consuming political passions that fired Kurt Schumacher as anyone in the SPD could be."[64] But if the SPD's de-ideologization made it more palatable and less scary to voters – and did indeed eventually lead to an expansion of the party's support and its participation in government – it also had its drawbacks. In particular, it "rendered [the SPD] unserviceable as a nexus for creating and reproducing utopian aspirations,"[65] alienating from the party those dissatisfied with the status quo and looking to transform it into something better.

By the 1960s, therefore, the SPD's reorientation had opened up a political space to the party's left, a trend furthered by its increasing intolerance of intra-party disputes and its own activists. The dilemma was only heightened by controversies over the Vietnam War, rearmament and the emergency laws, and the SPD's participation in a grand coalition with the Christian Democratic Union and the Christian Socialist Union in 1966. The coalition was a major milestone for the party, representing its first taste of power in the Federal Republic. Willy Brandt, who succeeded Ollenhauer as leader in 1964, made clear that despite the less-than-perfect conditions, the SPD could not afford to shy away from power now that it was offered, lest it once again convince Germans that it was unable or unwilling to govern. And indeed the SPD continued to gain acceptance, reaching its greatest electoral result ever in 1969, garnering 42.7 percent of the vote and forming its own government with the help of the Liberals. Yet the "reform euphoria" that accompanied Brandt's and the SPD's rise to power

---

[63] Bad Godesberg program, reprinted in Miller and Potthoff, *A History of German Social Democracy*, 275.

[64] Parness, *The SPD and the Challenge of Mass Politics*, 60.

[65] Philip Gorski and Andrei Markovits, *The German Left: Red, Green and Beyond* (New York: Oxford University Press, 1993), 44.

was short lived, with Brandt forced to resign as a result of scandals and his replacement by the more pragmatic and centrist Helmut Schmidt.

In many ways, Schmidt represented the culmination of the SPD's postwar transformation. Competent and determined, but lacking transformative goals or an ideological temperament, he focused on proving that his government, and the SPD more generally, was the most capable caretaker of Germany's domestic economy and international standing. Schmidt committed himself to maintaining and improving the living standards of Germany's citizens and committed the country to accepting NATO missiles on European soil. If successful on their own terms, however, these stances further alienated the left and, by tying the party's fortunes ever closer to the country's economy, made the SPD vulnerable to the economic downturn that began in the 1970s. As one observer notes, the flaw in Schmidt's plan "was the assumption of unlimited economic growth. The economic woes caused by the substantial increase in the price of oil as a consequence of the Yom Kippur war . . . and the global recession of 1977 undermined the theoretical premises and material bases of the social democratic reform program."[66]

By the 1970s, in short, the SPD had become so integrated into the system, and so inflexible and ideologically exhausted, that the partial discrediting of its leadership by economic doldrums dealt it a blow from which it has yet to recover. Over the next generation, the party hemorrhaged members and increasingly became a home for the elderly and beneficiaries of the status quo. It lost the support of the young and the radical, as well as many of the poor, unemployed, and alienated. Many of the former turned left to the Greens, and some of the latter have lately turned to right and left-wing populism. Lacking anything distinctive to offer, the hollowed-out SPD now finds itself electorally vulnerable, subject to internal dissension, and increasingly unable to generate either enthusiasm or commitment from anybody.

In Italy and France, the left's trajectories were not entirely dissimilar, although it took even longer for socialists in both countries to make their peace with reality. In Italy, for example, the socialists "jettisoned what remained of [their] Marxist heritage" only in the 1970s.[67] When the PSI reestablished itself after the war, it quickly returned, like the SPD, to many of the same patterns and practices that had doomed it to irrelevance in the 1920s. Its initial postwar leader, Pietro Nenni, sought to ally, and even merge, with the Communists (the PCI), and believed that the party's foremost goal should be the immediate formation of a "socialist Republic." Such stances alienated the party's more moderate and social democratic elements, leaving the PSI weakened by infighting.

---

[66] Gorski and Markovits, *The German Left*, 80. These problems were only compounded by Schmidt's leadership style, which further dried up the party's base and alienated its activists. Miller and Potthoff, *A History of German Social Democracy*, 203.

[67] Alexander De Grand, *The Italian Left in the Twentieth Century* (Indianapolis, IN: Indiana University Press, 1989), 161–2.

By 1947, Nenni's opponents had split off, leaving him free to dally with the Communists and reorganize the party along Leninist lines, thereby turning it into probably "most radical and, in a Marxist sense, fundamentalist, of all European socialist movements."[68] Watching these events unfold, one perspicacious observer noted that "[Nenni's strategy] is very silly … but the Italian Socialist Party is a remarkably silly party. It is living in a world of its own making, using language coined in the 20s and doomed to be eaten up by the much more astute Communist party."[69] Which is precisely what happened. The PCI soon overwhelmed the hapless PSI, becoming the main party of the left and wresting away control of many of the affiliated organizations of the labor movement.[70] This left the Italian center up for grabs, a situation that the Christian Democrats took full advantage of to become Italy's dominant party.

After many years of political irrelevance, the PSI was finally turned around by Bettino Craxi, who transformed it into a moderate reformist center-left party by the 1970s. At least initially, this strategy paid off and Craxi became the first socialist prime minister of Italy in 1983. Yet the party proved unable to build on this success and construct a distinctive and dynamic movement with broad appeal. It proved "too late to wrench the PCI's strong grip from the masses,"[71] and in any case the PSI now lacked the type of clear ideological profile that might attract committed followers and engender real enthusiasm. Making matters worse, Craxi proved prone to the same weaknesses as other Italian politicians, and in the 1990s was convicted of accepting bribes and kickbacks. With a discredited leader and no particular raison d'etre, Italian socialism's renewal proved short-lived.

French socialism, finally, offers yet another dreary version of the same theme. After the war, the SFIO abandoned many of its traditional policy stances and positions, and most importantly ended its long-standing internal battles over whether to accept a position as junior partner in a governing coalition. Nevertheless, despite such changes, the party proved unable to make a full break with its past or drop its Marxist rhetoric. Its most prominent member, Léon Blum, vociferously urged a change of course and pushed for a socialism based on evolutionary rather than revolutionary change, one committed to appealing to "people in every walk of life" rather than one steeped in class warfare and worker exclusivity.[72] Yet his pleas were rejected, and at its first postwar congress in August 1945, the SFIO proclaimed:

[68] Laqueur, *Europe Since Hitler*, 155.

[69] Quoted in Sassoon, *One Hundred Years of Socialism*, 89.

[70] Di Scala, *Italy: From Revolution to Republic*, 280.

[71] Simona Colarizi, "Socialist Constraints Following the War," in Spencer Di Scala, ed., *Italian Socialism* (Amherst, MA: University of Massachusetts Press, 1996), 151.

[72] Bruce Graham, *Choice and Democratic Order: The French Socialist Party* (New York: Cambridge University Press, 1994), 271–6; S. William Halperin, "Leon Blum and Contemporary French Socialism," *Journal of Modern History*, 18, 3, September 1946.

The Socialist party is by its nature a revolutionary party. It aims at replacing capitalist private property by a society in which natural resources and the means of production are socially owned and classes have been abolished. Such a revolutionary transformation, though in the interest of all mankind, is to be achieved only by the working class. . . . The Socialist party is a party of class struggle founded on the organized working class.[73]

During the following years, the orthodox faction of the party continued to gain in strength. At the party's 1946 congress, for example, this wing, under the leadership of Guy Mollet (who soon became the party's general secretary), attacked Blum's "watering down" of the party's principles and condemned "all attempts at revisionism, notably those which are inspired by a false humanism whose true significance is to mask fundamental realities – that is, the class struggle."[74]

Unsurprisingly, as a result the party's membership declined from 354,000 in 1946 to 60,000 in 1960, while its share of the vote dropped from 23 percent in 1945 to 12.6 percent in 1962. Its bastions of support, furthermore, ended up being not the working classes, the young, or the more dynamic sectors of the economy, but rather middle-aged civil servants and professionals along with those who stood to lose from rapid social and economic change (such as textile workers and small farmers). As one observer put it, in the decades after the war, the SFIO became a party of "unimaginative, superannuated functionaries" in "terminal decline." "The gulf between its daily practice as a party of the center, devoid of the faintest whiff of radicalism, and its blood curdling socialist rhetoric was enormous; its own parliamentary group, an assortment of mediocre Fourth Republic notables . . . defined itself as 'essentially a revolutionary party . . . a party of the class struggle.'"[75] As in Germany and Italy, meanwhile, one consequence of the SFIO's rhetorical radicalism was that it provided an opening for the center-right – here in the form of Gaullism – to capture those groups alienated by the left and form a true cross-class coalition on the other side of the aisle, thereby becoming the dominant force in French political life.

The SFIO remained stuck in a rut up through the 1960s; as one deputy put it, "The party doctrine is now like the Bible; we refuse either to change it or to believe in it."[76] Continual electoral defeats, however, culminating in routs in 1968 and 1969, finally led to change. Mollet retired in 1969 and a new, more pragmatic organization, the *Parti socialiste* (PS), arose in 1971. It insisted on maintaining a clear left-wing profile, at least in part so it could form an alliance with the Communists. Indeed, the two forces eventually agreed on a unity program, the *Programme commun*, which committed the Communists to democracy and pluralism and the socialists to economic radicalism, including

[73] Julius Braunthal, *History of the International 1864–1914* (New York: Praeger, 1967), 24.

[74] Joel Colton, *Léon Blum* (New York: Alfred Knopf, 1966), 459.

[75] Albert Lindemann, *A History of European Socialism* (New Haven, CT: Yale University Press, 1983), 342, and Sassoon, *One Hundred Years of Socialism*, 297.

[76] Frank Wilson, *The French Democratic Left 1963–1969* (Stanford, CA: Stanford University Press, 1971), 66.

large-scale nationalizations. This combined front came to power in 1981 during an economic downturn by convincing voters it had the most promising and innovative solutions to France's contemporary problems.

Unfortunately, the socialists' economic program did not work out as hoped and the long-awaited socialist government soon found itself overseeing an economy in turmoil. Forced to act but with little else to fall back on, the socialists ended up making a dramatic volte face: By 1982, the PS had moved from advocating one of the most radical economic programs of any socialist party in Europe to implementing deflationary measures and dramatically cutting public spending. As one observer puts it, this shift signaled "the end of [the PS's] ambition, the termination of passion, the beginning of routine. The PS became 'a grey party looking for colour.'"[77] By the end of the twentieth century, in other words, the French socialists, like their German and Italian counterparts, had shown themselves able to win elections but could no longer explain to themselves or others why anyone should care.

Not all socialist parties suffered the same fate, of course. As usual, for example, the Swedes did very well – largely because, unlike most of their counterparts elsewhere, they understood and believed in what they were doing. The SAP was able both to prosper at the polls and maintain its distinctiveness by recognizing that the two tasks were, in fact, complementary: The party's ability to integrate individual policy initiatives into a larger social democratic whole ensured that it remained more vibrant and successful than most of its counterparts in the rest of Europe.

To be sure, the Swedish social democrats started off the postwar era in a better position than their counterparts elsewhere. They could build on their own governing record rather than struggle to reestablish their very existence as a party, and their country emerged in better shape from the war than did most others. But even more than luck and a head start, their success was due to the fact that they had fully internalized the core elements of social democratic ideology and devoted themselves to developing creative policies for putting them into practice.

Politically, the SAP worked during the postwar years to strengthen its hold over a broad cross-section of the Swedish electorate. Continuing the strategy it had embraced during the interwar years, the party directed its appeals not to workers alone but to the Swedish "people" (*Folk*) in general. In doing so, it exploited its wartime leadership role, loudly proclaiming its commitment to social solidarity and the national interest. There was no conflict between such positions and social democracy, the party insisted, because properly understood social democracy was all about advancing collective interests rather than those of a particular group or class. SAP appeals were saturated with references to "solidarity," "cooperation," and "togetherness." This was especially true in discussions of plans for an expanded welfare state, which was presented as part of the SAP's strategy for creating a "strong society" (*starka samhället*) and protecting the public from the uncertainties and insecurities inherent in

---

[77] Sassoon, *One Hundred Years of Socialism*, 559.

modern capitalism. As Tage Erlander, prime minister from 1946–69, put it, the SAP's social policy grew out of a recognition that "security is too big a problem for the individual to solve with only his own power.... The problems of modern society demand an increasing measure of cooperation, collaboration, and solidarity."[78]

Economically, meanwhile, the SAP also continued along its prewar path of using state intervention to manage the economy and sever the link between individuals' market position and their broader life chances. What made these efforts so distinctive was not only the sizable amount of intervention and decommodification they involved, but also the way they were presented as part of a larger, transformative project. The Rehn-Meidner model, for example, was sold not merely as a practical package of wage regulations but as a case study in the party's strategy of increasing "social control" over the economy without resorting to full-scale nationalization.[79] It both exemplified and furthered the SAP's attempts to shift the definition of socialization from "common ownership of the means of production" to increasing "democratic influence over the economy."[80] As Gunnar Adler-Karlsson noted – picking up where Nils Karleby had left off a generation earlier – Swedish social democrats had begun to look upon our capitalists

...in the same way as we have looked upon our kings in Scandinavia. A hundred years ago a Scandinavian king carried a lot of power. 50 years ago he still had considerable power. According to our constitutions the king still has equally as much formal power as a hundred years ago, but in reality we have undressed him of all his power functions so that today he is in fact powerless. We have done this without dangerous and disruptive internal fights. Let us in the same manner avoid the even more dangerous contests that are unavoidable if we enter the road of formal socialization. Let us instead strip and divest our present capitalists of one after another of their ownership functions. Let us even give them a new dress, but one similar to that of the famous emperor in H.C. Anderson's tale. After a few decades they will then remain, perhaps formally as kings, but in reality as naked symbols of a passed and inferior development state.[81]

The Swedish welfare state was understood in a similar way. Its comprehensiveness and universalism helped "manufacture broad class (even cross-class) solidarity and social democratic consensus," while at the same time marginalizing "the market as the principal agent of distribution and the chief determinant of peoples' life chances."[82] The party consciously used social policy to expand its hold over the electorate and to develop a sense of common interests across classes. As one commentator noted, "the central mission of the [Swedish social

[78] Tage Erlander, 1956 SAP congress protokoll, in *Från Palm to Palme: Den Svenska Socialdemokratins Program* (Stockholm: Rabén and Sjögren), 258–9.
[79] Rudolf Meidner, "Why Did the Swedish Model Fail?" *Socialist Register*, 1993, 211. Also, Sven Steinmo, "Social Democracy vs. Socialism," *Politics and Society*, 16, December 1988.
[80] Diane Sainsbury, *Swedish Social Democratic Ideology* (Stockholm: Almqvist and Wiksell, 1980), 166.
[81] Gunnar Adler-Karlsson, *Functional Socialism* (Stockholm: Prisma, 1967), 101–2.
[82] Esping-Andersen, *Politics Against Markets*, 245.

democratic welfare state] is to increase solidarity between citizens by creating a foundation for national rallying (*samling*)."[83]

Recognizing the growing importance of white-collar workers, for example, the SAP explicitly designed social policies that would appeal to them and tie their interests to those of other workers. This was particularly clear in the fight over supplemental pensions at the end of the 1950s, when the SAP "stressed the common interests of manual and white-collar workers [in such pensions] and the struggle for the[m] as of vital interest for all wage-earners."[84] As with increased economic management, moreover, welfare state enhancements were presented as valuable not only on their own terms but also as steps toward a better future. The party insisted that the welfare state itself represented a form of socialism, since under it "the total income of the people was regarded as a common resource and a portion of it was transferred to those with inadequate incomes." Ernst Wigforss was a well-known proponent of this view, arguing, for example, that the Swedish welfare state was doing the "work of social transformation" and was a critical "means of creating the good society."[85]

All these strategies proved quite successful, and in the years after the war, the SAP was able to remain firmly anchored in the working class while strengthening its support well beyond it. It remained by far the largest party in the Swedish political system, used its dominance to shift the country's center of political gravity to the left, and built the greatest record of political hegemony of any party in a democratic country during the twentieth century.

Even this remarkable string of triumphs, of course, did not allow the party to escape unscathed from some of the problems that set back its counterparts elsewhere. As in the rest of Europe, for example, by the early 1970s economic challenges were mounting, although they took on a distinct aspect in Sweden due to the particular nature of the Swedish model. As noted previously, one consequence of Rehn-Meidner was to create "excess" profits in some firms, as wages in particularly efficient industries were kept artificially low. This led over time to frustration from both workers in those industries (who felt they were being shortchanged) and unions more generally (which worried that the mounting pressures would ultimately lead to abandonment of the entire scheme to delink wages from market forces).[86] The government appointed a committee headed by Meidner to study the problem, and its proposed solution – the so-called "wage-earner" funds (*löntagarfonder*) – represented both the culmination, and something of a repudiation, of the SAP's approach to social democracy.

Essentially, Meidner's committee recommended gradually transferring the excess profits to funds controlled by the efficient industries' workers, so they

[83] Fredrika Lagergren, *På Andra Sidan Välfardsstaaten* (Stockholm: Brutus Östlings, 1999), 167.
[84] Torsten Svensson, "Socialdemokratins Dominans" (Ph.D. Dissertation, University of Uppsala, 1994), 272.
[85] Sainsbury, *Swedish Social Democratic Ideology*, 66.
[86] Sassoon, *One Hundred Years of Socialism*, 706ff.

could be reinvested. Such a solution would help satisfy the workers whose wages were being kept artificially low, the thinking ran, without causing any loss of productivity. This was consistent with the party's strategy of maintaining both growth and a solidaristic wage policy while at the same time increasing "democratic" control over the economy. On the other hand, to the extent that the transfer of money to such workers' funds continued over time, it would gradually eliminate private ownership across much of the Swedish economy – a goal that the SAP had in fact long since rejected as unnecessary as well as politically counterproductive.

Although the story of the funds is complicated, this last characteristic proved to be critical. Recognizing that the wage-earner funds threatened the very existence of capitalism and therefore an end to the implicit trade-off that social democrats had long offered the private sector (that is, markets and private property remain but are tempered and directed by the state), the Swedish business community and its political allies mounted an unprecedented effort to block them. Having no burning desire to kill off capitalism itself, and realizing that it had landed on what was destined to be the losing side of a bruising political battle, the SAP soon backed away from the idea and allowed the funds to be watered down and then essentially eliminated. The controversy took its toll, however, and, in conjunction with other fights over issues such as nuclear power, helped lead to the SAP's first real loss of governing power in four decades.

The setbacks that the SAP suffered in the 1970s forced it, like its counterparts elsewhere, to reevaluate some of its traditional tactics and even strategies. It even went through a period in the late 1980s when it appeared to be drifting intellectually and politically.[87] But because it had strong reserves of political, ideological, and intellectual capital to draw on, and had reshaped the political and social structure of Swedish society so extensively, in the end the party was able to weather the storm better than others. It bounced back politically, recaptured power in the 1980s, and remains the dominant party in the Swedish political system (although it is not as hegemonic as before). It has maintained its ability to appeal to voters across much of the political spectrum and has managed to coopt many new "postmaterialist" issues (such as environmentalism and women's rights). And economically it recovered from the wage-earner funds fiasco by essentially promising the electorate that it would maintain traditional social democratic policies while updating them as appropriate to deal with contemporary challenges – something at which it has been relatively successful, overseeing impressive economic growth in recent years while still maintaining high levels of social spending and a commitment to egalitarianism and social solidarity.

Perhaps the SAP's greatest success, however, has been to preserve a sense of social democratic distinctiveness in Sweden.[88] Despite all the changes that have

---

[87] Mark Blyth, *Great Transformations* (New York: Cambridge University Press, 2002).

[88] Francis Castles, *The Social Democratic Image of Society* (London: Routledge and Kegan Paul, 1978).

occurred in both the domestic and international economy over recent decades, that is, the vast majority of Swedes acknowledge and accept the SAP's basic ideas about the virtues of social solidarity, egalitarianism, and political control over the economy. Rather than questioning whether such social democratic concepts are worthwhile, political debate in Sweden has tended to be about whether the socialists or the bourgeois parties are best able to implement them together with steady growth.

9

Conclusion

The preceding chapters of this book have shown that, correctly understood, social democracy is far more than the defender of particular policies or values such as the welfare state, equality, or solidarity. Nor is it merely watered-down Marxism or bulked-up liberalism, but rather, at least as originally conceived, a distinctive ideology and political movement all its own.

Social democracy's foundations were laid in the late nineteenth century when Eduard Bernstein and other democratic revisionists began attacking the main pillars of orthodox Marxism, historical materialism, and class struggle, and arguing for an alternative based on new principles, the primacy of politics, and cross-class cooperation. These democratic revisionists at first insisted that they were merely "revising" or "updating" Marxism, but here it was their fiercest critics – the defenders of orthodoxy – who saw more accurately what the revisionists themselves were loath to admit: that they were actually replacing Marxism with something entirely different. Just what that thing was became clear a generation later. In response to the challenges of the interwar years, socialist dissidents across Europe built on the principles laid out by Bernstein and others and developed a whole new practical program for the left based on state control of markets, communitarianism, and a "people's party" strategy. By the 1930s, in other words, the project begun by the democratic revisionists in the nineteenth century had been completed: A new political movement that embodied its own principles and policies had been born. Social democracy represented the final and full severing of socialism from Marxism.

After the Second World War, social democratic principles and policies became broadly accepted across the continent and served as the foundation of Europe's vaunted postwar settlement. In particular, the primacy of politics and communitarianism were translated into policies that insulated individuals and communities from the harsh effects of capitalism and to a new emphasis on social solidarity and stability. The postwar order entailed, in other words, a dramatic revision of the relationship that existed among states, markets, and society up through the early twentieth century. This was a far cry from what liberals had long advocated (namely, as free a rein for markets and individual liberty as possible) as it was from what orthodox Marxists and communists wanted (namely, an end to capitalism). Referring to this order as an "embedded liberal" one – as an "updated" or "softer" version of the liberal regime that reigned up through the early twentieth century – is therefore a misreading of the nature and significance of the shift that occurred after 1945. Instead, we must recognize this order as a fundamentally social democratic one. In addition, therefore, to being seen as a distinctive ideology and movement all its own, social democracy should thus also be seen as the most successful ideology and movement of the twentieth century. Its principles and policies undergirded the most prosperous and harmonious period in European history by reconciling things that had hitherto seemed incompatible: a well-functioning capitalist system, democracy, and social stability.

Understanding social democracy's roots and rationale and gaining a renewed appreciation for its role in twentieth century political development are reasons enough for reconsidering the movement's history. There are other pressing reasons for doing so as well. For students of twentieth century history, an examination of social democracy provides an example of the ideological market in action, a case study of how structural factors create a demand for new intellectual frameworks, which political agents then supply and particular national contexts extensively shape. They can also take from it a new understanding of the relationships among the great ideologies of the twentieth century, and in particular an appreciation of the common genealogy of social democracy, fascism, and national socialism. As we have seen, social democracy, fascism, and national socialism promoted surprisingly similar solutions to the problems unleashed by modernity and capitalism, with the crucial distinction that only the former managed to come up with a project that placed democracy front and center. Finally, social democracy's story is not merely of historical interest. Far from being a spent force, as conventional wisdom would have it, social democracy, when interpreted correctly, offers an impressive twenty-first century road map for politicians in advanced industrial countries and the developing world alike. This is because for all its purported novelty, the issue at the heart of contemporary globalization debates – whether states can and should dominate market forces or must bow before them – is in fact very old. Indeed, social democracy emerged from similar debates within the international socialist movement a century ago. It is only because such debates have been forgotten or misunderstood that contemporary discussions of social democracy are so superficial and intellectually impoverished, and why it is so important to refresh the democratic left's collective memory about its past.

Understanding the Ideological Market: Structure and Agency

Ideology is one of the most important yet least understood political phenomena. One problem is that those who study ideology tend to focus on either agency or structure. Intellectual historians, for example, tend to focus on the role played by key individuals and their local contexts, giving the misleading impression that ideologies emerge largely from the internal debates and efforts of particular thinkers, writers, and activists. Those political scientists who bother to study ideology at all, meanwhile, tend to focus on the influence of broad environmental and structural factors, giving the equally misleading impression that ideologies emerge merely in response to new external circumstances. In practice, of course, structure and agency work together to shape the development of ideologies, and therefore a true understanding of the ebb and flow of political history must take both into account.

The study of social democracy is a case in point. Social democracy, as we have seen, had its origins in several structural and environmental changes that came together during the late nineteenth century to undermine the main tenets of orthodox Marxism and open a space for ideological challengers. Capitalism simply wasn't collapsing; small businesses and agriculture weren't disappearing; society wasn't becoming divided into two implacably opposed groups. Socialist parties, moreover, were gaining strength in various countries and found themselves confronting dilemmas about whether and how to use their new-found power to press for change – a topic about which orthodox Marxism had little to say. The immense social dislocation caused by capitalism, finally, had generated a rise in communitarian and nationalist sentiment across the continent, a hunger for belonging that the chilly strictures of Marxist orthodoxy could do little to satisfy. The result, as we saw, was that challenges to orthodox Marxism arose in all West European countries during the fin-de-siècle. The similarity of these challenges and their cross-national nature indicates that their origin and development requires looking at factors outside the borders of any particular country.

But if the demand for alternatives to orthodox Marxism was driven largely by environmental and structural changes, the supply side of the equation was not. To understand why particular challenges emerged and fared differently in each country, one must focus on individuals and the precise contexts within which they operated.

In France, for example, the early arrival of a democratic political system and the continued importance of the peasantry created strong incentives to challenge orthodoxy early on. The notions that democracy was no better than its alternatives, that socialists should remain aloof from political alliances and cross-class cooperation, or that small farmers should be either ignored or encouraged to recognize that their days were numbered were particularly ludicrous in the French context. Such factors help to explain why the first practical challenges to orthodoxy arose in France. Germany, on the other hand, was the home of the most important theoretical challenge to orthodoxy, and to understand this we must also turn to a study of individuals and country-level variables, in particular Eduard Bernstein and his milieu. No ordinary socialist, Bernstein was the executor of Engels' will, a close friend of Kautsky, and a major figure within both the international socialist movement and its most important national party. It was his personal stature, along with the force and comprehensiveness of his theoretical critiques, and the critical importance of the German SPD as the standard-bearer of Marxist ideology, that gave his challenge to orthodoxy such power and bite.

What was true of the origins and early development of revisionism was true of the transition to social democracy as well. Although attacks on orthodoxy grew increasingly powerful during the late nineteenth and early twentieth centuries, it took the immense structural and environmental changes wrought by the First World War to turn revisionism into social democracy. The internationalist and revolutionary credentials of socialist parties across the continent were permanently tarnished by their decisions to support their national war efforts and even in some cases to join national unity governments, and many were overwhelmed by the nationalist upsurge accompanying the war. Many socialists' faith in the inevitability or even the desirability of class struggle never recovered from these blows. After the war, trends continued to push many socialists away from orthodoxy. Newly established democratic political systems, for example, provided socialist parties with new opportunities to share governing power, a development that led many to recognize that the orthodox insistence on the inevitability of class conflict and the undesirability of cross-class cooperation was a recipe for political irrelevance. The onset of the Great Depression put the final nail in the coffin of historical materialism and class struggle, as it became clear to many that orthodoxy's insistence that economic forces could not and should not be tampered with, and that the needs and fears of groups outside the proletariat were of no concern to socialists, was tantamount to political suicide.

Yet if to understand why social democracy emerged during the interwar period one must look at cross-national structural and environmental trends, to understand the precise form that these new movements took and their varying degrees of success, one must look within individual countries themselves. In Germany, the story of social democracy was one of abject failure. The unwillingness of the SPD to heed calls for a shift to a "people's party" strategy and its rejection of an activist, Keynesian-style response to the Depression were consequences of the actions of key individuals (such as Rudolf Hilferding) as well as a widespread belief that a social democratic course shift was simply too great a break with the past. In Sweden, on the other hand, precisely the opposite outcome emerged: the victory of social democracy and the adoption of a "people party" appeal and a new economic strategy, thanks to the actions of key individuals and pecularities of the Swedish situation. The SAP's leader during this period, Per Albin Hansson, was savvy and charismatic and worked with others to coopt themes and appeals from the right – in particular, the idea of Sweden as the "people's home" – and to position his party as the champion not merely of the proletariat, but of the "little people" more generally, the "common good," and even the nation. Similarly, the SAP's adoption of "Keynesianism before Keynes" depended on the actions of key individuals such as Nils Karleby and Ernst Wigforss, who worked throughout the interwar years to build an acceptance of, and practical strategies for, using the state to control

economic developments. The relative ease with which the final transition to
social democracy was made in Sweden depended on the party's prewar acceptance of revisionism: By the 1930s, the intellectual and practical groundwork
for a course shift had long been in place. And finally, unlike the SPD, which
both felt itself and was considered by others to be the standard-bearer of orthodoxy, the Swedes, on the periphery of Europe, could move increasingly away
from Marxism without having to worry very much about condemnation from
abroad.

In addition to amplifying our appreciation for the role of both structure
and agency in shaping the development of ideologies, this reexamination of
social democracy has also reminded us of the critical role that political parties
have played as "carriers" of ideology during the twentieth century. Ideologies
do not achieve resonance or political power on their own; instead, they must
be "carried" by political actors capable of implementing political projects and
changing the way that people think and act. This was precisely the role that
political parties played. As we have seen, the distinctive ideologies of the twentieth century – social democracy, fascism, and national socialism – not only had
critical roots in debates that began within existing parties (most importantly,
socialist ones), but they were then carried to political prominence and in some
cases put into practice by party leaders and party organizations. In addition, we
have also seen how ideologies shaped the political parties that carried them. The
organizations, political strategies, and electoral coalitions that defined twentieth century political parties were all critically shaped by the ideological projects
that they championed. As we saw, the cross-class coalitions, "people's party"
strategies and "principled pragmatism" that characterized social democrats,
fascists, and national socialists are impossible to understand without reference
to their distinctive ideologies.

Understanding the Twentieth Century
Social democrats were not the only ones to break with liberals and orthodox
Marxists and argue for the primacy of politics over economics and the value
of communitarianism over individualism or class conflict. Fascists and national
socialists came to similar conclusions. Part of the reason for this, as scholars
such as Zeev Sternhell and A. James Gregor have pointed out, is that fascism
and social democracy both had their roots in the revisionist controversy of the
fin-de-siècle. While Bernstein and other democratic revisionists were laying the
groundwork for one alternative socialist vision, Georges Sorel and other revolutionary revisionsts were laying the groundwork for another. Both revisionist groups believed in the primacy of politics and communitarianism. Where
they differed was in their assessments of liberalism and democracy. Democratic revisionists saw socialism as liberalism's spiritual and practical heir, and
democracy as both the best means of attaining their objective and a fundamental component of it. Their rivals, however, viewed liberalism as an anathema
and democracy as a disruptive and degenerative influence. Rather than hoping
for a gradual evolutionary transformation of the existing liberal order, they

thought change would come only through a violent and revolutionary break with it.

These revolutionary revisionists became a significant force in both Italy and France during the late nineteenth and early twentieth centuries. Their emphasis on the primacy of politics and communitarianism attracted interest from both the left and right, particularly from the growing nationalist movement, and provided a foundation that fascists could build on a generation later. Revolutionary revisionism did not enjoy the same popularity in Germany, but a not dissimilar dynamic unfolded there nonetheless, as nationalists developed a powerful critique of capitalism and called for a socialist alternative to Marxism. By the late nineteenth century, such people had begun referring to themselves as national socialists.

The parallels among social democrats, fascists, and national socialists deepened during the interwar years. The groups' commitment to similar principles led them to develop and advocate similar policies and appeals, with all of them championing a "third way" between laissez-faire liberalism and Soviet communism and working hard to cultivate cross-class support. Once in power, the parallels continued, with the Italian Fascists and German National Socialists being even more vociferous than the Swedish social democrats in their insistence that it was the state's right and duty to control capitalism. And indeed, Fascists and National Socialists pioneered a range of policies including state control over investment, nationalized industries, and corporatism that helped do just that. Since, as already noted, many of these principles and policies were incorporated into the postwar order, it is fair to say that fascists and national socialists as well as social democrats deserve to be included in its family tree.

If one can make a case for recognizing the economic bequest of fascism and national socialism to the postwar order, however, it seems perverse to argue for any lasting political legacy. Indeed, these movements were implacably opposed to the postwar order's most striking political feature: stable democracy. Yet even here fascism and national socialism can be seen to have played at least an indirect role, not only by providing the first example of modern "people's parties" in countries such as Italy and Germany, but also by breaking down many social structures and institutions that had hitherto hindered the development of stable democracy.[1]

Fascists, national socialists, and social democrats, in short, shared important similarities that other scholars have not recognized – namely a belief in the primacy of politics and communitarianism. They differed, however, in their views of how the former should be carried out and in what the latter really meant.[2]

---

[1] This case has been made particularly strongly by Ralf Dahrendorf, *Society and Democracy in Germany* (New York: W. W. Norton, 1967), and David Schoenbaum, *Hitler's Social Revolution* (New York: W. W. Norton, 1966).

[2] Given this analysis, the assertion by many scholars that fascism and national socialism had no ideological core, that they lacked firm principles and were willing to adopt any position or policy if it held out the promise of increasing their power, seems flawed. Certainly these movements were pragmatic, responsive, and hell-bent on gaining power. But at the core of both, from their origins

For social democrats, the primacy of politics meant using a democratic state to institutionalize policies that would protect society from capitalism's harshest effects and promote the well-being and security of its weakest and most vulnerable members in particular. For fascists and national socialists, the primacy of politics meant using a tyrannical state to control markets, ostensibly for the good of society, but really in order to ensure the hegemony of the state (or the party). Social democrats translated communitarianism, meanwhile, into an emphasis on social solidarity and policies designed to strengthen social unity and solidarity. Fascists translated it into an emphasis on the nation and policies designed to further national interests. National Socialists in Germany translated it into a biological and exclusionary view of national identity, as well as policies that aimed at eliminating a host of internal and external enemies. However critical these differences turned out to be, it is important to recognize that shared commitments to the primacy of politics and community fundamentally differentiated social democrats, fascists, and national socialists from contemporary liberals and orthodox Marxists.

The most important dividing line between social democrats, on the one hand, and fascists and national socialists on the other is that the former were committed to democracy and aspects of liberalism while the latter rejected them entirely. As we have seen, democratic revisionists and social democrats saw democracy as both a means and an end and were willing to subordinate other goals to the achievement and maintenance of democracy.[3] They also, for the

to their conquest of power, was a commitment to the primacy of politics and communitarianism. (It is worth noting that throughout the twentieth century, liberals and Marxists have supported a wide range of policies and positions without anyone questioning whether liberalism and Marxism deserved the status of ideologies.) Another finding that this analysis challenges is the view that fascism and national socialism represented fundamentally different phenomena. Zeev Sternhell, for example, claims that, "Fascism can in no way be identified with Nazism," while Renzo De Felice maintains that "there are few points in common" between them. Renzo De Felice, *Interpretations of Fascism* (Cambridge, MA: Harvard University Press, 1977); Zeev Sternhell, *The Birth of Fascist Ideology* (Princeton, NJ: Princeton University Press, 1994), 4. Once again, however, from the perspective of this book, such claims do not compute. Both drew a large part of their inspiration and appeal from a desire to combine communitarian nationalism with some kind of non-Marxist "socialism," one that sought to address capitalism's insistence on the primacy of economics and its destruction of *Gemeinschaft*. And after abandoning unsuccessful attempts to target urban workers, both ended up appealing to the "people," the nation, and the "common good"; sought to assemble cross-class coalitions; and achieved the status of true "people's parties." To say that these movements had fundamental similarities, of course, is not to say that they were identical in all respects. In particular, as many scholars have noted, racism and violence were far more central to national socialism than to fascism. Yet even this difference looms less large in theory than it did in practice. It is hardly a stretch, for example, to see the racism at the heart of national socialism as the most radical and extreme form of a communitarianism that characterized fascism as well, and even social democracy.

[3] As noted in Chapter 1 (footnote 17), there is a lively debate among social scientists regarding the actors and groups that have been the most important backers of democracy. As this book has made clear, to argue that the left or socialist parties were in general strong advocates of democracy is somewhat misleading. Many within the left who were under the spell of orthodox Marxism (not to mention Leninism/communism) were unwilling to sacrifice much for democracy. Democratic

most part, viewed social democracy as the logical "second act" of or successor to liberalism. To paraphrase Bernstein, social democracy should be understood as liberalism's "legitimate heir, not only chronologically, but also intellectually."[4] Or as Carlo Rosselli put it a generation later, the task of social democrats was to "liberate" liberalism from its attachment to the free market and spread its "revolutionary potential" not merely to the well-off but to all of society.[5]

Yet even though social democrats were committed to democracy and aspects of liberalism, their emphasis on the primacy of politics and communitarianism could lead them astray as well. As we saw in Chapters 5 and 6, for example, some prominent intellectuals did lose their faith in democracy and liberalism, and this, combined with their commitment to the primacy of politics and communitarianism, facilitated a journey from revisionist left to fascist or national socialist right during the interwar years.[6] But even those who retained their commitment to democracy and aspects of liberalism could be led astray by their dedication to the primacy of politics and communitarianism. For example, the belief in a powerful state standing above the interests of society that had the right, indeed the duty, to protect and foster the "common good" facilitated the integration of eugenics into the interwar social democratic vision, just as it did into the vision of fascists and National Socialists. Thus in Sweden – as always, the social democratic standard-bearer – widespread sterilizations were presented as "justifiable and desirable from society's point of view,"[7] and as a manifestation of the state's responsibility to "protect people against themselves."[8] Some of the most well-known figures in the SAP, such as Alva and Gunnar Myrdal, were associated with these policies, which they viewed as a natural part of the party's strategy for improving the health and welfare of the Swedish *folk*[9] and producing "better, healthier children."[10]

revisionists and social democrats, on the other hand, were strong and consistent advocates of democracy.

[4] Eduard Bernstein, *The Preconditions of Socialism*, Henry Tudor, ed. (New York: Cambridge University Press, 1993), 147. On Bernstein's relationship to liberalism, see Roger Fletcher, *Revisionism and Empire* (London: George Allen and Unwin, 1984); Peter Gay, *The Dilemma of Democratic Socialism* (New York: Columbia University Press, 1952); Manfred Steger, *The Quest for Evolutionary Socialism* (New York: Cambridge University Press, 1997).
[5] Carlo Rosselli, *Liberal Socialism* (Princeton, NJ: Princeton University Press, 1994), 86–7.
[6] Many have found this journey puzzling, but from the perspective of this study, it makes perfect sense. Donald Sasson, *One Hundred Years of Socialism* (New York: New Press, 1996), chapter 3, and Dan S. White, *Lost Comrades: Socialists of the Front Generation, 1918–1945* (Cambridge, MA: Harvard University Press, 1992).
[7] Quoting a sterilization commission, Nils Roll-Hansen, "Geneticists and the Eugenics Movement in Scandinavia," *Journal for the History of Science*, 22, 1989, 342.
[8] Gunnar Myrdal, quoted in Yvone Hirdman, *Att Lägga Livet till Rätta* (Stockholm: Carlssons, 1989), 100.
[9] Gunnar Broberg and Mattias Tyden, "Eugenics in Sweden," idem, eds., *Eugenics and the Welfare State: Sterilization Policy in Denmark, Sweden, Norway and Finland* (East Lansing, MI: Michigan University Press, 1996), and idem, *Oönskade i Folkhemmet* (Stockholm: Gidlunds, 1991).
[10] Hirdman, *Att Lägga Livet till Rätta*, 84, 86.

What made the Myrdals as well as many other Swedish social democrats sympathetic to such policies was a belief in "endless possibilities to change, form and improve people,"[11] as well as a conviction that "society had the right to intervene not with any aim to improve the race, but for social reasons and for the common interest."[12] Hence although the Myrdals and others took pains to differentiate the Swedish eugenics program from the type of the things going on in Germany – noting, for example, that the former had little to do with racism and was voluntary[13] – such policies must be seen as a blot on the record of the SAP and as a warning of the risks that are run whenever states are viewed as somehow standing above or "embodying" society and whenever collective goods are given precedence over individual rights and liberties.

The Once and Future Ideology

This book has suggested a new way of understanding the relationships among the great ideologies of the twentieth century. Two narratives dominate current debates on that topic. The first focuses on the struggle between democracy and its alternatives, pitting liberalism against fascism, national socialism, and Marxist-Leninism. The second focuses on the competition between capitalism and its alternatives, pitting liberals against socialists and communists.[14] Both help illuminate critical features of twentieth century history, but both are also incomplete and thus misleading – for both ignore the third struggle that was taking place, between those who believed in the primacy of economics and those who believed in the primacy of politics. From this perspective, classical liberalism and orthodox Marxism stand together on the losing side of history, while fascism, national socialism, and social democracy stand opposite. Each of the tyrannical systems met with early success, but all were so violent and destructive that they ultimately crashed and burned. It was thus social democracy – the least heralded and understood of all the contenders – that was left holding the field.

This new understanding of the ideological and political dynamics of the twentieth century would be reason enough to refresh our understanding of the roots and rationale of social democracy. It turns out, however, that there are

---

[11] Ibid., 86

[12] Broberg and Roll-Hansen, *Eugenics and the Welfare State*, 105.

[13] This point was perhaps more true in theory than practice since it is unclear that many of the affected truly understood that to which they were agreeing.

[14] The somewhat more scholarly totalitarianism perspective encompasses elements of both of these perspectives. Hannah Arendt, *Origins of Totalitarianism* (New York: Harcourt and Brace, 1966); Albert Chandler, *Totalitarianism* (New York: Appelton, 1940); Carl Friedrich, *Totalitarianism* (New York: Grosset and Dunlap, 1964); Carl Friedrich and Zbigniew Brzezinski, *Totalitarian Dictatorship and Autocracy* (Cambridge, MA: Harvard University Press, 1956); A. James Gregor, *Contemporary Radical Ideologies: Totalitarian Thought in the Twentieth Century* (New York: Random House, 1968); Wolfgang Wippermann, *Totalitarismusttheorien* (Darmstadt: Primus, 1997).

pressing contemporary reasons to do so as well, since many of the hard-earned insights of earlier ideological battles have been forgotten in recent years, as a shallow version of neoliberalism has come to exert an almost Gramscian hegemony over mainstream public debate.

Thanks to globalization, it is often said, the world is at the dawn of a new era. The spread of markets across the globe, and the deepening and quickening of economic interconnections accompanying it, is creating a fundamentally new situation for leaders and publics, imposing burdens while constraining choices. You can either opt out of the system and languish, or put on what Thomas Friedman has called neoliberalism's "Golden Straitjacket," at which point "two things tend to happen: your economy grows and your politics shrinks."[15]

Globalization's onward march has produced a backlash too, of course, and antiglobalization protests have become a regular feature of contemporary life. Yet today's market boosters find it hard to understand what all the fuss is about. They point to the very real economic benefits that capitalism brings and the poor economic track record of non-market–based approaches to economic affairs, shake their heads, and dismiss the protesters as ignorant fools or adolescents acting out some personal psychodrama. If only the marchers could learn some math, they scoff, or learn to care about increasing the aggregate wealth of society as a whole rather than coddling a few special interests, everything would be fine.

What neoliberals fail to recognize is that such narrow economistic attitudes miss the point. Yes, capitalism is easily the best system for producing growth. But that has never been, and is not today, the only issue. The real debate about markets has focused not simply, or even primarily, on their economic potential, but also on the broader impact they have on the lives of individuals and societies. Critics have worried, and still worry, not about whether unleashing markets will lead to economic growth, but about whether markets themselves will unleash morally and socially irresponsible behavior while eviscerating long-standing communities, traditions, and cultures.

We have seen that it was in response to precisely such concerns that social democracy first began to emerge a century ago. Democratic revisionists such as Bernstein saw that capitalism was not collapsing and seemed likely to be around for at least the medium term. They decided, accordingly, to try to reform and reshape it rather than destroy it. Democratic revisionists also recognized the need to counter the immense mobilizing power of nationalism and to offer something to the vast majority of people suffering from the injustices and dislocations of capitalism. Their successors a generation later built upon this

[15] Thomas Friedman, *The Lexus and the Olive Tree: Understanding Globalization* (New York: Farrar, Straus, and Giroux, 1999), 87. This is not to say that this view is correct; indeed, much scholarly literature now shows that claims about globalization's remaking of the world are very overblown. Nonetheless, this view is very common, indeed dominant, in popular discourse and debate and is often used by neoliberals to justify their policy positions. See Mark Blyth, *Great Transformations* (New York: Cambridge University Press, 2002), and John Ravenhill, ed., *Global Political Economy* (New York: Oxford University Press, 2004).

foundation, arguing that the time had come to put aside calls for capitalism's collapse and focus on managing and directing markets instead. By the 1930s, social democrats recognized that markets and capitalism were not only here to stay, but were also an invaluable tool for producing growth and wealth. At the same time, they never wavered in their insistence that while markets made great servants, they also made terrible masters. Capitalism might be necessary to ensure an ever-increasing economic pie, but it had to be carefully regulated by states so that its negative social and political consequences could be kept in check. During the 1930s, social democrats came to see as never before how widespread and powerful was the longing for some sort of communal identity and social solidarity, and that if they did not come up with some convincing response to this longing, other more nefarious movements would.

Whether or not the participants recognize it, in other words, today's battles over globalization are best viewed as simply the latest chapter in an ongoing debate about the implications and consequences of capitalism and whether and how it can be reconciled with democracy and social stability. Now as before, liberals who venerate markets uncritically and old-style leftists who are unwilling to recognize any good in them have little to offer the vast majority of people who recognize and want to share in capitalism's material benefits but who fear its social and political consequences. And now as before, social democrats have principles at hand to help navigate just these shoals.

This is not a common view, I realize. In recent decades, the social democratic movement in Europe has become a shadow of its former self. Identified by both supporters and critics with a particular set of statist welfare policies designed for mid-century conditions, it stumbled when conditions changed and those policies fell out of favor. The increasing mobility and internationalization of capital have complicated state efforts to regulate business decisions and development, while international competition, some argue, has made generous welfare states and high tax rates luxuries that can no longer be afforded.[16] Immigration and the changing nature of European societies, others contend, have undermined the sense of common purpose and willingness to sacrifice necessary to sustain broad universalistic policies. And the collapse of the Soviet Union, however irrelevant it may have been to the social democratic project, is said to have dashed some people's hopes that any significant leftist alternative to unregulated capitalism might exist.

Yet none of these are reasons for despair, since none of them affect the basic problem of modernity – the tension among capitalism, democracy, and social stability – to which social democracy was and remains the only durable solution. Upon close examination, in fact, the most significant obstacles to a

[16] Geoffrey Garrett and Peter Lange, "Political Responses to Interdependence: What's Left for the Left?" *International Organization*, 45, 4, Autumn, 1991; Jonathon Moses, "Abdication from National Policy Autonomy," *Politics and Society*, 22, June 1994; Fritz Scharpf, *Crisis and Choice in European Social Democracy* (Ithaca, NY: Cornell University Press, 1991); Wolfgang Streeck, *Internationale Wirtschaft, Nationale Demokratie* (Frankfurt: Campus Verlag 1998).

social democratic revival turn out to come not from structural or environmental factors, nor from the vibrancy of alternative ideological approaches, but from intellectual fallacies and a loss of will on the part of the left itself.

Perhaps the most prominent attempt to refashion the democratic left for the contemporary era has come from the so-called "third way" associated with British Prime Minister Tony Blair and sociologist Anthony Giddens.[17] Even though its very name is designed to indicate continuity with traditional social democratic politics,[18] its proponents appear not to understand that one of the core principles of social democracy has always been a belief in the primacy of politics and a commitment to using democratically acquired power to direct economic forces in the service of the collective good.

Supporters of the "third way" want to bring efficiency to the fore; they seek to retain the communitarian aspects of social democracy while rejecting the idea that market forces may need to be redirected or even overruled in order to achieve some more fundamental societal goal. Not wanting to transform or transcend capitalism in any fundamental way, they favor policies that may provide a "safety net" for the poor and underprivileged, for example, but want to avoid challenging market principles whenever possible. (This is also true, of course, of almost all American Democrats.)

Yet for true social democrats, efficiency may be an important criterion for judging policy, but it is not the only or even the most important one. Social democrats have traditionally accepted the market because of its ability to provide the material basis upon which the good life can be built, but have been unwilling to accept its primacy in social or political life. What the "third way" is really resuscitating and updating is thus not social democracy, but a strand of liberal revisionism (as opposed to socialist revisionism) that was particularly popular in Great Britain around the turn of the twentieth century.[19] That may be all well and good, but it should hardly be held to constitute the outer reaches of contemporary progressive aspiration.

If "third way" devotees have lost touch with the primacy of politics, meanwhile, many from the New Left have lost touch with social democracy's other core principle, communitarianism. Convinced that group identities are fundamental and that societal prejudices are deep-seated and possibly ineradicable, these multicultural leftists have come to reject the very idea of national solidarity – seeing it as yet another way for majorities to rob minorities of their particular identities while imposing their own values upon them.[20] In the

[17] Anthony Giddens, *Beyond Left and Right: The Future of Radical Politics* (Stanford, CA: Stanford University Press, 1994), and idem, *The Third Way: The Renewal of Social Democracy* (London: Polity Press, 1998).
[18] Indeed, note that the subtitle of Giddens' book is *The Renewal of Social Democracy*.
[19] Richard Bellamy, *Liberalism and Modern Society* (University Park, PA: Penn State Press, 1992), and James T. Kloppenberg, *Uncertain Victory* (New York: Oxford University Press, 1986).
[20] E.g., Bikhu Parekh, *Rethinking Multiculturalism* (Cambridge, MA: Harvard University Press, 2002), and Bikhu Parekh et al., *Commission on the Future of a Multiethnic Britain* (London: Profile, 2000). But see Brian Barry, *Culture and Equality* (Cambridge, MA: Harvard University Press, 2002).

process, the multiculturalists have abandoned the broad outreach and emphasis on common needs and responsibilities that made social democracy such a
powerful and attractive force in the first place. As one observer laments:

The decline of the Left can be measured by the slackening of its ability to speak on
behalf of a common humanity. Between left and right there has been a curious reversal.
[In the past] the Left stood for the equality of persons, the mainline of the Right for
distinctions and privileges of birth, position, nation. [Yet at the beginning of the twenty-
first century] it is the Right that affects a language of general rights, while the Left, if
it can be addressed with a singular noun, insists on the primacy and irreducibility of
difference.... To be on the Left [today] is to doubt that one can speak of humanity at
all."[21]

The Road Ahead

The prerequisite for a social democratic revival is a rediscovery of the movement's own founding principles. To begin to solve contemporary problems, in
other words, social democrats need to remember that their movement has long
been characterized by a desire to use markets to drive growth while at the
same time using the state to protect citizens from the collateral damage that
markets inflict, and by a commitment to work earnestly on behalf of the entire
community rather than at the service of its individual components or special
interests.

At the twenty-first congress of the Socialist International in 1999, former
French socialist leader Lionel Jospin reminded the assembled delegates that
"The market is an instrument that is effective and important, but it is nothing
more than an instrument."[22] This, rather than the kindler, gentler neoliberalism
of New Labour (or the U.S. Democratic Party), is what the starting point of a
contemporary social democratic strategy should be. But what Jospin and many
others who champion such sentiments rarely if ever acknowledge is that making
this idea relevant to twenty-first century conditions will require a significant
overhaul of the movement's current policy agenda.

The analysis presented here suggests some clear guidelines for those undertaking the task of spelling out the details of a viable new political program.
In keeping with their movement's best traditions, twenty-first century social
democrats should reject both the globaphilia of neoliberalism and the globa-
phobia of many current leftists. They should strive instead to promote what has
been called "progressive globalization,"[23] harnessing the productive potential
of expanding markets while managing the process so that it works to the benefit
of all.

---

[21] Todd Gitlin, "The Left's Lost Universalism," in Arthur Melzer, Jerry Weinberger, and M.
Richard Zimmerman, eds., *Politics at the Turn of the Century*, (New York: Rowan and Littfield,
2001), 3.

[22] Quoted in *Die Zeit*, 46, November 11, 1999, 2.

[23] Michael Jacobs, Adam Lent, and Kevin Watkins, *Progressive Globalisation: Towards International Social Democracy* (London: Fabian Society, 2003).

The notion that without proper supervision unfettered markets can generate a variety of social and political ills but that with it they can produce miracles should not be so hard to understand or communicate. After all, it has irrefutable evidence on its side – it was at the heart of the most successful period in Western Europe's history. But much of this has been forgotten during the last decades. Indeed, the nature and extent of the shift that occurred after 1945 with the institutionalization of the postwar order seems to have faded from our collective memory, with critical implications for how we think about contemporary problems.

Participants in today's globalization debates need to be reminded that it was only with the postwar order that Europe managed to combine capitalism's ability to generate untold riches with functioning democracy and social stability. Before the second half of the twentieth century, these things had indeed been incompatible and almost everyone believed that there was little that could be done to change this: Liberals felt this way because they believed democracy "would lead by necessity to tyranny and expropriation by the poor and uneducated"[24]; Marxists felt this way because they believed that giving the poor and workers the vote would lead inexorably to the end of bourgeois society; and fascists and national socialists felt this way because they believed that democracy stood in direct contradiction to national cohesion and social solidarity. It was social democracy that most forcefully argued for the compatibility of capitalism, democracy, and social stability and that developed a practical program that to a surprising degree actually made them compatible. One of the great ironies of the twentieth century, therefore, is that the very success of this social democratic compromise has led us to forget what a historic accomplishment it was.[25]

Indeed, today even many on the left question this accomplishment, wondering, for example, whether "capitalism with a human face" is something worth fighting for. Such arguments reveal a profound misunderstanding of the original impetus and rationale underpinning the postwar order, as well as a lack of appreciation for how different is was from what came before. For social democrats, the goal was not merely to create a "kinder, gentler capitalism," but rather a world where the market's impact on social and political life was limited as much as possible.[26] This was, in many ways, a revolutionary goal: it went against profound tendencies inherent within the capitalist system as well as the traditional arguments of liberals (both of which push toward an expansion of

---

[24] Clas Offe, "Competitive Party Democracy and the Keynesian Welfare State: Factors of Stability and Disorganization," *Policy Sciences*, 15, 1983, 225–6.

[25] On the social democratic "genius" for compromise, see A. Bergounioux and B. Manin, *Le Régime Social-Démocratie* (Paris: Presses Universitaires de France, 1989), and B. Manin and A. Bergouniux, *La Social-Démocratie ou le Compromis* (Paris: Presses Universitaires de France, 1979).

[26] Or to put it another way, social democrats strived to achieve as great a degree of decommodification as possible – that is, a world in which the political and social lives of individuals depended as little as possible on their position in the marketplace.

the market's scope and reach),[27] and it was, to an impressive degree, realized during the postwar era.

But if social democracy should trumpet its accomplishments and stay true to its principles, it must also be pragmatic. To the extent that capitalism has changed, so too must social democracy's approach to managing it. In particular, to the extent that the nation-state – the instrument that social democrats have traditionally relied on to manage capitalism – has lost some of its autonomy and power, social democrats must now shift their attention to the international arena. This is more easily said than done, since no global political authority comparable to the nation-state currently exists. Yet there are international organizations that could be pressed into service, if social democrats concentrated their intellectual and political firepower on doing so.

The logical place to begin would be with the European Union (EU), and indeed a number of intellectuals have argued that Europe can and should provide the oversight and control over capitalism that the nation-state once did.[28] Others have pointed to the International Monetary Fund (IMF), the World Bank, and the World Trade Organization (WTO) as institutions that could potentially be used to manage global capitalism. Now as in the past, however, the prerequisite for turning these institutions into an instrument for achieving social democratic goals is democratization. Historically, social democrats championed democracy at the national level because they saw it as both a means and an end. The contemporary form of this argument is that institutions such as the EU and the IMF should be made more accountable to the people whom they are purportedly serving both because democratization is a good in and of itself and because by doing so the public at large, rather than merely a few powerful segments of it, can have a say in the management of global capitalism.

If twenty-first century social democrats must reiterate their commitment to the primacy of politics, they must also rediscover the value of communitarianism. The movement emerged partly in response to liberalism's obsession with individualism and orthodox Marxism's obsession with class conflict. What the masses stressed by capitalism really wanted, its founders recognized, was to be addressed as part of some overarching political community; only such an appeal could begin to restore the sense of *Gemeinschaft* that had been lost with the transition to capitalism. Communitarianism, like democracy, was also seen as both an end and a means: It was valuable not only as a counterweight to the atomization, divisiveness, and discord generated by capitalism, but also as a facilitator of other aspects of the social democratic program. Both a strong, interventionist state and generous, universalistic welfare policies, for example, depend on the support of a citizenry driven by a high

---

[27] The best discussion of this dynamic remains Karl Polanyi, *The Great Transformation* (Boston: Beacon Press, 1947).

[28] E.g., Jürgen Habermas, "Why Europe Needs a Constitution," *New Left Review*, 11, September–October 2001.

degree of fellow feeling and a sense of shared purpose. As Michael Walzer has put it:

Membership is important because of what the members of a political community owe to one another and to no one else, or to no one else to the same degree. And the first thing they owe is the communal provision of security and welfare. This claim might be reversed: communal provision is important because it teaches us the value of membership. If we did not provide for one another, if we recognized no distinction between members and strangers, we would have no reason to form and maintain political communities.[29]

The fact that Europe was composed of independent states with relatively homogenous societies made an emphasis on communal and social solidarity rather unproblematic during the first two-thirds of the twentieth century. Today, however, immigration and interdependence have made such appeals more difficult to sustain – at least for those unwilling to flirt with chauvinism and xenophobia. Yet it is crucial that social democrats find a way of doing so, for neither individualism nor multiculturalism can provide a basis for a long-lasting political success.

In an increasingly diverse Europe, basing a call for social solidarity on shared ethnic or religious background is no longer a viable or attractive strategy. Social democracy's refashioned communitarian appeal will therefore have to be built upon more inclusive grounds – namely, shared values and responsibilities. Social democrats must make clear, in other words, that since twenty-first century citizenship cannot be built on some fellowship of blood, it must be based upon the acceptance of certain rules and norms. As one observer has put it, "The glue of ethnicity ('people who look and talk like us') has to be replaced with the glue of values ('people who think and behave like us')."[30] Social democrats must insist on the non-negotiable nature of certain political, social, and cultural values while at the same time asserting that the integration of immigrants is both a moral good and a practical necessity.

To the charge that this smacks of coerced conformity, social democrats must respond that, with the theme of community once again becoming the provenance of the populist right (as has already begun to happen with groups ranging from the French National Front to the Austrian Freedom Party), the alternative is far worse. As the founders of the social democratic movement understood, people have a deep-seated and ineradicable psychological need to feel part of a larger community – a need that the expanding reach of markets only intensifies, as all that is solid melts into air. That need will be met one way or another, and if the democratic left cannot figure out how to do so, less savory forces will be more than glad to step into the breach.

Although finding an attractive and realistic approach to dealing with the changing nature of European societies has proven no easier than finding a way to

[29] Michael Walzer, *Spheres of Justice* (New York: Basic Books, 1983), 64.
[30] Ibid., 32.

deal with the changing global economy, here too there is reason to be optimistic. Across Europe there are increasingly calls from those on the left for a new "third way" between the xenophobia of some of those on the right and the relativism and multiculturalism of some on the left. Perhaps not surprisingly, some of the strongest such calls have been coming recently from those parts of Europe where the problems of unassimiliated immigrants and deeply divided societies have exploded into violence. In the Netherlands, for example, where the killings of Pim Fortuyn and Theo van Gogh have spurred immense soul searching, Wouter Bos, leader of the Dutch Labour Party, has recently argued that maintaining the sense of solidarity upon which well-functioning democracies and welfare states are built requires addressing "the absence of common cultural values" that has accompanied growing ethnic and religious diversity in Europe. Bos argues that, in order to address this problem, all citizens, regardless of background, need to accept fully the core principles upon which Dutch society is built, and that migration will, in the future, need to be restricted "because our capacity to integrate and emancipate is not limitless." As Bos notes:

... leaving this debate (about diversity, values, and the future of Europe) to conservatives may feel comfortable because we will not have to disappoint anybody.... But let's not fool ourselves. This will not help those who count on us. It won't help the newcomers to our society who are promised a future that we cannot provide. And it won't help the long-term citizens who either fool themselves that diversity causes no problems at all or who will suffer from the slow erosion of collective arrangements.... This debate cannot be ignored by the progressive side of politics. It is our debate too.[31]

Even in Sweden, the SAP, which has long successfully exploited communitarian themes, has had difficulty dealing with this issue. When the SAP came to power over seventy years ago, Sweden was a remarkably homogeneous country; now, more than 17 percent of all Swedish children have at least one foreign-born parent. Not surprisingly, this shift has created widespread social problems and prompted worries about xenophobia. In response, the SAP has taken some steps to reformulate its long-standing communitarian traditions for the contemporary era. A recent government paper on "Immigration and Diversity," for example, calls for "social cohesion built on diversity" and "social development characterized by mutual respect within the boundaries following from society's fundamental democratic values in which everyone, irrespective of background, should participate and share a sense of commitment."[32] Several prominent Swedish politicians, meanwhile, have made it clear that immigrants are welcome in Swedish society but must adapt to the country's ruling norms in order to partake of the full benefits of citizenship. Such policy stances have led some to accuse the SAP of being a nationalistic or even anti-immigrant party,[33]

---

[31] Wouter Bos, "After Van Gogh," *Prospect*, January 2005.

[32] Swedish government, "Integration and Diversity," available online at http://www.sweden.gov. se/sb/d/2188/a/19443.

[33] Mauricio Rojas and Merit Wagner, "S är en Invandrarfientlight Parti," *Dagens Nyheter*, July 9, 2002.

but such criticisms are off the mark. The moves are better seen as potentially early gropings toward a new form of communitarianism based on ideas and behavior rather than identity politics, and thus a sign of progress rather than of regression. The SAP as well as other social democratic parties would do well to follow along on this path.

At the end of the day, in this area as in others, there is good reason to hope that technocrats and political entrepreneurs will eventually come up with passable solutions for the various policy problems currently bedeviling the social democratic left. Even if they do so, however, it will lead to a true revival of the movement's fortunes only if activists can regain their optimism and vision. Perhaps the greatest failing of social democratic parties today, in fact, is their loss of the idealism that has sustained the movement from the beginning.

It is possible to win elections without proclaiming any commitment to ideology or a desire to change the world. But over time, the parties that do so become dead men walking, losing momentum, enthusiasm, and the ability to weather difficulties. This is precisely what is happening across Europe today: Social democratic parties continue to do reasonably well at the polls and join governments, but their membership figures are down dramatically and few think that they can do more than offer a kinder, gentler version of their opponents' platforms.

Given the movement's history, such a situation is simply astonishing. However pragmatic and flexible social democrats have been over the years in formulating their practical appeals and tailoring their programs to particular circumstances, they have always been driven by the conviction that a better world was possible and that it was their task to bring it about. From Eduard Bernstein to Henrik de Man, Carlo Rosselli to Per Albin Hansson, true social democrats have always thought (in contrast to their reformist cousins) of particular policies not merely as ends in themselves, but also as steps toward a better future. They believed, in other words, not only that there was no contradiction between present-oriented policies and future-oriented goals, but that in fact you could not (or should not) have one without the other. Social democracy, at least as originally envisioned, was based on the view that integrating theory and praxis was the key to political victory and that transforming the existing world was the ultimate goal.

All this began to change during the postwar era, as the movement lost touch with its ideological heritage and began basing its appeal on its ability to manage the system successfully rather than to transform it. "Up through the 1980s," as one observer has noted, "politics on the left was enchanted – not by spirits, but by radical idealism; the belief that the world could be fundamentally different. But cold, hard political realism has now done for radical idealism what rationality did for pre-Enlightenment spirituality. Politics has been disenchanted." Many have welcomed this shift, believing that transformative projects are passé or even dangerous. But it is even more true that this loss of faith in transformation "has been profoundly damaging, not just for the causes of progressive politics but for a wider sense of public engagement with the political process."[34]

As the great social democrats of the late nineteenth and early twentieth century recognized, the most important thing politics can provide is a sense of the possible. Against Marxist determinism and liberal laissez-fairism, accordingly, they pleaded for the development of a political ideology based on the idea that, in spite of everything, people working together could and should make the world a better place: the result was the most successful political movement of the twentieth century. The problems of the twenty-first century may be different in form, but they are not different in kind; there is no reason that the accomplishment cannot be repeated.

[34] Michael Jacobs, "Reason to Believe," *Prospect*, October 2002.

Index

Boulanger, Georges, 29
Boulanger crisis of 1889, 29
Boulangism, 82–3
Brandt, Willy, 191
Branting, Hjalmar, 152–8, 160–1, 164,
    167
Breslau congress (1895), SPD, 37–8
Bretton Woods conference, 179
Brno (Brünn) program (1899), 64
Brousse, Paul, 29
Brüning, Heinrich, 109–12, 142
Bülow, Bernhard von, 58

Cabrini, Angiolo, 75
Capital (Marx), 23, 69
capitalism, 2–8, 109–15
    de Man Plan, 115, 118–19, 186
    in postwar era, 187
Catholic Mouvement Républican
    Populaire, 178
Catholic Popular Party (Italy), 103,
    130
Centre Confédéral d'Études Ouvrières
    de la C. G. T., 121
Cercle Proudhon, 85
Christian Democratic Union (CDU)
    (Germany), 178, 191
Christian Socialist Union (CSU)
    (Germany), 191
Christian Social Party (Austria), 93–5
class struggle, 12–15, 20–1, 26, 33, 42,
    48, 51, 96–7, 99, 116, 126
communism, 22–3, 67, 206
    in France, 122, 194
    in Germany, 109, 114
    in Italy, 105, 192–3
Communist International, 105
Communist Manifesto, 61
Communist Party of Germany (KPD),
    137, 139, 141, 143
communitarianism, 8, 15, 120, 125–6,
    200, 204–7, 211, 214, 217
Confederazione Generale dell'Industria
    Italiana (Confindustrio) (CGII),
    133
conservative revolution (Germany),
    137
Conservatives, Italian, 130

Copenhagen congress (1910), Socialist
    International, 64–5
corporatism, 133–6
Corradini, Enrico, 78–9
Craxi, Bettino, 193
Crispi, Francesco, 52
Croce, Benedetto, 51, 74, 78
Croix de Feu (CF), 149, 151
Crosland, C. A. R., 181, 187
cross-class cooperation, 11, 14–16, 20,
    34, 52, 56, 60, 74, 88, 97, 116,
    150, 155, 160, 200, 203
Czech nationalism, 64–5

D'Annunzio, Gabriele, 127
D'Aragona, Ludovico, 104
Daladier, Edouard, 101, 120
Danielsson, Axel, 154–5, 157–8
Darwinism, 25
Das Dritte Reich (The Third Reich)
    (Moeller), 137
Daudet, Léon, 84
David, Eduard, 37, 158
de Man Plan, 115, 118–19, 186
Déat, Marcel, 120–1, 125–6
decommodification, 181, 185, 196, 213
Delegation des Gauches, 49
democratic revisionism, 14–16, 204, 209
    in Austria, 59–65
    in France, 28–35, 48–50
    in Germany, 54–9
    in Italy, 50–4
    origins in Germany, 35–46
    in Sweden, 152–9
depression, 10, 13, 26
Der Moderne Kapitalismus (Sombart),
    90
Deutsche Demokratische Partei (DDP)
    (German Democratic Party)
    (Germany), 140
Deutschnationale Volkspartei (DNVP)
    (German National People's Party)
    (Germany), 140
dictatorship of the proletariat, 102–3
Dresden congress (1903), SPD, 55–6
Dresden resolution, 55–6
Dreyfus, Alfred, 31
Dreyfus Affair, 31–2, 83–4

For EU product safety concerns, contact us at Calle de José Abascal, 56–1°,
28003 Madrid, Spain or eugpsr@cambridge.org.

www.ingramcontent.com/pod-product-compliance
Ingram Content Group UK Ltd.
Pitfield, Milton Keynes, MK11 3LW, UK
UKHW020807190625
459647UK00032B/2363